After Blair

Conservatism Beyond Thatcher

After Blair

Conservatism Beyond Thatcher

Kieron O'Hara

ICON BOOKS

Published in the UK in 2005
by Icon Books Ltd., The Old Dairy,
Brook Road, Thriplow,
Cambridge SG8 7RG
email: info@iconbooks.co.uk
www.iconbooks.co.uk

Sold in the UK, Europe, South Africa
and Asia by Faber and Faber Ltd.,
3 Queen Square, London WC1N 3AU
or their agents

Distributed in the UK, Europe, South Africa
and Asia by TBS Ltd., Frating Distribution Centre,
Colchester Road, Frating Green, Colchester CO7 7DW

Published in Australia in 2005
by Allen & Unwin Pty. Ltd.,
PO Box 8500, 83 Alexander Street,
Crows Nest, NSW 2065

Distributed in Canada by
Penguin Books Canada,
10 Alcorn Avenue, Suite 300,
Toronto, Ontario M4V 3B2

ISBN 1 84046 594 8

Typesetting by Hands Fotoset

Printed and bound in the UK by
Clays of Bungay

CONTENTS

List of Figures and Tables

Figures

Tables

ACKNOWLEDGEMENTS

This book has developed out of some research I have been doing in my spare time with members of the School of Politics at the University of Nottingham. In particular, I would like to thank David Stevens, Andrew Denham, Mat Humphrey and Pru Hobson-West for giving their time and expertise very freely, and helping me greatly along the way.

Many thanks also to David Willetts, who has been very generous with his comments and criticisms. Icon Books has been very encouraging of this project, and I am particularly grateful to Peter Pugh, who has taken a firm interest in the book from the beginning, Andrew Furlow and Tansy Hiner; and by thanking Ruth Nelson, whose deft editing led to many improvements, I can dispel the guilt that has burdened me since I forgot to acknowledge her important work on my previous book for Icon, *Trust*.

The School of Electronics and Computer Science at the University of Southampton has as ever been a delightful employer, and has given me plenty of space to pursue what must seem very recondite research interests. Particular thanks to Nigel Shadbolt and Wendy Hall for providing that research environment, and to Susan Davies for helping in countless ways.

Conversations with Rebecca Hughes and Yorick Wilks have been very influential on certain sections of the book. And I would also like to acknowledge the often intangible but nonetheless real contributions of various people with whom I have discussed this project, including: Sri Dasmahapatra, Hugo de Burgh, Mark Garnett, Louise Maskill, Andy Robinson, Tom Scutt and Simon Tormey.

For NW, smallest of small 'c' conservatives

There is nothing like a theory for blinding the wise.
George Meredith, *The Ordeal of Richard Feverel*

The French are famous for the clarity of their thought and the lucidity of their prose, yet in whatever they do, they never fail to bring chaos, filth, and hubbub, as witness the mess on board the ship. Relying on man's ingenuity and entrusted with his hopes, but loaded with his clutter, the ship sailed along amidst the noise and bustle; each minute it returned one small stretch of water, polluted with the smell of man, back to the indifferent, boundless, and never-ending ocean.
Qian Zhongshu [Ch'ien Chung-Shu], *Fortress Besieged*
Translated by Jeanne Kelly and Nathan K. Mao

PREFACE

Where do the Tories go from here?

Since Tony Blair became leader of the Labour Party in 1994, he has won two landslides, and seen off three Conservative leaders. At the time of writing, he is on course for his third election victory, which would in all likelihood mean the end of Michael Howard. Not since the beginning of the last century have the Tories been in such doldrums.

And that is bad for all of us, even those who could never vote Conservative as long as they live. A more effective opposition means a more effective government, properly scrutinised legislation, and a realistic choice for voters come election time.

The Tories are not finished by any means. No one would rule out the rebirth of such a resilient political force, the oldest political party in the world. The question is: how can they do it?

There have been many suggestions, including changing the party's name, changing its colour, restructuring it to give more power to the members, and restructuring it to take power *away* from its members. Some urge a move to the right, to shore up the core vote. Others want a leftward move, to get back those who defected to Mr Blair. Still others worry less about political direction, and instead want new, youthful, exciting faces on the front bench.

There are many aspects to a political party's success or failure, including personalities, presentation and marketing, and competence. No doubt the Tories could benefit from looking at all of these. But in this book, I want to focus on the question of *ideology*.

In a nutshell, I want to argue that the Tories are victims of their success in the 1980s. The Thatcherite programme was a masterpiece of practical liberal thought that shook up rusting industries and transformed the face of Britain. But Thatcherism cannot be the answer to the Tories' problems today, for three reasons.

First of all, Thatcherism was accepted by the British voter relatively grudgingly, as a nasty medicine to get rid of unionitis and all the other diseases of the corporate state. Now the disease is cured, we don't want to continue to take it. The Tory take on liberalism focused very much on the economy; most people now recognise that economics is only part of the story.

Second, if the Tories are to take votes from Labour, they need to move back towards the centre; they are currently perceived to be the most extreme of the three major national parties. That entails a move *away* from Thatcherism – though there is no need to repudiate Mrs Thatcher's legacy. The Tories can claim with justice that her policies were essential in the 1980s, and indeed that they have become the basis for a consensus in British politics. But nowadays there are other issues to address, other dragons to slay.

Third, without undoing Mrs Thatcher's work, Mr Blair has undeniably moved the centre of British politics leftward in his years of power. The average British voter now considers him- or herself to be slightly to the left of Mr Blair. So not only do the Tories have to move leftward, but the target at which they aim is moving away from them all the time.

The ideological problem, then, is that the Tories need to get back to the centre, currently occupied by Mr Blair. They need a message that is centrist and yet will differentiate them from New Labour. Which, given Mr Blair's ability to pinch Tory ideas and make them his own, is far more easily said than done.

In this book, I want to suggest a possible route for their journey. The Conservative Party has not always been a free market liberal party; as a broad coalition of interests it has usually sheltered a number of ideological tendencies. One such tendency, very prominent until the rise of Mrs Thatcher, was the philosophy that gave the party its name: conservatism.

But surely conservatism is unrealistic in a fast-moving, complex world, where technological change is unravelling the social weave all the time, and where the presence of many different cultures and ethnic groups undermines attempts to specify common values? Can there *really* be any mileage in fogeyish relapse into nostalgia? The past isn't what it was.

True enough. But conservatism, as a philosophy, is less to do with nostalgia and more to do with understanding how little we know about the world. It is a claim about knowledge, and about human frailty. In short, it is a philosophy that might well be a great boon in the uncertain conditions in which we find ourselves.

As we trace the history of conservatism as a philosophy of *knowledge*, from Socrates and the Greek sceptics, to the giant figure of Montaigne, and on to the great 18th-century thinkers Burke and Hume, we rediscover a tradition of tolerance and humility. Tracing this history enables us to distil the philosophy of conservatism to its essence.

Which isn't just an exercise in intellectual history. This distillation, applied to the problems of the 21st century, produces a very interesting policy profile, eminently centrist, eminently up to date. When we think about the real meaning of conservatism, we can chip away the unpalatable accretions of racism, hanging and flogging, the defence of privilege against merit.

Instead, conservatism can help defend tolerance against prejudice, support pragmatism against dogmatism, and provide security in an uncertain and disorienting world. It is a civilised tradition from whose restatement and revival we would all benefit.

CHAPTER ONE

MESSAGE IN A BOTTLE FROM THE SLOUGH OF DESPOND

How long shall mine enemy be exalted over me?

Psalm 13:2

A dire situation

The British Conservative Party is the most successful party, and the oldest, in the history of democracy. For a party whose instincts have not been terribly democratic, that's an amazing feat. It spent the 19th century going up and down, out of power for long periods, yet always influential and important. It reigned supreme in the 20th century, often with no serious rivals. But now it's the 21st century, and the winning machine seems to have broken down more than somewhat.

Figure 1 shows the poll ratings of the Tories since Mrs Thatcher's victory in 1979. The Tories were brilliantly success-ful, particularly in the Thatcher years. They did (and still do) a lot better in general elections than opinion polls, which is the right way round.[1] Mrs Thatcher's initial unpopularity (ten points down in January 1981) was soon wiped out by the effect of her victory in the Falklands, in the teeth of liberal/left wing opposition at home. And after Mrs Thatcher's declining fortunes led to a large Labour lead in 1990, her defenestration and replacement by John Major restored the status quo.

But at the beginning of the new century, the Tories seem to be in worse trouble, and changing leaders, shifting the tone of debate, seems not to be effective in restoring them to their traditional pre-eminence. A key event in this apparently more permanent decline was Black Wednesday, the day in September 1992 when the pound sterling was ejected from the Exchange Rate Mechanism, and the Tories lost their reputation for economic competence. As can be seen in Figure 1, the Labour lead went from being marginal in August, to double digits by October, and has rarely been much below that since. The British electorate fell out of love with the Tories at that point, and have shown little or no enthusiasm for the party ever since. The Tories seem not to have moved with the times, and appear hopelessly out of touch, more concerned with attacking each other than bothering with the seemingly invincible Tony Blair and Gordon Brown (who often seems to be the real leader of the opposition). The activist membership seems even less in step with the *Zeitgeist*. The end of the Tory party as a serious political force is often predicted.[2]

The situation is actually even worse for the Tories than these figures suggest. If, in the election that we can expect in 2005, the Tories get, say, 37.5 per cent of the vote (and we can see from Figure 1 that that has not happened in polls since Black Wednesday), and Labour get exactly the same number (and they have not been that low since the 1992 election), Labour would win about 140 more seats than the Tories, and have an absolute majority of around 70 (thanks to over-representation of Wales and Scotland, smaller Labour seats, smaller turnout in Labour seats, and the ingrained habit of tactical voting by Labour and Liberal Democrats). To win a majority of one seat, the Tories would need a lead of 11.5 per cent (last seen in the months following the 1987 election victory).[3]

What is very clear is that the Tories need to move towards the centre to reclaim as many voters as they possibly can. Their problem, of course, is that the giant figure of Tony Blair is squatting squarely on the centre ground, and they are naturally struggling to squeeze out a message that is centrist enough to attract their traditionally large vote, yet distinct enough from Mr Blair's bland managerialism. The fact that Mr Blair has stolen many of the Tories' clothes, and is often seen, fairly or unfairly, as a 'closet Tory', is no help.

6

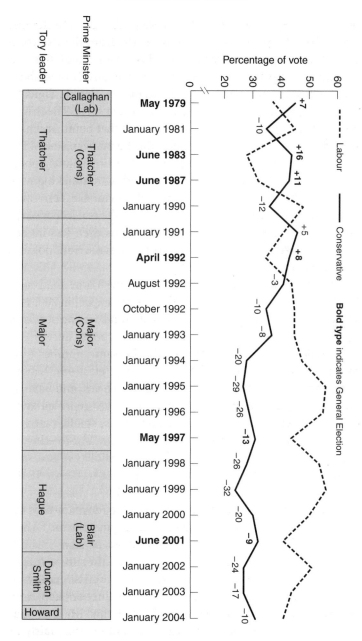

Figure 1: The petering out of the Conservative century[4]

I should also mention at the outset that the notions of 'left', 'right' and therefore 'centre' are much more problematic than this diagnosis suggests. Spotting whether a policy is left wing, or is a move to the right, depends on many things, including subtle shifts in political context, and the complex process of dialectic between politicians and parties. The interface between the philosophical, the pragmatic and the inevitable is very difficult to understand; I hope to make some of the implications of my argument clearer in Part Two.

The trick, then, for the Tories is to move towards the centre, avoiding sounding like Mr Blair, while also retaining continuity with their traditions. My aim in this book is to suggest one way of pulling that trick off, producing a distinctively Tory message that could be attractive to voters, by plundering the party's past for some ideological support that makes sense in the complex, uncertain and tense world of the 21st century.

Plus ça change

Of course, this is not the only serious political party in living memory to implode. The Labour Party managed the same trick in the 1980s. Between 1964 and 1974, Harold Wilson won four out of five elections against the Tories, albeit only once having a comfortable majority, and so in the period 1964–79 there were only three and a half years of Tory government. Wilson's surprise and still unexplained resignation of 1976 brought Jim Callaghan to Number 10 for an unhappy coda to Labour's first period of hegemony.

Aristocracy, in the correct meaning of the term, is government by the best. By that definition, Wilson's governments were perhaps the most aristocratic Britain has ever known; the brainpower he was able to deploy could produce enough wattage to power a small town. At cabinet level, he could draw upon the services of Roy Jenkins, Barbara Castle, Anthony Crosland, Richard Crossman, Tony Benn, Denis Healey and George Brown, and in later years Shirley Williams, David Owen and Michael Foot. Below the cabinet, and on the backbenches, could be found luminaries such as C.P. Snow, David Marquand and John Mackintosh. This is a stellar line-up that would grace any governing party (or indeed any senior common room).

What stuns the observer of the time is how disastrously these governments performed. Their second shot at power in 1974, given grudgingly by a disillusioned electorate, came about only because Edward Heath's Tories were even more inept. Into the power vacuum had stepped the trade unions, orchestrated by Jack Jones and Hugh Scanlon.

Labour responded to their defeat in 1979 by dithering. Mrs Thatcher had taken the British government firmly to the right, abandoning the centre; her aims were to reduce both the government's responsibility for the economy, and the political power of the unions. That left Labour with two alternatives: it could try to move towards the vacant centre, or it could match Mrs Thatcher's atavism with a red-in-tooth-and-claw socialism of its own. The initial battles were won by the left, with Tony Benn as their champion. Even the removal of Mr Callaghan, whose avuncular brand of common-man unionism had lost whatever lustre it had during the Winter of Discontent, a prolonged period of union militancy in 1978–9, and his replacement by fiery intellectual Michael Foot, did not satisfy the militants. In the unflattering glare of publicity, Mr Benn attempted to reorganise the Labour Party in order to maximise the voting strength of the left. Some policy stances – pro-Europeanism, opposition to Clause 4 nationalisation and unilateral disarmament – were demonised, and party conferences became bear pits. Voters left in droves, the party split and Mrs Thatcher, though never receiving particularly high numbers of votes, was left to govern unhindered by the opposition. The move away from pragmatism to ideology had merely secured the exact opposite of what the left had hoped for.

Kinnock, Smith, Blair – and the gang of four

However, the Labour experience had a happy ending: they were dragged out of the wilderness by a fortunate combination of leaders, political theorists and activists. The leaders who followed Michael Foot gradually moved rightward, and in doing so ended the toleration of the left's antics. Neil Kinnock was the first of these leaders, from 1983 to 1992; his contribution was to attack the Militant Tendency in the party, and thus to do the essential groundwork. Like Moses, he was not to see the promised land of Number 10; he was never a convincing opponent for Mrs Thatcher, and an ill-advised triumphal rally in Sheffield days before the 1992 election probably shifted enough votes away from Labour to deny him a victory at the second attempt.* However, the symbolism of Kinnock, a man of the left, taking on the ideologues of the hard left, undoubtedly stiffened spines at a key time. He also, with the help of Bryan Gould, began the process of trying to match the Tories' new professionalism.

Kinnock was succeeded by John Smith, a Scot of almost palpable rectitude, whose manner, essentially that of a super-conservative solicitor of impeccable Presbyterian tendencies, contrasted effectively not only with the wild-eyed demeanour of Labour politicians (of left *and* right) of the previous decade, but also with the circus that the post-Thatcher Tory Party was becoming. He had also, despite having been a member of Mr Callaghan's cabinet, managed to avoid being tainted with the failures of the past. As a result, he was trusted in a way that Kinnock would never be; whereas Kinnock strengthened Labour, Smith was able to attract voters from other parties. His premature death in 1994 prevented us from discovering how his government might have functioned; what is virtually certain is that, by the time of his death, he had holed John Major's government below the waterline, and pretty well ensured victory for his successor in 1997.

Mr Blair followed, and though Mr Smith had left a winning hand on the table, it can safely be said that Mr Blair's contribution was to render a Tory victory in either 1997 or 2001 as unthinkable as a Labour victory in 1983 or 1987. He achieved

---

* Indeed, one Labour MP opined to a friend of mine that the Sheffield rally had given people the excuse they were looking for not to vote Labour!

this through a number of methods. First, there has been a dramatic increase in the professionalism of the Labour Party's operation – symptomatically, they are now resented for their slickness, whereas twenty years ago they were despised as a ramshackle, argumentative shower. Second, Mr Blair, like Bill Clinton, has a flair for finding formulae for bringing people together. In his early days, particularly in opposition, this was mistaken for indecisiveness and shiftiness (the Tories' 1997 'demon eyes' election campaign sought to portray Mr Blair as being secretly in hock to left wing ideals and ideology – a charge that, from the perspective of 2004, looks even more ludicrous than it did then).

But third – and this is his great achievement – he was the first serious politician of the left to appreciate the legacy of Mrs Thatcher. He was able, unlike any of his predecessors, to operate in the post-Thatcher world. Mrs Thatcher had dragged the political consensus to the right during her period in office, and (see below) had ultimately overbalanced and taken the Tories too far. Mr Blair recognised where the new centre was located, and promptly occupied it.

This miniature stroke of genius has been mistaken for Mr Blair's 'selling out'. He is often accused of being a 'closet Tory'. This is actually not true, as plenty of Mr Blair's policies – pumping money into public services, setting up a minimum wage, constitutional reform, setting stiff targets for eliminating child poverty, meeting the UK's targets on the Kyoto environmental protocol, increasing international aid – are particular totems of the left. Indeed, it is striking how far Mr Blair has got with the implementation of a traditional left wing slate; certainly much further than any previous Labour Prime Minister, with the possible exception of Clement Attlee.

Mr Blair has recognised that Mrs Thatcher deliberately changed Britain to rid it of socialism. She failed; but what Mr Blair represents is the mutation of socialism to function in the post-Thatcher ecosystem. And function it does. This mutation was supported, in the early days at least, by a series of political theorists who were able to create an ideology, the so-called 'Third

Way', that stripped socialism of the unacceptable baggage – economic restriction, punitive taxation, anti-Americanism, pacifism, corporatism – that characterised the pre-1979 Labour Party. Such theorists, who are not all necessarily satisfied by the results of their champion's period of office, include Will Hutton, Anthony Giddens, Geoff Mulgan and Charles Lead-beater.[5] Many a wonk-hour was spent in seminars trying to discover what the Third Way actually was.

Finally, Mr Blair has received the support of most of his MPs, and most Labour Party members, if often grudgingly. Even when he was attacking nostrums about which the party was sentimental, he got away with it. He has done that because, after four consecutive and decisive election defeats, the party gradually got fed up with losing. It wants to win, and Mr Blair is a winner. The party does not love Mr Blair, and if the feeling that Gordon Brown would also be a winner spreads much further, Mr Blair may have difficulty holding on to office. But be that as it may, four defeats (and two landslide victories) have meant that the party is willing to hold its nose and go along with Mr Blair – for now.

The three leaders, all essential in their various ways for the spectacular Labour revival, took the party rightward, so that it now not only occupies the political centre, but actually stands in a position that, in the pre-Thatcher world of the 1970s, would be seen as really rather right wing. This was not an easy task, and it is not clear that any of the three leaders could have done it on his own. But another lesson that stands out from Labour's recovery is the role played by the so-called 'gang of four': David Owen, Roy Jenkins, Shirley Williams and, er, the other one.*

Their aim was to realign British politics, to provide a new party of the centre left that would command the anti-Thatcher majority and turn the Labour Party into a retirement home for the leftie rump. They left Labour in a brilliant blaze of publicity, and set up the Social Democratic Party, which, in alliance with

---

* Actually William Rodgers, a respected cabinet minister, but undeniably much less stellar than his three comrades.

the Liberals, ran Labour a very close third in 1983. The effect, though, as with the ideologues of the left, was the very opposite of what they intended. They cemented Mrs Thatcher, whose radicalism they deplored, in power, and the Labour Party reacted strongly against the splitters. Labour were eventually dragged towards the centre, as we have seen, but the process took much longer than it might have done without the SDP to provide opposition against it from the centre, pushing it, for a few years, in the wrong direction. The mistake – a terrible and irresponsible mistake, in retrospect – that Owen et al. made was not to stay within Labour and work to pull it back to the centre.* It would have taken time, and would have been tiring and unglamorous work; splitting, on the other hand, gave them the luxury of centrist politics and the limelight immediately. But the SDP lacked the organisation to sustain a serious bid for power.

So, in the context of the Tories' current malaise, the Labour Party's recent history provides a few interesting pointers to consider (see Table 1). No doubt not all these will end up being germane to a putative Tory recovery, but learning from others' experiences is a useful trait, in politics as elsewhere.

The glory days

Ironically, the Tories' troubles stem from their post-war glory days, Mrs Thatcher's period of office from 1979–90. Her style of government was famously robust, and many malign forces that had plagued Britain as its post-war consensus declined were taken on and beaten, notably the trade unions. They lost out largely as a result of creeping legislation, although the psychological damage inflicted by Mrs Thatcher on Arthur Scargill's NUM during the great strike of 1984–5 should not be underplayed. Mrs Thatcher was certainly pugnacious, but she was also skilful in her choices of fights to pick.

---

* As a less good but still plausible alternative, they could have waited for Labour to drift centrewards and re-merged with them. The merger with the Liberals was the final nail in the coffin of the gang of four's project.

Table 1: Labour's problems in the 80s, and their solutions

	Problem	Solution
1	Unpopularity	Kinnock diagnosed the electoral problem with the party, and acted unsentimentally to remove it.
2	Lack of trust	Smith managed to personify something completely different from what had gone before (despite having been a prominent Labour politician throughout its wilderness years). As a result, he was able to generate trust; he attracted voters from other parties.
3	Organisational defects	Blair continued the work of Kinnock before him to improve organisation.
4	Causing division	Blair deliberately aims for maximal inclusion, even when his policies are at their most divisive. It is impossible to imagine Mrs Thatcher spending as much time and effort as Mr Blair drumming up support in the country and in the United Nations for the Iraq War, say.
5	Inept positioning	Blair has pulled the party back towards the centre.
6	Failure to understand history and context	But also note that Blair, unlike virtually anyone else in his party, has recognised that, post-Thatcher, the centre has moved.
7	Lack of unity	The nuclear option, taken by the gang of four in forming the SDP, does not work. The process of moving a giant party towards the centre of politics is a gradual one, and there is no short cut.
8	Lack of pragmatism	The party as a whole needed to want to win, and to stop being precious over its favoured ideologies.
9	Lack of intellectual clout	There was a requirement for strong theoretical ideological backing, provided by Hutton, Giddens, Mulgan et al.

The Tories had had one other spell of sustained post-war government, from 1951–64, under four Prime Ministers, Churchill, Eden, Macmillan and Home. The policies of that long period, however, were largely dictated by Attlee's left wing government of 1945–51. The experience of the 1930s depression (under Tory government and policy), the war (under Labour-style economic controls), and Attlee's government which implemented the recommendations of the popular Beveridge report on welfare (in the teeth of Churchill's opposition) had shifted the consensus leftward, and so the moderate Tories of the 50s, seeking the centre, moved left too. Butskellism, the nickname given to this consensus, owed rather more to Labour's Hugh Gaitskell than to Tory Rab Butler, though it should be noted that there was always a strong free market strand in Tory thought at this time, perhaps most strongly under Churchill, most repressed under Macmillan. Macmillan's rejection of free market solutions led to some opposition from the right, most notably when Chancellor Peter Thorneycroft and two of his junior ministers, Nigel Birch and Enoch Powell, resigned in 1958 over the level of public spending; Powell continued a guerrilla campaign throughout the 1960s against Tory acquiescence in government attempts to set income levels.[6] Tories do not tend to look back particularly fondly on 1951–64.

After the mildly left wing corporate consensus broke down in the 1970s under a tidal wave of strikes and poor economic performance, Mrs Thatcher acted decisively to shift Britain's politics rightward. Thatcherism was born, though maybe accidentally.[7] Various experiments, such as monetarism, the idea that the quantity of money in an economy determines the inflation rate, were tried, though they never provided the government with the level of control it sought. Thatcherism settled down in the end to being a programme of the removal of government influence from industry, the introduction of market-based methods of incentive in those public services that could not, for philosophical, economic or political reasons, be privatised, and a shift of the onus of care from the state to individuals or, as a second best, voluntary organisations. Mrs Thatcher's ascent to the leadership in 1975 does not represent a big discontinuity in Tory ideas; in many ways she continued Mr Heath's early rhetorical programme, and exploited currents of ideas that had been influential in Tory circles since the war, for example with the writings of Hayek.* But on the other hand, the effect of her repositioning of Britain is clear when we compare the political consensus in Britain with, say, those of France or Germany, whose corporatist assumptions appear outdated to British eyes.

Thatcherite policies were intended to capture or recreate the spirit of public service and self-reliance that characterised the Victorian era, which throughout the 20th century had been a deeply unfashionable time. The irony, though, is that in so far as Mrs Thatcher genuinely recreated the Victorian ethos, it was the policies of the Victorian Liberal Party that she brought in, not those of the Tories of the day.[8] And indeed, had Gladstone by some miracle been drafted into her cabinet, even he would have been derided, with Francis Pym, Norman St John-Stevas and James Prior, as a 'wet'. (Disraeli might well, oddly, have made it to the inner circle, as Mrs Thatcher, like Queen Victoria, was always susceptible to the charms of a smooth flatterer – as well as being impeccably free of anti-Semitism.)

Post-Thatcher blues

The Tory slide began in Mrs Thatcher's third term, after 1987, when her previously sure touch seemed to desert her. As well as a number of odd incidents ('we are a grandmother'), she seemed to alienate most of the people of real talent around her, notably Nigel Lawson and Sir Geoffrey Howe. Her policy instincts also went awry, with the disaster of the poll tax being only the most prominent. Finally, a boom engineered in the run-up to the 1987 general election became a recession after it. The Tories began to lose council elections, and the party lost grass roots members; it began to 'hollow out'.

The Tories, sliding in the polls, were faced with the classic twist-or-stick dilemma: should they carry on with Mrs Thatcher as leader, hoping that she would get back on track and continue her exemplary record of winning elections, or make a change?

* As David Willetts has pointed out to me, her views were formed in the pre-Macmillan 50s, when free market thought was in a period of exciting development. Contrast this with Macmillan himself, who reached political maturity in the 30s, when the ideological right seemed to have failed.

One attempt to change the leadership went off half-cocked in 1989, but after Howe's devastating resignation speech in the Commons in 1990 (in Mrs Thatcher's own words, 'cool, forensic, light at points, and poisonous. ... this final act of bile and treachery'[9]), Michael Heseltine was emboldened to strike, wounding her fatally.

Since then, the Tories have been divided largely between those who regret that incident, and those who thought it necessary for victory in 1992. Whatever the truth of that, the succession has been a disaster, and it is only since the ascent of Michael Howard that the lancing of the boil has looked possible.

John Major's problem was that he was neither as combative as Mrs Thatcher, nor as ideologically driven. He had the advantages of being (a) not a toff, like Douglas Hurd for instance, and therefore supposedly more acceptable in our egalitarian age, (b) untainted by plotting or faction membership, having risen from pretty well nowhere, and (c) not Michael Heseltine. But it soon went wrong. Mrs Thatcher unhelpfully (and arguably inaccurately[10]) decided that Mr Major had betrayed the ideological cause. He proved incapable of steering a course between the pro-Europeans and the Eurosceptics, whose antagonism was multiplied tenfold as Europe was the ostensible issue that brought Mrs Thatcher down. Major's Chancellor Norman Lamont became a laughing stock after Black Wednesday. And, as we have seen, Labour came up with not one but two consecutive electable leaders. After the euphoria of Mr Major's 1992 election victory, his experience of the premiership became very sour, and he resigned immediately after his heavy defeat in 1997. The long period of unpopular Tory government had merely cemented their bad reputation with the voters.

In opposition, the only tangible note of progress has been the laying to rest of the European issue; a thoroughgoing yet moderate Euroscepticism has prevailed. But William Hague otherwise failed to dispel the general dislike of the Tories. Having tried to make the Tories inclusive and 'modern', he panicked in the face of poor poll ratings and moved the party sharply to the right.[11] Big mistake.[12] He also managed to wound the party still further by introducing a truly terrible method of electing the leader, who can be fired by the parliamentary party but is hired by the grass roots members.[13]

The first – and so far only – 'beneficiary' of this system was Iain Duncan Smith. He had difficulty not only commanding the support of the parliamentary party, but also in improving the Tories' organisation, and was widely derided as an inept leader. His years as a rebel against John Major made it impossible for him to appeal to loyalty. So, despite his producing an interesting and thoughtful set of policies,[14] he was eventually deposed after poor opinion polls and allegations of financial scandal involving his wife (of which they were exonerated). The parliamentary party then – for the first time since 1990 – showed evidence of the traditional Tory will to win[15] by by-passing the party membership and ensuring that only a single candidate stood.[16] Michael Howard has only a small amount of time to motivate his team and chip away at Mr Blair; victory in 2005/6 may be too much to expect, but he should at a minimum hope to put the Tories within striking distance of Labour.

So, how do the Tories shape up against the lessons from Labour's renaissance which we set out in Table 1?

Table 2: Have the Tories learned from Labour?

	Problem	Tory progress
1	Unpopularity	Much of the Tories' problem with the electorate stems from their social illiberalism in a liberal age. Michael Portillo, the most liberal of the serious candidates for the leadership, has been decisively rejected, and is leaving the Commons. Indeed, there is a question as to his suitability; the Tories have to be pulled and persuaded in a liberal direction, not pushed against their will. Mr Howard and Oliver Letwin have made some of the right noises; we shall have to see.
2	Lack of trust	It is not yet clear that Mr Howard is untainted by the years of Tory strife. He, as a savage Home Secretary, was at one time probably the most unpopular (and illiberal) politician in the land.

Table 2: Continued

	Problem	Tory progress
3	Organisational defects	After the wasted Hague and Duncan Smith years,[17] Mr Howard has acted to improve the party organisation.[18]
4	Causing division	The Tories are beginning to sound like a coalition of interests once more, rather than a narrow ideologically driven clique.
5	Inept positioning	Mr Howard has talked of taking the Tories back to the centre. As yet, it is not clear how – if he manages it – he will differentiate himself from Mr Blair.
6	Failure to understand history and context	As yet, we do not know if Mr Howard has understood and accepted the changes that Mr Blair has made in Britain.
7	Lack of unity	The very good news is that the Tories, after a few wobbly moments, are in no danger of splitting. But they are feeling the pressure from the UK Independence Party, and need to resist the temptation to move right to combat that threat.
8	Lack of pragmatism	Again good news: the unopposed re-election of Mr Howard (despite there being no shortage of hungry candidates) showed the desire to avoid another damaging and protracted campaign, and therefore the will to put differences aside and focus on Labour.
9	Lack of intellectual clout	There is, as yet, no obvious ideological underpinning to the Tories; many of their intellectual leaders of the 70s and 80s (e.g. Oakeshott, Friedman, Nozick) have been somewhat marginalised since then. Their damaging dithering over student fees is symptomatic.[19] Although the ideas that students take responsibility for their own education (responsibility being empowering), and that fees should vary according to the quality of the course they take, seem central to virtually every strand of Tory thought, the Tories under both Mr Duncan Smith and Mr Howard preferred to oppose these ideas to discomfit Mr Blair in the short term (and to enable a juicy bribe for the middle classes).

This is a book about ideology, specifically about the conservative ideology. Ideology is not the whole solution to the Tory malaise. But it has to be part of any long-term fix. About half the issues listed above concern ideology, and the Tories' problems in creating and sustaining an ideology acceptable to the voters of the 21st century. In particular, we can look at the arguments germane to points 1, 4, 5, 6 and 9.

Our aim in this book, then, is to try to suggest how, ideologically, the Tories can appeal to uncommitted voters, while simultaneously capturing enough of their history and tradition to sustain continuity with the great figures of their past. This is not an easy trick to pull: a backward-looking party, as the Tories have often been, risks looking increasingly anachronistic as time moves on; the conservative response to modernity is of necessity problematic. This book will try to suggest one way that the trick can be carried off. We must begin by examining past reasons for Tory success.

The Conservative century

The Tories began the 20th century as they left it, in fairly bad shape. The long Victorian twilight of Lord Salisbury[20] ended with political failure; he was succeeded in 1902 by Arthur Balfour, a philosopher of some note but not a man of great political skill. Balfour, incidentally, was Salisbury's nephew, and his rapid rise was attributed less to his genius and more to his family connections (Salisbury's given name was Robert Cecil, and his uninhibited promotion of his nephew gave rise to the expression 'Bob's your uncle!').

The Tories fell apart over the issue of tariff reform, rather as they fell apart over Europe in more recent memory. As with monetary union today, the issue was central to economic and political affairs, although the recondite arguments, fanatical certainties and lack of consensus left voters cold. It took the Tories a decade to become electable again, after which, although they didn't always furnish the Prime Minister, it was the Tory majority in the Commons that underpinned a number of coalitions. The Tories dominated the inter-war years, in both election results and policy, and even when the appeasement-minded Tory governments of Baldwin and Chamberlain in the 30s were discredited, it was the opposition of brilliant up-and-coming Tories that propelled another Tory (of liberal instincts), Churchill, to the position of war leader.

The period 1945–79 was driven by a dialectic of corporatist doctrine (an extension of wartime measures of control and management) with the new libertarian free market ideas being developed by thinkers such as Hayek.[21] Even when corporatism flourished, and a roughly left wing consensus seemed in the ascendancy, as often as not the nation trusted the Tories to administer such policies. Since 1979, the Tories have set the intellectual agenda (indeed, it was from about this time that business-oriented terminology, like 'agenda', became so sadly *de rigeur* in political discourse, reaching its apotheosis in the dreary functionaries of New Labour). As noted above, Mr Blair is attempting to reconfigure socialism for existence in the new Thatcherite world.

It is an impressive record of success. Indeed, the 20th century has been called 'the Conservative Century'.[22] Why was that the case, and why have they lost their golden touch so spectacularly?

The unideological party

In their revues of the 1950s, Flanders and Swann poked gentle fun at middle-class mores of the day. One of Michael Flanders' introductory monologues (improbably to a song about a gnu) included the following passage:

> Well, I wrote to the local council about this. Very nice about it, you know, elections coming up and so on. We have got a jolly decent lot of old burghers on our council. Get them sticking up flags on the town hall, I'll tell you that much. But then our council is, of course, strictly non-political. They're all Conservatives.[23]

In our own time, after Mrs Thatcher and Sir Keith Joseph, after the infatuations with monetarism and Hayek, this is not a joke that one could make. Far from bumbling along, the Tories have often made a point of maintaining that much was wrong with Britain and that they knew what was right; they have torn up many long-standing institutions and replaced them with new ways of doing things.

Historically, this is a very odd situation. The 19th-century progressive philosopher John Stuart Mill famously called the Tories the 'stupid party'. What an insult that was intended to be, redolent of Thackeray's *Vanity Fair*, of fat claret-swilling swells living off the income of giant swathes of inherited land, their tenants working hard for long hours to support their consumption, their travels, their gambling and their snobbery. How surprised Mill and his intellectual descendants have been, then, to see the Tories not only not be offended by his insult, but almost welcome it positively. Many Tories' self-image, at least until 1975, was that of a group of sensible and responsible people unconcerned with political ideas, because ideas were the causes of trouble. They had ideas in France, which was why they had revolution and tyranny. They had ideas in Germany; indeed the German language furnishes them with lots of big abstract nouns, all made to look even more important by beginning with capital letters. No wonder they bequeathed to us such disruptive thinkers as Hegel, Marx and Nietzsche. Their undoubted brilliance hardly compensates for the trouble they caused. And the same was true nearer home: those few Tories who tried to be clever, like Iain MacLeod or Enoch Powell, were much more trouble than they were worth.*

The Tories were conservative, with a small 'c'. The wisdom of Britain, such people thought, was contained not in its books or universities, but in its ramshackle system that had grown up piecemeal over a thousand years, embodied in the parish church, in the pattern of agriculture, in the Briton's practical inventiveness, and in the judgements laid down – the same

---

* MacLeod was famously dismissed as being 'too clever by half'.

judgements, to rich and poor alike – by its judges. No doubt the system was not perfect, but the perfect is so often the enemy of the good. The system worked, conflict was rare, and that in itself was valuable. It was the duty of the British politician, on the Tory view, to make sure that everything continued to trundle on in its own way.

Commentators have long been dubious about these claims to be unideological. For example, Michael Freeden argues:

> Remarkably, proponents of conservatism have shared this deep-rooted image of anti-intellectualism. As one of them, F.J.C. Hearnshaw, remarked without a hint of apology: 'It is commonly sufficient for practical purposes if conservatives, without saying anything, just sit and think, or even if they merely sit.' Supporters and opponents notwithstanding, this line of argument cannot be adopted. Like any other concatenation of political ideas that refer to the real worlds of politics, conservatism *is* an identifiable ideology, exhibiting awareness among its producers and amenable to intelligent analysis.[24]

Political scientist Robert Eccleshall concurs.

> Nor should much credence be given to the suggestion that conservatism is different from other political doctrines because it belongs outside the realm of ideology. Those who characterise conservatism as a frame of mind often denigrate ideology as a perverted or 'alien' form of knowledge ... consisting of speculative notions which foster the illusion that the political order can be dramatically improved. Conservatives, in contrast, allegedly attain genuine understanding of human affairs because of their pragmatic attachment to existing institutions. This insistence that conservatism is not an ideology is itself an ideological ploy by those sympathetic to the doctrine, part of the rough-and-tumble of political argument rather than an analytical exercise.[25]

I think Freeden and Eccleshall are right. Conservatism is an identifiable ideology, and I am going to try to describe it, and discuss how it might function in a rapidly changing world. As will become clear, I do not agree with them about how conservatism should properly be described. I also think conservatism is a special kind of ideology, in a way that I will try to explicate later on, and which will explain why conservatives have traditionally been able to pretend disingenuously that they are such unideological creatures.

The party of stability – and free markets

So the Tories are traditionally the party of stability. They abhor uncertainty, and they are suspicious of innovation. There are many reasons for this. First, stability and certainty are good for planning ahead. Everyone needs to plan, because people take such big risks in the normal course of events. Second, if a society functions reasonably well – as the Tories claim most Western societies do – then one should have a very good reason to change the way that it works. Third, industry and wealth depend on sensible, timely and lucrative investment, and investment is higher, other things being equal, when there are fewer uncertainties about the future. Fourth, co-operation between people (and organisations such as firms, charities or governments) is greater if everyone behaves predictably, and does business along familiar lines.

The institutions that Tories have traditionally looked towards in order to promote stability in Britain are a relatively small set, although that is no reason why they shouldn't look for more in the future. They fall into two groups: the institutions over which their governments have had control; and the independent institutions of which they approve.[26]

Institutions that Tory governments have traditionally used include the financial system; in particular, the currency. Tories look for a stable pound (and if we join the euro, with or without their support, they will look for a stable euro). Governments usually spend more money than they can really afford, and in order to pay for the excess they are often tempted to print more money. This is an inflationary pressure, and the value of one's cash, one's investments and one's debts will vary unpredictably, making planning and investment hard. Sound money is one important Tory credo.

Another is the rule of law. Clear laws, applied to rich and poor, strong and weak alike, which have the support of most people, make social interaction stable, and – if crafted well – promote the kind of behaviour Tories instinctively approve of. Lawbreaking is a serious issue for Tories, and just because a law is thought to be unjust, for example, that is no reason to break it out of some adherence to a policy of civil disobedience (this in complete opposition to the liberal idea that civil disobedience is one of the institutions of the rule of law). The wrong caused by the disobedience will almost always, says the Tory, outweigh the wrong caused by the unjust law, because the former will undermine the rule of law in its entirety.

A third is the defence of the realm. The Tories are wary of disruption from within, but are also mindful of the dangers of disruption from without. Hence a strong defence capability is essential – and indeed military muscle is very important to project Britain's voice on the world stage. The real peace dividend at the end of the Cold War was not that a country could spend less on defence, but that the money it *did* spend would buy more power internationally. The Tories are keen to ensure that the system of international relations enables Britain's interests to be pursued successfully.

A fourth is property. It is essential, for the Tories, that everyone feels included in a society, and that as few people as possible should think it worth their while to change it. Property is a key element in making people feel that they are part of a society, that they benefit from being in the society, and so the Tories have generally supported a mild materialism, often expressed through the ownership of one's own home.

The independent institutions of which the Tories approve include the Church (specifically the Church of England, which used to be known as the Tory Party at prayer), the family, and business. However, these are proving disappointing. The Anglican Church is becoming a pretty left wing organisation, to the left of the Labour Party, never mind the Tories. Even when it takes a moral lead, it is often not the moral lead that the Tories would be interested in. And its adherents are smaller in number every year (for the Tory, these facts are not unconnected).

Fewer and fewer people live in the stable family units that the Tories prefer, and more families than ever are dysfunctional. Business, which likes a winner, has also migrated to the hegemonic Labour Party, creating a rather vicious circle for the Tories. The Tories need money to make inroads into the Labour majority, but as long as that majority looks invincible, the people with lots of money will continue to back the winning horse, and ignore the also-rans, however ideologically agreeable. However, some types of business retain Tory support, for example private health care organisations and private schooling.

Given all this, a major problem for the Tories, which we will discuss in Chapter Five, and throughout Part Two of this book, is how their philosophy can function in a world that is changing all the time, that appears to be inherently unstable and uncertain, and in which the Tories' traditional allies no longer share their basic instincts.

Another interesting issue, which we will discuss in Chapter Six, is the Tories' long-standing support for free markets. There are many good reasons for such support. But one thing that has to be said about free markets is that they are not inherently stable. Indeed, stability has been substantially greater under the Chancellorship of Gordon Brown than under the eighteen years of Tory government that preceded it, which began with an engineered bust, then proceeded with an engineered boom, which turned to bust once more; since 1997, in contrast, growth has been steady, and for good measure better than most of the UK's competitors most of the time.

Indeed, one commentator has gone so far as to claim, at some length, that the adoption of the free market ideology, and the rapid altering and reconfiguring of many of the institutions of government under the Thatcher and Major governments, have destroyed the traditional Tory philosophy. The institutions which provide the continuity essential for stability have all gone, and the comfortable middle-class life, to which the upwardly mobile Tory voters of the Thatcher years aspired, has gone with them. There is, no doubt, more money to be made for the enterprising, but that requires entrepreneurial energy – and the spectre of bankruptcy and insecurity makes the effort of climbing the greasy pole seem less worthwhile. Tory policy during the 80s and 90s, according to this analysis, was self-undermining. It relied on aspirational Tories for votes, at the same time that the lifestyle to which they aspired was being destroyed by Thatcherite reforms.[27]

Party and ideology

The attentive reader will have noticed that I have so far referred to the Conservative Party as the Tory Party, to Conservatives as Tories. There is a reason for that, which has become clearer in the above discussion. Conservatism is a philosophy, an ideology, and those who profess it are conservatives. In general, conservatives are members of the Conservative Party; that is, conservatives are Conservatives. Conservatives (with a small 'c'), as their name suggests, prefer where possible to conserve; they are not radical, they distrust innovation. This is not always true of Conservatives with a big 'C' (= members of the Conservative Party); Mrs Thatcher's free market policies changed the political landscape (sometimes even the physical landscape) of Britain, for better or worse, dramatically. She was a radical, of the liberal tradition (which the Conservative Party has continued to an extent since her deposition).[28] Her instinct was not at all to conserve, not at all to avoid disruption.

There is nothing wrong with this *per se* – the Conservative Party is and always has been a broad church. It contains not only liberals and conservatives, but also libertarians, businessmen and women, and moral atavists among others. Understandably, practising Conservative politicians have been keen to emphasise the ideas they hold in common.[29] But there has been a tendency to equate conservatism with 'that which the Conservative Party does', which seems to miss the point, given all these different views.

Michael Freeden calls the idea of several ideologies within the Conservative Party a 'chimera',[30] though one might be forgiven for thinking that the chimera in this case was the hybrid 'ideology' he specifies. Similarly, political theorist W.H. Greenleaf wrote in 1983 about the 'twin inheritance of Conservatism' – though note how the issue is confused when the capital letter is used; does that mean an ideological follower of conservatism, or a member of the Conservative Party? The twin inheritance is that of Tory paternalism and free market liberalism, the two particularly prominent views held within the Conservative Party.

> There remains the continuing assertion that there *must* be common characteristics in Conservatism (or any other ideology) of a meaningful and distinguishing kind. But, whatever its superficial appeal, this claim must be denied, and the counter-question asked: What *are* the aims, arguments and assumptions that are shared by Stafford Northcote and R.A. Butler, Joseph Chamberlain and Enoch Powell, Mallock and Macmillan, a Central Office pamphlet issued in (say) 1927 and the notions of Sir Keith Joseph? They do not even necessarily oppose the same things.[31]

Greenleaf is wary of distinguishing between party and ideology (although then what is Enoch Powell, who had by then left the Conservative Party in disgust, doing in his list?). And he is of course correct that ideologues of different periods may well have different priorities, depending, among other things, on who their perceived enemies may be. But claiming that conservatism means being a member of the Conservative Party, and *vice versa*, glosses over many interesting phenomena, as well as playing fast and loose with the original definition of 'conservative' – someone wanting to conserve.

Political researcher Bruce Pilbeam thinks that if conservatism is understood in this relatively straightforward sense, the result-ing class is too wide, and so the definition is flawed.

> Taking a bare attitude towards change as defining of con-servatism leads, on the one hand, to denying the label to the very many avowed conservatives who have actively sought change (such as advocates of dismantling the welfare state), and, on the other, to the inclusion within the ideology's boundaries of many who would not ordinarily be con-sidered conservatives (such as Soviet communists who defended their regime during the Cold War).[32]

To be honest, it doesn't seem absurd to me to lump together people of different positions who try to avoid change, be they English barons, Soviet generals or Iranian mullahs. But when we examine conservatism a little more closely, as we will in Part One below, we will find an interesting theme running through its history of a robust scepticism, and this in itself will rule out many who simply try to avoid change because they are doing rather well out of the status quo. Such a position is a natural selfishness, rather than anything ideological.

The point I have been belabouring in this section is that there is a distinction between conservatives (with a small 'c') and Conservatives. The former occupy an ideological position which I will specify; the latter are members of a particular political party. Many conservatives are Conservatives, and *vice versa*, but it is perfectly possible to be one without the other. The Conservative Party is the natural custodian of the ideology of conservatism, but has rather neglected it for the last 30 years. My argument in this book will be that attempting to re-establish conservatism as a viable philosophy for the 21st century may well be a way for the Conservative Party to regain the political centre while simultaneously providing differentiation from Blairism. But equally, it would be possible for members of other parties to be conservatives in the sense I will describe; when Mr Blair railed against the forces of conservatism, he did not mean to restrict his bile to members of the Tory Party.[33] It is perfectly possible to be a conservative of the left (for example, defending the current structures of our public services against Blairite reform).

So, in this book, orthography (and proof-reading!) are all-important. When I write 'conservative' with a small 'c' I specifically mean someone who holds the conservative ideology, whichever party he is in, or even if not in any party at all. When I write 'Conservative' with a capital 'C', I mean a member of the party, whatever ideological stance he takes. If there's an ambiguity, because the word appears at the beginning of a sentence for example, I'll take care to disambiguate. That small 'c' is vital to meaning.

With a small 'c'

Our enquiry, like Caesar's Gaul, is divided into three parts. The first part will raid history and philosophy to gather materials for a firm definition, and intellectual tradition, of conservatism, up to the point at which the Conservative Party became the representative in Britain of the conservative interest. We shall trace conservatism as an attitude to theory and knowledge, from the Ancient Greeks, via the transmission of their work to Renaissance Europe, and thence to Britain, showing how scepticism became a political attitude (Chapter Two). Next, we will follow conservatism in the Conservative Party, and try to show how a version of 19th-century liberalism took the party over, eventually replacing its conservative host in 1975 (Chapter Three). Given that intellectual and political history, we will then try to develop a definition of conservatism that is consistent with it, drawing in passing on the work of more recent conservative thinkers like Michael Oakeshott and Roger Scruton (Chapter Four). The final task of this opening part is to counter arguments, from commentators such as Anthony Giddens and John Gray, that conservatism, along the lines we have defined it, is necessarily dead in the rapidly changing post-Thatcher world (Chapter Five).

The second part of our enquiry looks at what would happen

were the Conservatives to make a committed attempt to replace their current liberal free market ideology with a conservatism such as we have described, as an attempt to take a non-Blairite central position. Three particular issues are examined: the key policy areas of economics and markets (Chapter Six), and social affairs (Chapter Seven); and an area where Conservatives currently score rather badly, but where – I shall argue – conservatives might actually do rather well: the collapse of public trust in authority (Chapter Eight).

The final part of the book will look at how the Tories have coped with the demands of opposition to one of the two most formidable Prime Ministers of the last half-century. We examine the ideological directions of the three leaders in opposition, William Hague and Iain Duncan Smith (Chapter Nine) and Michael Howard (Chapter Ten). How have they dealt with the difficult mix between Thatcherite liberal radicalism and traditional conservatism? Is the mix sound? Or attractive? On such questions, I shall argue, the fortunes of the Conservative Party will ride.

PART ONE

WHAT IS CONSERVATISM?

When, he'd say, we study the various types of industrial-ization in advanced countries, for example, we find they're like revolutions imposed on those societies from above; they're the work of ruthless minorities who aren't to be swayed from the goals they've set, and regard all obstacles to progress as solvable by technical and rational means. He found this imposed rationalism disturbing, because its advocates chose to view society as being susceptible to rational arrangement through a mixture of acumen and power, and any irrational elements discovered within the societal foundations had to be resolutely mastered and changed in accordance with the needs of the advocates of rationalism themselves.

Jabra Ibrahim Jabra, *In Search of Walid Masoud*
Translated by Roger Allen and Adnan Haydar

People, I have seen the doubt:
the lovely ambiguities of light and dusk.
Who wouldn't wish to share
this cherished jamais vu
of knowing next to nothing?

Peter Armstrong, 'Homage to Joe English'

CHAPTER TWO

THE IDEA OF HUMAN IMPERFECTION: A WHISTLESTOP TOUR

Socrates, morality and knowledge

The question this book addresses was posed in Chapter One: how can the Conservative Party regain the centre ground in British politics while retaining the essential continuity with its ideological roots? Of course this is a hard problem! It is easy to see political debate as being obsessed with the affairs of the moment – tuition fees, the Iraq War, congestion charging, tax cuts or whatever – because that is what politicians argue about. But, for a principled politician, ideological considerations always underlie the crude day-to-day parliamentary knock-about. Hence, straightening out those considerations, perhaps altering, perhaps merely coming to understand them properly, could well lead to a breakthrough in understanding how a political party, whose fortunes might be waning, could make itself relevant in a new context. It was such a first-principles examination of the socialist tradition that enabled Tony Blair to revitalise the left, for instance by unpicking the neat assumption, formulated during the Second World War, that the state was the essential architect of measures to redistribute wealth and to ensure equitable access to resources.

To pull a similar trick for the Conservative Party, we need a similar examination of their ideological traditions, though the task is complicated by the different ideological strands present within the party. It is of course a matter of taste as to which strand one thinks is most useful and important; I propose to examine its small 'c' conservative strand. To unpick this tradition, in the same way as Mr Blair's examination of socialism, requires stripping away the interests of the moment from conservative writings and rhetoric, and understanding what are their basic elements. Surprisingly, the basic ideas of conservatism are concerned not with morality, or economics, or human nature, or any of the standard subject matters of ideologies: conservatism is actually a claim made about human understanding and knowledge of the world, a plea for humility in the face of the widely differing sources of knowledge in the world.

The story of conservatism – the strand of conservatism with which we are particularly concerned – is a long one. We must travel back two and a half millennia, to the Ancient Greeks, to see its beginnings. The Greeks were a fascinating people, gregarious, curious, disputatious. They studied everything, and had theories about everything, many of which were horribly wide of the mark.[1] But that did not stop them arguing about them.

Our interest begins with Socrates (469–399 BC), a philosopher who wrote nothing; he merely argued (for this he was executed). There are first-hand accounts of him still extant, which paint incompatible pictures of him. But the abiding view of him is shaped by Plato, in whose philosophical dialogues Socrates is the main character.[2] In these brilliant vignettes, Socrates is witty, original and devastatingly destructive. The only thing he knows, he says, is that he knows nothing. He then takes on his interlocutors – all of whom claim knowledge about some philosophical concept, justice, say, or beauty – and demonstrates, merely by asking suggestive questions, that they actually know as little as he (except that they do not know that they do not know). Doubt everything, says Socrates; take nothing on authority.

We can only guess how much of the historical Socrates has survived in these portraits. But what does seem as certain as anything is that he was concerned with *questioning*. If someone claimed to have knowledge, Socrates would leap in and try to unravel what the content of that knowledge was. Presumably he would often discover that there was nothing to the supposed 'knowledge' at all; it was all meaningless jargon and puffery. No

doubt on occasion he punctured assiduously cultivated reputations for wisdom. As a modern parallel, recall the general
attitude towards the counter-cultural professors in the universities exhorting their students to revolt in 1968. Socrates was
perhaps the earliest exponent of a sceptical attitude towards
authority, demanding to know what the basis of the authority
was. He would simply ask questions, and lead his opponent into
various admissions that were either inconsistent with each other,
or deeply implausible, or otherwise unconvincing, earning him
great admiration from those thinkers who had grown impatient
with the fantastic proliferation of views, theories and ideas in
Greek intellectual life.

The schools of ancient scepticism

Socrates was not as deep a sceptic as it is possible to be, however.
Like some of his fellows (Xenophanes, Empedocles or Democritus, for instance), his view seems to have been that knowledge
is desirable, and that man had up till then failed to achieve it. If
knowledge was necessarily and completely unattainable, that
was a matter of regret. Socrates always remained an important
role model for sceptics, but he was essentially pessimistic.
Scepticism proper began when some philosophers started to
think not only that knowledge was unattainable, but that that
was a *good* thing; it was not a symptom of man's bleak fate in a
world that was doomed to be for ever foreign to him, but rather
a liberation from certain types of desire, certain types of error,
and certain types of pressure.[3]

The philosopher who is credited with this discovery is Pyrrho
of Elis (c. 365–c. 275 BC). Like Socrates, he wrote nothing, and all
we have of him are some near-first-hand accounts of which we
possess only fragments.[4] Pyrrho thought that knowledge about
the world was impossible, that the world was, in his reported
words, undifferentiated, unmeasurable and unjudgeable. Hence
enquiry about the world was pointless; Pyrrho's follower Timon
praised him for releasing mankind from the slavery of opinion
and the bonds of deceit and persuasion.

Pyrrho's ideas fell into obscurity after the death of Timon, but his name was spectacularly revived by a philosopher called Aenesidemus (who lived sometime at the beginning of the 1st century BC). Falling out with the 'official' sceptics, the intellectual followers of Socrates in the Academy originally founded by Plato, he stalked out, taking his new philosophy with him. In honour of his great predecessor, he called it *Pyrrhonism*.[5] This was focused on methods for creating doubt and uncertainty, ways to show that a dogmatically held theory was false. In particular, he thought that even the sceptics themselves were too dogmatic, not sceptical enough. They asserted dogmatically that knowledge was impossible. Aenesidemus wouldn't even have that. In his version of Pyrrhonism, no doubt some bits of knowledge might be true, but no one could ever know which. Maybe true knowledge was impossible, maybe not; the Pyrrhonist was agnostic over such questions. He wouldn't even claim that Pyrrhonism was true, only that the methods it espoused induced a spiritual calm.

Aenesidemus' work is completely lost, and the intellectual trail of Pyrrhonism goes cold for a while. But with the appearance in the 2nd century AD of an obscure doctor called Sextus Empiricus, Pyrrhonism becomes highly visible indeed.

Sextus Empiricus

Sextus Empiricus was not a great philosopher; nor did he claim to be one. But he does have a giant place in intellectual history, thanks to the ironies of fate. Whereas Aenesidemus, an original figure, remains obscure, Sextus is important because of the historical accident that his work has *survived*.

No doubt much of Sextus' work has been lost,[6] but there is still a decent quantity left. Most crucially, there is a piece called *Outlines of Pyrrhonism*;[7] this work was intended as an introduction for the layman, a textbook of the philosophy of Aenesidemus. It is this that has ensured that Pyrrhonism survived into the modern era, its textbook qualities ensuring that the work got read much more than the originals.

Despite this relative wealth of material, there are many doubts about what Pyrrhonism actually involved. Some maintain that Sextus' argument is that knowledge of *any* type is impossible, that no one can really know anything.[8] Others say that Sextus was really only railing against the wild Greek theories of science, about the speculations of the professors who claimed to have knowledge of, say, how the human body worked, when in reality they didn't. Our ordinary common-sense knowledge of the world is perfectly OK; it is only when we try to go beyond the obvious, to postulate hidden causes, deep mysteries, that we tie ourselves in silly speculative knots.[9] Still others say that Sextus inconsistently flip-flopped between these two views.[10] Others detect a more sophisticated argument in Sextus that has to do with justification; we are never justified in believing what we believe (and hence we should never be tempted to be dogmatic).[11] Indeed, as Sextus was not a philosopher of the first rank, and was bringing together material from several sources, all of these may be the case at different places.

What is Pyrrhonism?

The actual form of Pyrrhonism is of less importance for our purposes than the reaction to it and its influences on later thinkers, which we will trace in this chapter. Sextus left us a method for analysing arguments, based on the philosophy of Aenesidemus,[12] which does contain a nugget of effectiveness.[13] Here is not the place to go into details, but in a nutshell, the basis of Pyrrhonism is this.

Suppose there is some contested issue, let's say the existence of God. This has been debated for centuries, and the various positions have become very well worn. Suppose I advance an argument that God in fact does exist, and that He has some particular nature. Then you will without doubt be able to find arguments, from thinkers greater than I, that God does not exist, and other arguments, from other great thinkers, that He does exist, but that He is very different from the being I supposed. And to your arguments, I will be able to find counter-arguments, and so on. The only result of our discussion is to demonstrate the equipollence, or equal strength (*isostheneia*), of the arguments, the fact that each point of view can muster convincing arguments in its favour, arguments moreover that come with the endorsement of great intellectual figures.

Furthermore, at most one of the theories about God can be correct, yet they all come with clever arguments attached – hence a clever argument (even one I am unable to refute) is not, in itself, evidence that a view is correct. In the face of the complexity and intractability of the world, cleverness will never be enough. On some deep issue, for example a social or philosophical issue, there may well be a fact of the matter about which we are speculating, but we are simply not equipped to find it. This sceptical insight is the essential thread that will take us from the Greeks through to the 21st century.

Why would I choose one point of view over the other? If more brilliant people than I have failed to show convincingly that they are right and that others are wrong, why would I be able to advance the position any? If, for example, such geniuses as St Thomas Aquinas or René Descartes cannot prove the existence of God, and other geniuses like Voltaire or Nietzsche cannot prove the opposite, what on earth can I add to the debate? Much better, says Sextus, to forget the question, to cease to worry about the issue. No doubt there is a right and a wrong side of the argument. No doubt either St Thomas or Voltaire is correct. But I don't and can't know which; furthermore, nor did St Thomas or Voltaire. I cannot decide the matter, so why should I let it bother me? I should suspend my belief (*epoche*), and this will lead to a feeling of well-being and relaxation (*ataraxia*) – and after all, isn't a feeling of well-being what we're all really after?

What about those who reply that the Pyrrhonist undermines his own argument by saying that no one can know the truth of these weighty matters? The Pyrrhonist replies that he also knows nothing about the decidability of the argument between St Thomas and Voltaire. He does not know that nothing is knowable (if he did claim that, then of course he would be contradicting himself: if he knew nothing could be known, then he would know something, viz., that nothing could be known, and therefore it could not be true that *nothing* could be known). It is only that he is unable to decide between the point of view that the original argument is decidable, and the opposite point of view that it is not decidable. And he can't decide that question for the same reason that he can't decide the original question, i.e. because lots of equally powerful arguments from great thinkers can be piled up on each side of the issue.

Such, then, is Pyrrhonism. Why should Sextus think that Pyrrhonism was attractive? We know very little of Sextus, but the clue is that he seems to have been a doctor. The Greeks had lots of medical theories of how the body worked. Some thought that it was made up of the hot, the cold, the wet and the dry; others that there were bodily humours, for example black bile, yellow bile, blood and phlegm, and so on. The treatment of disease involved rebalancing these humours, for example by purgatives, emetics or bloodletting.[14] There was much, and fierce, argument about exactly what treatment should accompany which symptoms.

We should not, of course, be ungenerous to the Greek physicians, but equally we can't help but note that these scientific theories are all incorrect, to put it mildly. And no doubt many of the treatments came closer to killing than curing. A movement arose in medicine called *empiricism*, which was based as far as possible on eschewing theories and just observing symptoms.[15] If a particular treatment had dealt well with a particular symptom in the past, then that was a *prima facie* reason to try it again – though the physician couldn't know for sure that it would work for a second time. The idea was to build up, slowly and steadily, a portfolio of case studies.

Sextus was almost certainly a physician of this sort of persuasion;[16] indeed the name Sextus Empiricus means 'Sextus the empiricist'. And there is obviously a close link between the empiricist rejection of theory on practical grounds, and the Pyrrhonist idea that there are always clever arguments, between which it is impossible to decide, for and against any theory.

41

Both philosophies were reactions to the intellectual cacophony of the Greeks, the interminable disputation that seemed essential to the Ancient Greek character.

Scepticism and conservatism

This type of scepticism about knowledge and authority, though it might seem revolutionary and even conducive to libertinism, actually promoted a rather acquiescent position. Pyrrho himself, for example, believed that, as no moral standard could be established by reason (or be self-evident), then the wise man should conform to the laws, norms and conventions of the society of the day.[17] Sextus also recommended conformity in a famous and influential passage.

> Adhering, then, to appearances we live in accordance with the normal rules of life, undogmatically, seeing that we cannot remain wholly inactive. And it would seem that this regulation of life is fourfold, and that one part of it lies in the guidance of Nature, another in the constraint of the passions, another in the tradition of laws and customs, another in the instruction of the arts. Nature's guidance is that by which we are naturally capable of sensation and thought; constraint of the passions is that whereby hunger drives us to food and thirst to drink; tradition of customs and laws, that whereby we regard piety in the conduct of life as good but impiety as evil; instruction of the arts, that whereby we are not inactive in such arts as we adopt. But we make all these statements undogmatically.[18]

In other words, we have to make moral choices in our daily lives, but we can never know which moral choice is correct. It is therefore sensible to adhere to the customs of one's society, which after all are as likely to be correct as any other position.

The wisdom of basing one's moral and political behaviour on the customs of the country was also confirmed from another source. The restless Greeks had explored far and wide, and had amassed quite a literature on other cultures (most notably the works of Herodotus[19]). The variety they found chimed in with the idea that social regularities were accidents, matters of taste rather than manifestations of any kind of moral law.[20]

Such accidents were worth attending to.

> For perchance the Sceptic, as compared with philosophers of other views, will be found in a safer position, since in conformity with his ancestral customs and the laws, he declares that the Gods exist, and performs everything which contributes to their worship and veneration, but, so far as regards philosophic investigation, declines to commit himself rashly.[21]

Note here what is very clear: that the sceptic conforms to the norms of his age for his own self-interest. It keeps him from being attacked for non-conformity, and it also saves him having to think too deeply about matters that he cannot resolve – it brings the positive benefits of *ataraxia*. The result is a *type* of conservatism, but the strong element of self-interest means that Pyrrhonism has yet to become the conservatism that we understand today.

Before we leave the ancient world, we might pause to defend Pyrrhonism against many who argue that Greek scepticism is irrelevant in our modern world of science and technology. In the context of the world of the 2nd century AD, Sextus was, in the detail, pretty well *right*. If we take a generous interpretation of Sextus' often inconsistent texts, he is saying that common-sense understanding of the world is more or less OK, while speculative theories are wrong.[22] Given the situation in Ancient Greece, when science was at best nascent, the theories adduced by philosophers and thinkers were almost always false. Even when correct, as with the atomic theory of matter developed by Democritus, they happened to be right accidentally, for the wrong reasons.[23] If my shot in the dark hits the target and yours doesn't, that does not mean that I am a better shot than you.

On the other hand, the Pyrrhonists never dogmatically

claimed that knowledge was *impossible*. It turns out that we have gradually developed ways of accumulating knowledge about non-evident things; most notably science is fairly reliable. Hence a Pyrrhonist could admit that (some) scientific theories might be usable for knowledge acquisition. Doubtless he would continue to be critical and sceptical of all but the most confirmed theories; but there is nothing in ancient Pyrrhonism that rules out accepting (parts of) modern science.

And therefore one could be a Pyrrhonist today.

The transmission of ancient scepticism to the Renaissance

Sextus gained some celebrity, but was the last of the major sceptics. The world was changing in the 2nd and 3rd centuries AD, and the sceptical, challenging frame of mind had little place in it. The dynamic tension of the Greek city states had been replaced by the bureaucratic vigour and murderous political strife of the Roman Empire. Such conditions do not reward adventurous thinking.

Furthermore, Christianity was on the march, becoming the dominant framework for thought and politics. Scepticism was out; the essence of Christianity was certainty, the word of God through the Bible. The insight of Pyrrhonism – that clever theories are not necessarily informative about the world – was made irrelevant by the increasing acceptance that you could scour your Bible, or works of respected churchmen, for telling evidence one way or the other. The heavy hand of religious authority suffocated scepticism, for the time being at least.

And so the Pyrrhonists were gradually forgotten. In Western Europe, there was no mention of Sextus Empiricus for a thousand years or so. During the long dark ages, many ancient texts were lost; there are no doubt major philosophers, mathematicians and thinkers of all stripes of whom we are totally ignorant. But fortunately some of Sextus' manuscripts were preserved in libraries in Byzantium; Sextus' knack of bringing together arguments from different people, and of summarising the positions of other philosophers, including those of whom he disapproved – the skill of the textbook writer – meant that his work was occasionally consulted by Greek-speaking Byzantines and Arab scholars,[24] while the more technical, and perhaps more philosophically correct, works of his predecessors were neglected. This occasional consultation was just enough to keep the flame burning low.

Three developments in the late medieval period conspired to rekindle scepticism. The first was the nature of the Church. In the centuries following Sextus, the Church was for Christians pretty well the only source of hope, of intellectual comfort – one might almost say, of civilisation were it not for the Moorish kingdoms in Spain. But by the middle ages, the Church had abused its monopoly so flagrantly that its authority (if not its political and military power) had declined dramatically. Intellectual rebellions against corruption, sales of indulgences and the dissolute lifestyles of supposedly abstemious men, rebellions that were ultimately to lead to the Reformation, were under way. Hence there was once more a space for philosophies that questioned authority.

Second, while Christianity and the Bible remained paramount, other methods of understanding the world were gaining currency. Science, or something like it, was beginning to emerge. Mathematics and logic seemed to provide ways of achieving absolute certainty. This led to an obvious question: would these other methods of acquiring knowledge lead the inquirer to a belief in God? In other words, could you use your reason to establish the truth about God? What if reason issued in the wrong results? There was scriptural justification for worry about this: St Paul, for example, had often argued that the Holy Word was more important than any learning ('knowledge puffeth up, but charity edifieth'[25]). But logical thought seems so compelling. Is it possible to find things out about God without reading the Bible, without prayer, without faith? This had always been a source of tension for the Church, but as the medieval thinkers gradually recovered their intellectual confidence, the question became more pressing.

Third, the greater curiosity of the age, and the greater stability which allowed more travel and trade, meant that thinkers from the West began to rediscover the classical thinkers once more, often via translations out of Greek, into Arabic and thence to Latin (though all Sextus' work survived in Greek). Interest in the ancients began to spread, an intellectual movement known as *humanism*.

Sextus was one of the posthumous beneficiaries of the fashion. The first interested Western owner of a manuscript of Sextus' work was Francesco Filelfo (1398–1481), a manuscript that is now probably in Florence.[26] The early Italian humanists were mainly interested in the work for its antiquarian value. But gradually, thinkers began to take more notice of what Sextus' work actually said, and began to re-evaluate Pyrrhonism on its own terms. A number of minor Italian philosophers began to use the destructive critical methods that his work contained, notably Gianfrancesco Pico della Mirandola (1469–1533).[27] But Pyrrhonism's second wind really arrived in the 1560s, when Latin translations began to appear, and the scene of the action switched from Italy to France.

Montaigne

Michel Eyquem de Montaigne (1533–92) was one of the greatest, one of the most likeable, and one of the most unsystematic of all European intellectuals. After studying law, and serving for thirteen years as a magistrate in Bordeaux, he retired in 1570, at the age of 37,* to his country estate to read, to think, and to escape the fraught political situation of the day.

As he thought, so he wrote; the result was three books of almost unparalleled brilliance and humanity.[28] His short discursive takes on many and various topics provided the original model for the literary form of the essay. Montaigne revelled in the unusual, and the immediate – he saw no need for consistency, and his idea was that by ranging over this vast collection of

---

* Lucky sod.

topics, he could portray a human mind in the hopeless task of extracting sense from a vast, complex, patternless world.

The France of Montaigne's adult life was very troubled. The Reformation had created immense tensions between Catholics and Huguenots (Protestants); at the same time the Crown was trying to centralise power. France was almost ungovernable – certainly governed badly – and from 1562 to 1595 it was more often than not in a state of outright religious war.

Montaigne, a Catholic, had no time for religious intolerance – indeed, many of his own family had converted to Protestantism. What appalled him was not just the inhumanity of the wars, but also the way that the inhumanity was provoked by a strong sense of certainty about religion. Both sides naturally assumed that God was on their side. Not for the first time in history, speculative philosophy and theology, subjects that were over most people's heads and whose truths were hard if not impossible to verify, were the excuse for savagery and destruction.

So when Montaigne discovered the joy of Sextus (so to speak), and read in the *Outlines* in Latin translation that nothing is certain, and that arguments on each side of a problem generally if not always cancel each other out, he was delighted. He even struck a medal to commemorate the event, and painted quotes from Sextus on the beams of his study. Much of Montaigne's work was influenced by Pyrrhonism. He also, like Sextus, loved piling up evidence that different societies valued different things, and that none was better than any other. He loved to find travellers' tales of paradoxical societies that functioned perfectly well, and retold the stories to great effect.[29]

Montaigne certainly disliked and distrusted change. His views on human ignorance and imperfection led him to castigate the presumption of those who thought they knew how best to govern.

> ... for my humour, there is no system so bad (provided it be old and durable) as not to be better than change and innovation. ...

I find that the worst aspect of the state we are in is our lack of stability and that our laws cannot adopt one fixed form any more than our fashions can. It is easy enough to condemn a polity as imperfect since all things mortal are full of imperfection; it is easy enough to generate in a nation contempt for its ancient customs: no man has ever tried to do so without reaching his goal; but as for replacing the conditions you have ruined by better ones, many who have tried to do that have come to grief.[30]

Hence scepticism has led to the idea that people simply aren't clever or brilliant enough to understand how a society functions, or how to draft a system that will function better. But whereas Sextus (and the other Greek sceptics) were chiefly concerned with knowledge, science and philosophy, and only tangentially interested in politics, Montaigne was the opposite; he came to find Pyrrhonism exciting precisely because of the political suggestions he thought it supported.

There is no doubt that Montaigne was a Pyrrhonist sceptic for at least some of his writing life. There has been much scholarly debate about whether he was a conservative. Peter Burke has argued, sensibly enough, that the debate is not terribly interesting. 'Conservative' (small 'c') has a specific meaning and a more general meaning; the former is somewhat anachronistic, the latter is devoid of significance in the 16th-century context.

His support of outward conformity may suggest that Montaigne was a conservative. The difficulty here is that if we want to use the term in a precise sense, we have to say that a conservative is someone who opposes the liberals. In this sense, no one was a conservative in the sixteenth century. Right and Left, as names of specific parties, were born together at the French revolution. If we resolve to use the term 'conservative' in a vaguer sense, we are faced with the opposite problem. In the weak sense of the word, everyone was a conservative in the sixteenth century, for everyone, Luther no less than the pope, defended his views by appealing to tradition.[31]

And David Lewis Schaefer argues that Montaigne supported many progressive ideas, and that he was a determined anti-religious radical;[32] there is plenty of textual evidence in the *Essays* for this view.

But this leads us to perhaps Montaigne's greatest contribution to the development of conservatism out of ancient scepticism. For – rarely among political thinkers – Montaigne seems to have recognised his own ignorance just as acutely as he did that of the rest of society. He is quite happy to acknowledge that Sextus' sceptical arguments applied just as much to his, Montaigne's own, political ideas as to anyone else's. Schaefer replies that this is an 'extremely shallow' point of view,[33] but shallow or not, this use of scepticism to argue for conservatism has the brilliance and flamboyance of a jewel thief returning a tiara to a pretty girl.

> To speak frankly, it seems to me that there is a great deal of self-love and arrogance in judging so highly of your opinions that you are obliged to disturb the public peace in order to establish them, thereby introducing those many unavoidable evils and that horrifying moral corruption which, in matters of great importance, civil wars and political upheavals bring in their wake – introducing them moreover into your own country. Is it not bad husbandry to encourage so many definite and acknowledged vices in order to combat alleged and disputable error? Is any kind of vice more wicked than those which trouble the naturally recognized sense of community?[34]

However radical he 'really' was, Montaigne's contribution to a humane and civilised conservatism is immense. He did not introduce Pyrrhonism to the West; nor was he the first to associate Pyrrhonism with conservatism. His major intellectual innovation was shifting the focus of scepticism. Ancient scepticism was centred on the well-being of the sceptic himself, in three ways. First of all, the sceptical methods set out by Sextus were to be used by the sceptic to triumph in debate; the aim was a public demonstration of the sceptic's argumentative ability. Second, the use of the sceptical methods was intended to aid the sceptic to rid himself of unsupported belief, and thereby to reach a state of contented wisdom, or *ataraxia*. Third, as can clearly be seen from the quotes from Sextus above, the conservatism that Pyrrhonism supported was intended to protect the sceptic from the bad opinion of a society; it was not intended to benefit the society in any direct way.

Montaigne switched the whole thing around. The aim of Pyrrhonism as he recreated it was to benefit *society*. It was society that suffered when unsupported opinions clashed, and society that suffered when opinions and theories were implemented to right presumed wrongs. Montaigne *externalised* Pyrrhonism; he turned it from an attitude about knowledge, and an attitude towards an interlocutor, into a political attitude towards political interests and purposes. Instead of helping untangle someone's *mind*, Pyrrhonism now became a tool to promote social stability, and protect society from uninformed and unwarranted interference.

Shakespeare and the Elizabethans

In the slightly morbid atmosphere of England at this time, Montaigne's counsel of imperfection would find plenty of nourishment. Edmund Spenser's (1552–99) epic poem *The Faerie Queene*, for example, contains many passages making the point that God alone could possibly know what was best, or what fortune would hold. In one episode, the virtuous Artegall confronts a giant who is trying to restore the 'balance' of the Earth, to recreate order out of the chaos of the time.

> Such heavenly justice doth among them reign,
> > That every one do know their certain bound,
> > In which they do these many years remain,
> > And mongst them all no change hath yet been found.

> But if thou now shouldst weigh them new in pound,
> We are not sure they would so long remain:
> All change is perilous and all chance unsound.
> Therefore leave off to weigh them all again,
> Till we may be assured that they their course retain.[35]

If you try to impose a fair balance on everything, says Artegall to the giant, you are more likely to upset the present balance than produce a fairer result.

Shakespeare (1564–1616) too wrestled with problems caused by human attempts to redraw the boundaries. Many of his works were concerned with the tribulations of authority and the rejection of legitimacy. Characters try to influence events, but when they do, they quickly lose control of the situation. Such machiavels (as they were called, in honour of the notorious Italian philosopher Machiavelli) could be evil (Richard III), misguided (Macbeth) or even well-intentioned (Brutus). But their intrigues always led in the same direction. First, the new order they created could not supply justice, stability or good government. And second (most graphically demonstrated in *King Lear*), once the threat of the machiavel had been repulsed, it was not possible to restore the old order. Once a traditional society, with a legitimate ruler, had been disrupted, the delicate balance was irreplaceable.[36]

The problems of human imperfection, the vagaries of fortune, the uncertain relationship between the actions of individuals and the tribulations of society; these are all problems that Montaigne wrestled with, under the influence of many authors, Sextus Empiricus prominent among them. Sceptical ideas were spreading around Europe. Had Shakespeare read Montaigne? There is some evidence that he had, and that in particular 'On the Cannibals' could well have been one of the sources for *The Tempest*.[37]

Whatever the truth of that, as England moved from the relative stability of the Elizabethan reign to the beginnings of union with Scotland, and the inept politicking of the Stuart century, a taste for scepticism was developing.

Sir Thomas Browne and the nature of human imperfection

By the 17th century, the scepticism that had begun in antiquity was all the rage in Europe.[38] Montaigne had been championed in England by the philosopher and civil servant Sir Francis Bacon. But perhaps the Englishman most like Montaigne was a relatively minor figure, Sir Thomas Browne (1605–82), a distinguished doctor from East Anglia who had a healthy sense of the variety, unpredictability and mystery of the world. Indeed, he was rather too Montaigne-like for his own equilibrium; a placid man, he felt moved enough by a review of his *Religio Medici* to reply waspishly to his critic:

> The learned Annotator-commentator hath parallel'd many passages with other of Mountaignes essayes, whereas to deale clearly, when I penned that peece I had never read 3 leaves of that Author & scarce any more ever since.[39]

Browne's *Religio Medici* (*The Religion of a Physician*)[40] is an enchanting work, written, like Montaigne's essays, during a period of great religious controversy and strife (in Browne's case, the mid-1630s – the work circulated in pirated copies until Browne published an authorised edition in 1643). It caused controversies of its own: Browne was accused of atheism, and *Religio* was placed on the Catholic Index of Prohibited Works for three years; extreme Protestants were no less scathing, with one critic punning on the Latin title to call it a description of the religion of the notorious Medici family.

Browne was certainly not an atheist, but a moderate Anglican, and his style was informal, tolerant, and mistrustful of clever reasoning when so much of the world is uncertain and paradoxical. Argument is no sensible way of reaching agreement.

> A man may be in as just possession of Truth as of a City, and yet be forced to surrender; 'tis therefore far better to enjoy her with peace than to hazard her on a battle.[41]

The Pyrrhonist insistence on the equal power of conflicting arguments was a constant theme.

> We do but learn to-day, what our better advanced judgements will unteach to-morrow ... the wisest heads prove, at last, almost all Scepticks, and stand like *Janus* in the field of knowledge.[42]

The wisest men and women are perpetually afflicted with doubt. This leaves room for faith – indeed, theologically it positively invites it – but that faith could never be so positive as to license the religious violence that was seen in France in the 16th century and in England in the 17th. Browne's faith was relatively unusual, whimsical even; he believed strongly in witches (here he was unlike Montaigne), and even testified to that end in a trial in 1664. Though characteristically he was unconvinced that witchcraft was responsible for the victims' woes in actual cases.

English Pyrrhonism

Religio Medici had a great vogue, in both England and Europe, for decades. With it, English scepticism takes on a characteristically Pyrrhonist form. The Pyrrhonism is of a mild strain; the English Pyrrhonist does not espouse the strong form of scepticism (found on the Continent) that says that all knowledge is impossible. Instead, he or she suggests mildly that advanced theories are likely to be incorrect (experience, after all, tells us this), and that a common-sense understanding of the world will be much more important. The implication of this is that we shouldn't sacrifice the actual and concrete for the abstract and speculative, except in extreme circumstances.

Society's ills have their roots in human imperfection. But the word 'imperfection' is ambiguous. We should not focus on man's *moral* imperfection, the fall from grace, the eviction from Eden. If we do, we will be liable to veer into authoritarianism (as if others' moral vices were any of our business anyway). The desire to improve or perfect people quickly becomes the urge to eliminate those who refuse or are unable to be improved to order. Our brief examination of Montaigne and Browne shows us that the sceptical conservatism I am describing has its roots in tolerance, and the avoidance of extremes.

The imperfection of mankind has little to do with moral imperfection, but rather is an *epistemological* imperfection (i.e. imperfection of our means of gaining knowledge). The world is complex, scruffy and difficult to understand. Both Montaigne and Browne thought that God at least could understand it, but that that certainty was vouchsafed to no mortal. Such uncertainty cries out for tolerance.

If we do not keep an eye on the difference between moral and epistemological imperfection, then we risk turning sceptical conservatism from a tolerant creed to an intolerant one. From the 21st-century perspective of a troubled world, riven once more with religious and political strife, we can begin the task of reinventing conservatism as a philosophical and political tool for promoting tolerance and humility, against the malevolent certainties of extremism.

CHAPTER THREE

THE CONSERVATIVE PARTY AS THE CUSTODIAN OF THE CONSERVATIVE TRADITION

Right and left

By the beginning of the 18th century, the British two party system was already in place. The identities of the parties have often changed; we have had Whigs and Tories, Liberals and Conservatives, Conservatives and Labour. There have often been third forces which have threatened to destabilise the dual hegemony; the Peelites, Irish Nationalists, Social Democrats, Liberal Democrats. Indeed, the Labour Party started out as a disruptive third force, but by displacing the Liberals preserved the traditional duality.

In such a system, ideology is one factor only in the great decisions of policy that parties have to make. Electoral advantage always has to be borne in mind, of course; that may mean bribery of key parts of the electorate, and sometimes the necessity of giving in to distasteful aspects of the *Zeitgeist*. Furthermore, governments (though not oppositions) are under all sorts of unwelcome constraints, such as binding international treaties, human rights law, and the realities of government finance. Finally, each big party must position itself relative to the other, opposing some things, urging more action elsewhere. In particular conservatives, who by and large are happy with the status quo, find much of their ideological content determined by the radical plans of the opposition, whoever the opposition (liberals, socialists, feminists, etc) might be at any one moment, a point that students of ideology have made much of.[1]

Hence a party cannot do all it wants, even if its members all agree on the wish list. In a two party system, in a nation with a rich and varied political life, parties can be nothing more than fluctuating coalitions of interests. The Conservative Party, for example, contains not only conservatives, whose traditions are our focus in this book, but also agricultural interests, business interests (at least from the end of the 19th century), Anglicans (up to the middle of the 20th century) and free marketeers (in the 20th century). It is not trivial to read off the conservative ideology from the actions of the Tories or the Conservative Party.

A further wrinkle, not often discussed in detail, is that the two British parties seem to occupy different points in *psychological* space. At least since Disraeli and Gladstone (of whom more below), certain psychological characteristics have been identifiable in many supporters of the two parties, the party of the right (Tories/Conservatives), and the party of the left (Whig/Liberal/Labour). If I may resort to caricature, on the right politics is a game, about which it is appropriate to nurture a sense of humour; the left approaches matters with much deeper moral seriousness.[2] The left has the confidence to propose solutions to problems; the right is sceptical. The right is proud of the past, trusting of the institutions of society, and sympathetic to the law-abiding, the unsung, the ordinary; the left wants to free the human spirit, and instinctively sides with rebels and outcasts, those who are pushing the boundaries. The left worries about encroachment from the government, the right from the mob. As Dr Johnson put it, the Tory favours establishment, the Whig innovation. If we were casting film stars as personified political forces, we might put David Niven on the right, and Jack Nicholson on the left, the electorate to decide top billing.

Hence, for all these reasons, it would be impossible to show very much about ideology in Britain without studying the history of political parties in very great detail. What I want to do in this chapter is to pick out some conservative episodes in Conservative history, while thinking too about the simultaneous development of the sceptical conservative ideology, rooted in

Pyrrhonism, which we left bubbling away at the close of Chapter Two. Ideologies and history are inseparable, and so this juxtaposition is essential. However, I am very alive to the fact that I am being of necessity extremely selective, and, though the discussion below *illustrates* my point that the conservatism I wish to describe has until recently been written through the Conservative Party like the message in a stick of Blackpool Conference rock, proof is a very different thing.

The emergence of the two party system

The left/right split in British politics was already implicit with the arrival of the Stuarts in 1603. Everyone could agree that the monarchy's legitimacy came from the proper succession, because during the long reign of Elizabeth I (1558–1603), the question as to what would happen with an unsuitable monarch did not have to be raised. Elizabeth had turned England decisively into a Protestant country, and Catholicism was disapproved of by virtually everybody. But the Stuart kings flirted openly with Catholicism; this changed everything.

Rebellion was in the air, and the founders of the Tory tradition began to emerge during the civil war of the 1640s; in particular men such as Viscount Falkland and Edward Hyde looked for a middle way between the absolutism that the foolish King Charles I demanded, and the radicalism of Cromwell's Roundheads, a middle political way that mirrored the middle way in the literature and religion of Sir Thomas Browne. Falkland even furnished conservatism with a splendid dictum, that if it is not necessary to change the state, then it is necessary *not* to change it.

The Tories were in something of a bind. They were Anglicans, supporting the politico-religious establishment; on the other hand, the kings whose legitimacy they defended toyed with undoing that establishment. The problem came to a head when it became obvious that Protestant King Charles II would have no (legitimate) issue, and would be succeeded by his overtly Catholic brother James, Duke of York. This led to a political crisis in 1679–81, the exclusion crisis, when the first attempt was made through parliament to prevent James from ascending to the throne. It was during this crisis that recognisable parties emerged (political cliques at that stage, rather than organised bodies). Their names were terms of abuse given by their opponents, later worn with pride: a 'Tory' was an Irish cattle thief, satirising the espousal of the cause of a Catholic prince; a 'Whig' a Scottish horse thief, hinting at nonconformity and the undermining of the settled way of the land.

Initially, the Tories were triumphant, seeing off the Whigs in 1681. We can get the measure of the times from the work of poet laureate John Dryden (1631–1700), who was very much in the mainstream that we are describing: sceptical, an admirer of Browne (the title of his poem *Religio Laici* deliberately apes *Religio Medici*), and a defender of the legitimacy of the Stuart kings.[3] Dryden's poetry often spells out the ideal of the constitutional monarchy, the middle way between French-style absolutism and Whiggish democracy, a middle way whose nature was determined by the stoical and phlegmatic nature of the English people.

> Our Temp'rate Isle will no extremes sustain
> Of pop'lar Sway or Arbitrary Reign:
> But slides between them both into the best;
> Secure in freedom, in a Monarch blest.[4]

His epic *Absalom and Achitophel*, written in 1682 reputedly at the behest of Charles II himself, describes the feverish years of the exclusion crisis with the good English sense of the solid roast-beef Tory. Even if people could legitimately get rid of their king, what Englishman would ever want to?

> Yet, grant our Lords the People, Kings can make,
> What prudent man a settled throne would shake?
> For whatsoe'r their Sufferings were before,
> That Change they Covet makes them suffer more.
> All other Errors but disturb a State;
> But Innovation is the Blow of Fate.[5]

But the Tory victory was hollow. James II, as the Duke of York became upon succeeding his brother in 1683, extended the tradition of Stuart incompetence to the point of imbecility, promoting Catholics without consideration of Anglican sensibilities, and making cynical arrangements with Whig non-conformists. He alienated his Tory supporters on almost every level, and consequently they made very little effort to stand in the way when he was overthrown by a *coup* in 1688. James had had a number of Anglican offspring, and the Tories could console themselves that these princesses at least were involved in government.

Actually, this involved some high-grade mental gymnastics, as not only had James been overthrown, but his son James Edward had also been thrown aside. The new king was the Dutch William III, who was married to James's daughter Mary (now Mary II); on such flimsy ground did the Tories convince themselves, if no one else, that they were remaining loyal simultaneously to their religious principles and the hereditary idea. When first Mary, then William died, James's surviving Protestant daughter Anne succeeded to the throne, but none of her twelve children survived her (six more were stillborn). Then came the crunch.

When Anne died, the only realistic option for a Stuart succession was James's Catholic son James Edward (the Old Pretender). Parliament, however, had ruled out the possibility of a Catholic monarch, and had appointed as heir the non-English-speaking Elector of Hanover, who duly became George I. This was too much for most Tories – and the Scottish Tories (the Jacobites) even moved into open rebellion in 1715, and then again in 1745 in favour of the Young Pretender, Bonnie Prince Charlie, against George II (George I's son). The contradiction between the requirements of legitimacy and religion had been exposed, and the Tories were finished, politically, for two generations. Neither George I nor George II forgave them, and they appointed Whigs exclusively to office; the joint period of their reigns, 1714–60, has been called 'the Whig supremacy'.[6]

Edmund Burke: the Whig who inspired the Tories

In time, the Hanover kings forgot their antipathy towards the Tories, and under George III, the first English-born king since James II, they became a serious political force once more. However, bizarrely, the most influential figure in British conservatism was not a Tory at all, but a renegade Whig, the Irishman Edmund Burke (1729–97).

For most of his career, Burke was a model Whig, who served under a number of Whig Prime Ministers, including Lord Rockingham and Charles James Fox, and was a prominent supporter of both the American Revolution, an important victory of the Enlightenment forces upholding the rights of man, and the English 'Glorious' Revolution against James II in 1688. But he is most famous for a sensational attack on the French Revolution of 1789; his *Reflections on the Revolution in France*,[7] published in 1790, has remained the leading work of conservative philosophy ever since.

It has never really been explained why Burke should support two revolutions and not the third; the feeling at the time was that he was bribed to oppose the French Revolution by George III himself (Burke was a somewhat Bohemian figure, perpetually surrounded by a large, loud and flamboyantly Irish extended family, and was regarded as slightly shifty). Burke's editor Conor Cruise O'Brien suggests that Burke harboured secret revolutionary thoughts, and had mild, though suppressed, Jacobite sympathies.[8] David Willetts, on the other hand, identifies an important difference which Burke may well have appreciated, which is that whereas 1688 and 1776 were conceivable (and conceived by their perpetrators) as organic changes repairing traditions which had been broken by authoritarian governments, 1789 was a conscious breaking of all traditions.[9] However that may be, Burke laid into the French Revolutionary parties with a will.

The French Revolution, initially at least, was popular in Britain; for some time it had generally been felt that the liberties and freedoms available in Britain contrasted favourably with the rigid hierarchies of French society. The French were storing up trouble for themselves, it was thought, and the Revolution seemed to prove the point. The British allowed themselves a smug snicker.

So, for the last few years of his life, Burke was not a popular man; his counter-revolutionary propagandising – for the *Reflections*, despite their laid-back, academic name, were in truth no more nor less than propaganda – was seen as extremist rabble-rousing. Much of this was because the Tories were in power at the time; no doubt he would have been more circumspect had the Whigs been required to dream up a policy to contain the revolutionary virus. But the net result was to alienate him from both sides in British politics. His own Whig party was generally in favour of the Revolution of 1789, as they were of those of 1688 and 1776; they thought they were prompted by human rationality in the face of superstition and tradition, classic victories of the spirit of Enlightenment over the forces of ignorance. Burke did not agree, and he and the Whigs parted company acrimoniously.

The Tories, on the other hand, never warmed to Burke, at least while he was alive, nor he to them. Burke thought that the French Revolution would bring down the established order with disastrous consequences, unless Britain was prepared for a long war to defeat the revolutionary movement. The Tories were quite happy for a war, but only a short one designed to secure Britain's interests, not to install a counter-revolution.

To the modern reader, Burke's prescience stands out compared with the misplaced optimism about the French Revolution of virtually all his British contemporaries; for instance, Tom Paine welcomed the bloodless revolution that would establish the rights of man.[10] We often forget, reading the *Reflections*, how early it was written, during the initial, relatively benign phase of the Revolution. Burke forecast that the overthrowing of the old order, corrupt and authoritarian though it was, would result in a complete lack of stability, a flourishing of violence, and the opposite of the rational Enlightened society that most commentators were expecting to follow. He recognised that the

French peasantry was unprepared for the difficult task of self-rule, that the compromise and humanity that such a task required were absent. It was French society that had been beheaded, not just the monarch.

Actually, when the *Reflections* were written, the monarch and his queen had *not* been executed. The September massacres and the Terror had yet to take place. Burke was generally thought to have been exaggerating, but events were to prove him correct. He even predicted that a militaristic despot would take over; Napoleon finally took control of France two years after Burke's death. In the event, the long war that Burke desired did happen, and did not end until Napoleon's final defeat at Waterloo in 1815.

Burke became a very fashionable figure in the Cold War, as his arguments seemed to apply quite nicely – for hawkish American purposes – to the Russian Revolution of 1917 as much as to the French one.[11] But it is an error to see Burke as a systematic political philosopher. The *Reflections*, and more so his later counter-revolutionary works, were explicitly propaganda, as noted above. Nevertheless, he develops many interesting themes that have been deeply influential on British conservative thought since, and that make their most commanding appearance in the *Reflections*.

First, there is the general worry about the violence of revolutions, that the forces unleashed by the sudden lifting of authority – even if that authority was not benign – will be worse than what they swept away.

Second, Burke much preferred the realities of practical politics to abstract theorising. The sceptical thread that we have been tracing through political history comes out strongly in Burke's preference for expediency and pragmatism over high-flown theories that may or may not apply to reality. People, not only as individuals, but also *en masse*, are unpredictable, and the real, unique circumstances of any situation count for more than abstract ideas of rationality, human nature, etc.

> I flatter myself that I love a manly, moral, regulated liberty as well as any gentleman of that society, be he who he will;

and perhaps I have given as good proofs of my attachment to that cause, in the whole course of my public conduct. I think I envy liberty as little as they do, to any other nation. But I cannot stand forward, and give praise or blame to any thing which relates to human actions, and human concerns, on a simple view of the object, as it stands stripped of every relation, in all the nakedness and solitude of metaphysical abstraction. Circumstances (which with some gentlemen pass for nothing) give in reality to every political principle its distinguishing colour, and discriminating effect. The circumstances are what render every civil and political scheme beneficial or noxious to mankind. Abstractedly speaking, government, as well as liberty, is good; yet could I, in common sense, ten years ago, have felicitated France on her enjoyment of a government (for she then had a government) without enquiry what the nature of that government was, or how it was administered? Can I now congratulate the same nation upon its freedom? Is it because liberty in the abstract may be classed amongst the blessings of mankind, that I am seriously to felicitate a madman, who has escaped from the protecting restraint and wholesome darkness of his cell, on his restoration to the enjoyment of light and liberty? Am I to congratulate an highwayman and murderer, who has broke prison, upon the recovery of his natural rights?[12]

Third, Burke supported moderation, as being a prerequisite for liberty to be properly enjoyed.

Men must have a certain fund of moderation to qualify them for freedom else it becomes noxious to themselves and a perfect nuisance to every body else.[13]

Fourth, a useful mechanism for securing stability is property. This argument has been transposed into the language of 'stakeholding' in New Labour ideology; people must feel they have a stake in society before they will act to preserve it. This 'stakeholding' is intergenerational; that is, it is expressed through inheritance; private property can be appropriated legitimately neither by the state (except via properly instituted tax law), nor by revolutionary forces.

> These professors of the rights of men are so busy in teaching others, that they have not leisure to learn any thing themselves; otherwise they would have known that it is to the property of the citizen, and not to the demands of the creditor of the state, that the first and original faith of civil society is pledged. The claim of the citizen is prior in time, paramount in title, superior in equity.[14]

Though property and moderation are important, and can be undermined by massive inequalities (as indeed happened in the top-heavy French society of the 18th century), this does not mean that equality should be pursued to the extreme. Equality, like liberty, is an abstract idea that no doubt is perfectly sensible in the privacy of the thinker's office, but whose imposition, in a real situation, onto real people, will inevitably cause injustice and strife. The best solution is to avoid centralisation, promote varied and disparate sources of power, and seek to limit the domination of government by big bureaucracies that enjoy a monopoly of effective information.

> The characteristic essence of property, formed out of the combined principles of its acquisition and conservation, is to be *unequal*.[15]

These principles, their careful balance between interests and support for stability and moderation, were an important, if unusual, contribution to 18th-century thought. Their general common sense, and evident usefulness to preserving the status quo, made Burke the hero of conservatives within a few decades. But he wasn't the only Enlightenment thinker who managed to articulate a philosophy of conservatism that went beyond the self-interest of the wealthy and powerful; in Scotland, the philosopher David Hume was thinking more explicitly in the Pyrrhonist tradition, and reaching similar conclusions from a more theoretical direction.

David Hume: Pyrrhonism in the 18th century

Pyrrhonism has always been controversial. Does it say that all knowledge is wrong, or just that we should accept what is evidently true while not going beyond the evidence? Does the sceptic break his or her own rules by stating that (some) knowledge is impossible? Is it possible to live life as a sceptic, or is scepticism just an intellectual pose?

As we have seen, Sextus Empiricus himself was ambiguous about the first question, and its interpretation has been a matter of dispute ever since. The second question caused an ancient split between the sceptics, with the Pyrrhonists following Aenesidemus in accusing the sceptics of the Academy of indeed breaking their own rules. The third question has always led to the charge of inconsistency being laid against sceptics, although Sextus, for one, used to say that living a sceptical life was not only possible, but the only means to a serene existence.

However, by the 18th century, scepticism had been used as a sharp philosophical tool, by sceptics such as Pierre Bayle (1647–1706) and non-sceptics such as René Descartes (1596–1650) alike. Such rigorous debate went far beyond the undogmatic moderation promoted by Sextus or Montaigne; Descartes went so far as to doubt everything, to wonder whether the external world existed at all.[16] A large literature developed, with many thinkers charging that scepticism was self-undermining. Pyrrhonism was paradoxical: do you *know* that knowledge is impossible? If yes, then you have contradicted yourself; if no, then by what right do you assert it? And Pyrrhonism was unbelievable: you claim to doubt everything, but when you are about to be run down by a carriage, you don't doubt its existence, you leap out of the way just like everyone else.

David Hume's (1711–76) contribution was to articulate a Pyrrhonist philosophy in the tradition of Sextus and Montaigne that defused such arguments. Being a man of the Enlightenment, he argued much more cogently and rigorously than the deliberately unsystematic Montaigne. In his great works,[17] Hume argued that our knowledge could never be grounded as definitely as we might hope; we could never assemble adequate evidence for us to be certain of our knowledge. We could, of course, assemble evidence, but a properly critical examination of the evidence would reveal that it was at least as uncertain as the propositions it was supposedly evidence for. Even mathematics and logic could let one down.

> In all demonstrative sciences the rules are certain and infallible; but when we apply them, our fallible and uncertain faculties are very apt to depart from them, and fall into error. ...
>
> There is no Algebraist nor Mathematician so expert in his science, as to place entire confidence in any truth immediately upon his discovery of it, or regard it as any thing, but a mere probability. Every time he runs over his proofs, his confidence encreases; but still more by the approbation of his friends; and is rais'd to its utmost perfection by the universal assent and applauses of the learned world. Now 'tis evident, that this gradual encrease of assurance is nothing but the addition of new probabilities, and is deriv'd from the constant union of causes and effects, according to past experience and observation.[18]

We no doubt reason; no doubt the realisation of some things is forced upon us (as Sextus pointed out, we notice that some food is sweet, or that the weather is cold). But we do not have solid foundations or *grounds* for such beliefs, not in the way that scientific rationalists would like to think.[19]

In this way, Hume ingeniously drew a distinction between a *reason* for believing something, and a *cause* of our believing it. I have no reason for thinking it is cold; but my belief that it is cold is caused by the wind and the rain (and the wiring of my nervous system). In this way, we actually go around believing things about the external world – because nature has wired us up to do so. As the critics of Pyrrhonism claimed, it is impossible to be sceptical about everything. But, says Hume, this is not because it is *incorrect* to be sceptical. Rather, it is because we are what we are that we believe things based on the input to our senses.

> It seems evident, that the dispute between the sceptics and the dogmatists is entirely verbal, or at least regards only the degrees of doubt and assurance, which we ought to indulge with regard to all reasoning. ... No philosophical dogmatist denies that there are difficulties both with regard to the senses and to all science, and that these difficulties are, in a regular, logical method, absolutely insolvable. No sceptic denies that we lie under an absolute necessity, notwithstanding these difficulties, of thinking, and believing, and reasoning, with regard to all kinds of subjects, and even of frequently assenting with confidence and security. The only difference, then, between these sects, if they merit that name, is that the sceptic, from habit, caprice, or inclination, insists most on the difficulties, the dogmatist, for like reasons, on the necessity.[20]

But this psychophysical necessity does not mean that the philosophical arguments adduced by sceptical Pyrrhonists are wrong. The Enlightenment dream of building an understanding of the world on an edifice of reason and self-evident axioms of human nature is undermined just as surely by this modified Pyrrhonist argument.[21]

So Pyrrhonist scepticism kills off the Enlightenment rationalist hope. But it does not prevent the sceptic himself or herself leading a perfectly normal life. How so? Because it would take a literally superhuman effort to worry about it, except when one was being a philosopher.

> Most fortunately it happens, that since reason is incapable of dispelling these clouds, nature herself suffices to that purpose, and cures me of this philosophical melancholy

and delirium, either by relaxing this bent of mind, or by some avocation, and lively impression of my senses, which obliterate all these chimeras. I dine, I play a game of back-gammon, I converse, and am merry with my friends; and when after three or four hour's amusement, I wou'd return to these speculations, they appear so cold, and strain'd, and ridiculous, that I cannot find in my heart to enter into them any farther.[22]

Even when Hume is trying to worry about knowledge, science, reason and the external world, a few hours' backgammon with his friends stops him, and he feels rather silly. Would that more academics had that reaction to their work.

Between them, Burke and Hume develop a distinctive conservative position from the tradition of Sextus and Montaigne. Abstract theorising is all very well, but society is not an abstract thing; nor are people abstractions. Political conditions are here and now, *sui generis*, with concrete benefits (and also concrete drawbacks). One should be very wary of attempting to substitute abstract benefits for concrete ones, because the trajectory of human society is inherently unpredictable (Burke), and abstract reasoning is usually flawed (Hume). Removing well-understood institutions will lead to the collapse of those elements of society that the institutions were meant to uphold; removal of sources of power will lead to power vacuums and violence; and all this in the name of some theory or other for which there can be no ultimately persuasive ground.

The moderation of ancient and Renaissance scepticism, that had been lost during the early Enlightenment, had now been restored to it. All that now remained was to translate these insights into political action.

Peel, corn, and the origins of the Conservative Party

The development of what we now know as the Conservative Party was pretty murky throughout the 18th century.[23] There are definite continuities from the Tories to the Conservatives, but also several false starts, stalls and dead ends. The inheritances of Burke and Hume, and indeed other thinkers such as Coleridge, were and are argued over. In this book, we have space only to sketch a tradition, and then to map it onto current ideological discourse; hence we will skip a lot of development and jump to the middle of the 19th century, to the premiership of Sir Robert Peel (1788–1850*), which illustrates some of our themes rather well.

Peel, although even now a household name, was not a successful party leader. He had to deal with a major shock to the political and economic system, and failed to carry his party with him. The problem was the notorious Corn Laws.

These had been introduced in the aftermath of the war against France in 1815. Wartime financial measures, including Britain's first income tax, were repealed. However, the landowning interests foresaw a fall in the price of corn from the high wartime prices (indeed, they were right – prices halved in the months after Waterloo), and ambushed the government of Lord Liverpool, a limited but long-serving Tory Prime Minister. They forced the Liverpool government, which they generally supported, to impose restrictions on imports of corn; not until corn prices reached 80 shillings per quarter[†24] could foreign corn be brought in. The effect, naturally, was to keep corn prices artificially high, to the benefit of landowners and the detriment of those who spent a large proportion of income on food, including the increasing working classes in the towns. The new manufacturers were indirectly hit as well, as the high food prices reduced demand for manufactured goods, and they began to campaign effectively and strongly against them. Prominent among them were the members of the Anti-Corn-Law League (founded 1838), Richard Cobden (1804–65) and John Bright (1811–89). And with the passing of the Reform Act of 1832, the

---

* Prime Minister 1834–5, 1841–6.
† 80 shillings is £4. A quarter is bizarrely difficult to define. A quarter in Liverpool was 480 lb; in London 496 lb; elsewhere 504 lb. Nowhere was it a quarter of a ton, which is 560 lb.

parliamentary influence of the landowners in whose interests the Corn Laws were passed was inevitably diluted.

The Reform Act prompted the reorganisation of the Tories; they emerged from the crisis with a new name, the 'Conservative Party', and a new organisational centre, the Carlton Club.[25] They were also forced to broaden their appeal, and their leader, the splendidly reactionary Duke of Wellington, recognised the talents of their best middle-class mind, Robert Peel. Peel was undoubtedly correct to recognise, as Prime Minister from 1841, that the Corn Laws were indefensible, not only morally and economically, but also in electoral terms. His calculation, further, was that the laws would be best repealed by the Conservatives, rather than the Liberals (as the Whigs had become) – who had always been hostile and would in all probability find additional ways to kick the Conservative landowning interests.

Party historian Lord Blake has suggested that the Conservatives, from 1832, really had three alternatives, each interestingly dramatising the complex dialectic between conservatism and modernity, between pragmatism and distaste for progress. First, they could become the party of solid reaction, opposing change and continuing their pre-1832 protection of landowners' interests. Second, there could be an anti-progressive alliance with the working class against the rising middle class, their liberal economics and 'dark satanic mills'; this would appeal to the Romantic strand in British politics. Third, the Conservatives could recognise the force of the middle class, accept the industrial revolution and the rapid change it brought, the liberalism of economic law, and try to broker acceptable compromises between the three social classes.[26] Peel was temperamentally disposed to the third option, which was probably also the only realistic one. Hence he moved to abolish the Corn Laws.

The result, though, was a catastrophic split in the Conservative Party that put it out of office for two decades. The measure was passed, but only with Liberal support; the 'ultras', hard Conservative reactionaries, voted against. The rebels left the party, though most of the office holders in Peel's government stayed loyal, and Peel kept command of the party machinery. The split toppled the government, and a disastrous election followed. In 1841, the Conservatives had won 367 seats; in the election of July 1847, the rebels won 243. Peel's support collapsed; there were just 89 'Peelite' MPs. The Peelite rump continued for another ten years or so, tending to side with the Liberals. The rebels took the brand name of 'Conservative' (after toying with others – the 'Protectionists' was popular), and started their party afresh. Blake maintains that 1846 is the best date to take as the beginning of the Conservative Party we know today.[27]

This incident is very interesting from our point of view. It shows the dangers of blanket opposition to change, the problems of deeply reactionary conservatism. There is no doubt that Peel, though tactically inept and personally aloof,[28] was right to repeal the Corn Laws. The party as a whole was wrong to reject change; change sometimes needs to happen, and conservatives need to recognise when we have reached such a time – not that that is always easy.

It also shows the danger of splitting the anti-progressive vote. The Conservative Party in 1846 was the country party, rural, communitarian, traditionalist, of orthodox religious views. These are all no doubt important interests in a country such as Britain, but they had never formed a majority of the electorate since the 1832 Act. If the Conservative interest is restricted to these groups, it cannot win elections; if the conservative ideology benefits only these groups, it stands no chance of influencing governmental policy. Wider coalitions need to be formed; without them, as in many countries in Continental Europe, anti-progressive forces will find themselves losing out to liberal or socialist parties.[29] A new alliance had to be forged, and the man who forged it was an outsider, Benjamin Disraeli.

Dizzy

Disraeli (1804–81*) is an outstanding figure of his day, comparable – in many ways – to Lloyd George or Churchill. After a

* Prime Minister 1868, 1874–80.

splendid start in life, helped by writing a series of best-selling novels and marriage to a wealthy widow, he became an MP in 1837. He was driven by pragmatism, personal dynamism and not a small quantity of bloody-mindedness, rather than ideology. He had flirted with the Whigs and radicalism, before settling on being a progressive Conservative.

But having made this choice, he didn't advance as quickly as he would have liked. Peel, in forming his government of 1841, overlooked Disraeli, despite his manifest talents. Disraeli, a man for whom revenge was a dish best eaten hot, then cold, then warmed over for breakfast next day, launched a ferocious campaign to destabilise Peel.

With some young Romantic aristocrats, he formed a group called Young England (of which Disraeli, a slightly moth-eaten 38 years old, was much the senior), which lived on a diet of nostalgia and escapism. Peel's stiffness, and the wit and charm of the Young Englanders, ensured that they remained a thorn in Peel's side. Disraeli brought his literary skills to bear, writing a 'state of the nation' novel called *Coningsby* (1844), in which the Young Englanders were lightly caricatured, and Peel mercilessly satirised.

> There was indeed considerable shouting about what they called Conservative principles; but the awkward question naturally arose, what will you conserve? The prerogatives of the Crown, provided they are not exercised; the independence of the House of Lords, provided it is not asserted; the Ecclesiastical estate provided it is regulated by a commission of laymen. Everything in short that is established, as long as it is a phrase and not a fact.[30]

A sequel, *Sybil* (1845), made more of the increasing divisions between rich and poor, and coined the idea of two nations within one.[31] 'One nation Conservatism' since then has become a coded phrase for Conservative politicians embarrassed by the gap between rich and poor.

The fall of Peel over the Corn Laws was no doubt a great

delight to Disraeli. The problem was that actually Peel had adopted the only realistic policy strategy, one that Disraeli might well have gone along with had there been a place for him in the Peel government. The Conservatives found themselves out of step. Furthermore, as most of the Conservatives' most experienced and talented people had been driven by the back-woods reaction into the arms of the Liberal Party (Gladstone was the most famous man to make that journey), virtually the only man of ability left was Disraeli – but his cosmopolitan background and his Jewishness were a massive turn-off for his colleagues, who overlooked his obvious claims to the leadership for over twenty years.

Had Disraeli died much earlier than he did, he would be remembered only as a talented maverick failure, a sort of Lord Randolph Churchill or Enoch Powell figure (whose torturing of the stiff, awkward, proud Edward Heath irresistibly recalls Disraeli's attacks on Peel). He had a couple of spells as a not-too-successful Chancellor in Lord Derby's brief administrations. But as the pilot of the 1867 Reform Act, he becomes a serious historical figure.

The history of the 1867 Act is complex, and makes little narrative sense.[32] In a nutshell, the Liberals attempted to get their Reform Bill through the House, to try to extend the franchise still further; they failed, thanks to a revolt by the right of the Liberal Party in alliance with the Conservatives, and the government fell. Derby was asked to form a minority administration, and Disraeli, in the Commons, developed a bill that was even more radical than the Liberals' measure, which passed! No one is really sure how this happened.[33] Trollope satirised the various *voltes faces* in his novel *Phineas Redux* (1873);[34] certainly Disraeli's about-turn was as glaring as that for which he excoriated Peel in 1846.

Nevertheless, the measure actually improved the fortunes of the Conservatives, if not immediately – Disraeli, upon the retirement of Derby, had finally become Prime Minister in 1868, and lost a general election under the new franchise a few months later – at least in the long run (*The Times* famously said that Disraeli saw the Conservative in the working man as Michelangelo saw the angel in the marble). The angels made their first appearance in the general election of 1874.

The Liberal Prime Minister Gladstone,* though concerned, like Disraeli, with the condition of the working man, was rather more concerned with what the working man *ought* to do, than with making it possible for the working man to do what he *wanted* to do. The Education Act of 1870 provided for genuine mass education, but also aggravated sectarian concerns. Trade union laws alienated the leaders of organised labour. And the Licensing Act, aimed more at keeping the working classes from drink, than the drinking classes at work, was not at all popular![35] Since then, brewing companies, at least until very recently, have traditionally been major donors to the Conservative Party.

Hence Disraeli, in the face of Gladstone's reforming zeal, was able to present the Conservatives, in a series of important speeches, as a party with a broad base covering the working classes and the propertied classes generally as well as its aristocratic core. The Liberals were interfering, constantly legislating, while the Conservatives were not. The Liberals 'knew best', while the Conservatives did not claim to. The result was that in 1874 the Conservatives turned a deficit of 100 seats into a majority of 52 over all parties. This method of opposition to an interfering, ideologically driven government that 'knows best' may well have relevance for small 'c' conservatives in the current political climate.

Disraeli's feat was to develop a set of conservative principles adapted for office, appealing beyond the Conservatives' natural constituency. First, he – as befits a follower of Burke – displayed a genuine commitment to various and dispersed centres of power, as opposed to the Gladstonian sentiments of centralisation. Second, he carefully ensured sufficient continuity of policy between his government and the government that preceded it (Gladstone's) to ensure that politics did not collapse into a left–right bunfight (or at least any more of a bunfight than

* Prime Minister 1868–74, 1880–85, 1886, 1892–4.

one would expect an antagonistic system to produce). Disraeli, in a quiet way, produced a series of social reforms that kept relations with the working class open; and though it goes without saying that these policies were much less thoroughgoing than a Gladstonian government would have produced, nevertheless the measures were civilised, just, justified, and as a bonus electorally sensible. The Sale of Food and Drugs Act, the Public Health Act, the Artisans' Dwellings Act, the Rivers' Pollution Act, and various Factory Acts and other labour legislation were all important measures to protect the weak against the strong.[36] Disraeli went with the flow of the times; he did not try to reverse it. In that way, he held the country together, re-established the Conservative Party as a party of government, accepted the shift in the political mainstream in the Gladstonian direction, and – as a happy by-product – is accepted as a major folk-hero in Tory history. Can Michael Howard, from a not dissimilar starting position, pull off the same trick?

Salisbury, man of inaction

Lord Randolph Churchill sketched Disraeli's career thus: 'failure, failure, failure, moderate success, renewed failure, sudden and absolute triumph.'[37] However, there was to be one more failure, if a relatively minor one: the Liberals turned their deficit of 52 into a majority of 52 in the 1880 election. Disraeli, now ennobled, died shortly afterwards. He was replaced by the enigmatic Lord Salisbury (1830–1903*).

Salisbury was a reactionary, who had had some difficulty in accepting the low-born Jew Disraeli as his leader. He had vaguely conspired against him in 1869 and again in 1870, was

---

* The greatest member of an impressive political family. This Salisbury was the 3rd Marquess. The 4th Marquess led the Conservatives in the Lords in 1925–31; the 5th Marquess in 1942–57. Lord Cranborne, who is heir to the seat, led the Conservatives in the Lords from 1994–9, before being summarily sacked by William Hague for independently negotiating a deal with the Labour government to phase out the majority of hereditary peers. The 3rd Marquess was Prime Minister 1885–6, 1886–92, 1895–1902.

often not on speaking terms with him, and described him in print as a 'mere political gamester'. He resigned from Derby's cabinet in 1867 over the Reform Act, though he served under Disraeli in the government of 1874–80. As leader of the party, Salisbury's record, though not unblemished, is impressive; several years of effective parity with the Liberals ended in 1895 after three years of miserable Liberal government which did the Liberals more harm than anyone else, and gave Salisbury the platform for a crushing victory, followed by a second in 1900.

It has been said that Salisbury is difficult to characterise.[38] He was certainly unusual. Politics is essentially a space for action. You go into politics if you want to change the world, to right a wrong. But Salisbury opposed action, tried to avoid intervention wherever he could; in this we can detect the authentic voice of an age-old scepticism in his writings.

The optimist view of politics assumes that there must be some remedy for every political ill, and rather than not find it, will make two hardships to cure one. If all equitable remedies have failed its votaries take it as proved without argument that the one-sided remedies, which alone are left, must needs succeed. But is not the other view barely possible? Is it not just conceivable that there is no remedy that we can apply to the Irish hatred of ourselves? that other loves or hates may possibly some day elbow it out of the Irish peasant's mind, that nothing we can do by any contrivance will hasten the advent of that period? May it not, on the contrary, be our incessant doctoring and meddling, awaking the passions now of this party, now of that, raising at every step a fresh crop of resentments by the side of the old growth, that puts off the day when these feelings will decay quietly away and be forgotten? One thing we know we can do in Ireland, for we have done it in India and elsewhere with populations more unmanageable and more bitter. We can keep the peace and we can root out organised crime. But there is no precedent in our history or any other, to teach us that political measures can conjure away hereditary antipathies which are fed by constant agitation. The free institutions that sustain the life of a free and united people, sustain also the hatreds of a divided people.[39]

Indeed, a tragedy early in his ministerial career when he was Secretary of State for India affected him deeply, not only personally, but as a warning against experts and claims for omnipotence of expertise. A famine in the Indian state of Orissa developed, despite the warning signs, which were ignored by the officials of the Raj. Salisbury always felt responsible for the failings of his department, and denounced the 'experts' and political economists roundly in the House. He remained sceptical of experts to the end of his life.[40]

Although Salisbury liked to give the impression that he did very little other than give the occasional touch on the tiller when the ship of state threatened to go off course, he actually continued the Disraelian strategy of cautious reform, accepting that a very weak concoction of the policies that might appeal to wavering Liberals would help drain their support (for example, Salisbury devoted a lot of effort to improving working-class housing[41]). This strategy of Disraeli's and Salisbury's we might call a *vaccination strategy*; a mild dose of what Salisbury certainly regarded as a virulent strain of political action would protect the nation from a more deadly outbreak in the future.

So historian John Ramsden is unfair when he accuses Salisbury of failing 'entirely to understand the political trends of his time',[42] though he does have Salisbury's own account on his side.

Salisbury himself found it hard to explain the trends of his political lifetime, for such Conservative dominance in the 1890s defied all the pessimistic, disintegrationist and class-conflictive predictions that had been his stock in trade ever since 1866–7, when he had defied Disraeli over the extension of the franchise; 'the result turned out exactly the other way', he confessed in 1895.[43]

But politicians often fail to understand their environment; Salisbury's incomprehension is hardly unknown elsewhere. In our own day, armed with batteries of opinion polls and platoons of media managers, it is often incredible how little politicians seem to understand of the people who vote for them. Economic or environmental disaster, even civil war, have regularly been forecast, by very bright people, to follow mass immigration, joining the Common Market, rising unemployment, not joining the euro, globalisation or the spread of technology.

That Salisbury, the grandest of grandees, should be taken aback that Disraeli's strategy of reform should work, that he should fail to see the angels in the marble where Disraeli succeeded, is no surprise. Rather, the inevitable condition of politics is surely that of uncertainty in the face of complexity. The issue, as Salisbury appreciated, is how best to navigate through such choppy waters.

Balfour the philosopher

Salisbury's nephew and successor A.J. Balfour (1848–1930*) is unusual – and helpful to us – for being the most intellectual of Prime Ministers, the author of a number of books of philosophy. These works are interesting not least because Salisbury himself took an interest in them, to the point of suggesting a change of title for the first book,[44] a work of 1879 originally called *A Defence of Philosophic Scepticism*, Salisbury's advice being to call it *A Defence of Philosophic Doubt*.

Balfour's *oeuvre* was not great philosophy, but interesting, building laconically on the work of David Hume. He discusses the idea of scepticism as a presence in the real world, as a philosophical (and political?) tool.

> I must point out that the word 'scepticism' taken without explanation is ambiguous. It may mean either the intellectual recognition of the want of evidence, or it may mean this together with its consequent unbelief. ...

* Prime Minister 1902–5.

If, then [as Balfour had argued], scepticism in the second sense be impossible, is scepticism in the first sense – scepticism which merely recognises the absence of philosophical proof or other logical defect in a system of belief – of any but a speculative interest? At first sight it would seem not. Scepticism which does not destroy belief, it is natural to suppose, does nothing. This, however, is by no means necessarily the case. If in the estimation of mankind all creeds stood on a philosophical equality, no doubt an attack which affected them all equally would probably have little or no practical result. The only result it could reasonably produce would be general unbelief, and, as I have just remarked, general unbelief can hardly be regarded as a possible frame of mind. But if in the estimation of mankind there is the greatest difference in the relative credibility of prevalent systems of belief, if now one system now another is raised to the dignity of a standard of certainty, it is plain that a sceptical attack, especially if it deals with the system that happens at the moment to be in favour, may have considerable consequences – consequences, at least, quite as considerable as any which considerations addressed merely to the reason are ever likely to produce.[45]

Balfour's message is implicit in much of Hume and Montaigne. Scepticism shouldn't be espoused to undermine belief; rather, its purpose is to ensure that the believer preserves a questioning attitude, never relaxes into a complacent certainty. He argues that a watertight set of reasons for adopting one system of beliefs over another – in his case, the systems he is interested in are Science and Religion (he capitalises them) – will never emerge, on the basis, more or less, of the arguments put forward by Hume. Brute and unpersuasive causes of belief remain, and these should, and can, be respected by others. This line of thought is the direct descendant of the tolerance of Montaigne.

In the absence then of reason to the contrary, I am content to regard the two great creeds [Religion and Science] by which we attempt to regulate our lives as resting in the main upon separate bases. So long, therefore, as neither of them can lay claim to philosophic probability, discrepancies which exist or may hereafter arise between them cannot be considered as bearing more heavily against the one than they do against the other. But if a really valid philosophy, which would support Science to the exclusion of Religion, or Religion to the exclusion of Science, were discovered, the case would be somewhat different, and it would undoubtedly be difficult for that creed which is not philosophically established to exist beside the other while in contradiction to it – difficult, I say, not absolutely impossible. In the meanwhile, unfortunately, this does not seem likely to become a practical question. What has to be determined now is the course which ought to be pursued with regard to discrepancies between systems, neither of which can be regarded as philosophically established, but neither of which we can consent to surrender; and on this subject, of course, it is only possible to make suggestions which may perhaps commend themselves to the practical instincts of the reader, though they cannot compel his intellectual assent. In my judgment, then, if these discrepancies are such that they can be smoothed away by concessions on either side which do not touch essentials, the concessions should be made; but if, which is not at present the case, consistency can only be purchased by practically destroying one or other of the conflicting creeds, I should elect in favour of inconsistency – not because I should be content with knowledge which being self-contradictory must needs be in some particulars false, but because a logical harmony obtained by the arbitrary destruction of all discordant elements may be bought at far too great a sacrifice of essential and necessary truth.[46]

Balfour was a religious man, and had a deep interest in science; like Hume (who could be dissuaded from his abstract scepticism by a game of backgammon), he was able to juggle the two belief systems, and because he felt that each of them contained a core of value and wisdom, he wished not to jettison either, even though he accepted their inconsistency.

Balfour's focus is on the social aspects of beliefs and belief systems. A later work, *The Foundations of Belief* of 1895, takes his survey somewhat further in the political direction, by introducing the idea of 'authority'.[47] This has the effect of bringing Burke into the mix (though Burke is never cited by Balfour). Reason, claims Balfour, actually supports few of our beliefs (and, *contra* many Christian accounts, nor does direct spiritual insight). Rather, we gain much from cultural absorption, inbred knowledge, custom, tradition. Reason cannot safely be permitted to provide the principal source of support for our convictions, because individual citizens have neither the time, energy nor brainpower to decide 'with open minds the claims which charity, temperance and honesty, murder, theft and adultery respectively have upon the approval or disapproval of mankind'. The Burkean concepts of prejudice, prescription and presumption will inevitably remain the most reliable guides to moral action.[48]

For Balfour, authority provides what he calls a 'psychological climate' where some beliefs seem impossible, others essential – though there may be no rationality to such processes. 'Do they follow, I mean, on reason *qua* reason? or are they, like a schoolboy's tears over a proposition of Euclid, consequences of reasoning, but not conclusions from it?' If we base our beliefs on authority – as we inevitably do – then if we also wish to produce convincing reasons for our beliefs, we may be disappointed.[49] Democrats may wish to support their beliefs by pointing to the 'rights of man', but these are abstractions, and will not convince non-democrats; similarly the myths of science, or religion, or environmentalism, or whatever, will fail to convince their opponents, though they will provide a nice comforting glow to their proponents. What the epistemological value of that glow is, is a moot point.[50]

What, then, is 'authority'? It contrasts with reason, and consists in the loose congregation of the non-rational causes of

belief, which may be moral, social, educational, or psychological. Authority will certainly get in the way of progress, and
will on many occasions propagate error. But, so valued has
reason become, that there is a temptation to postulate reasons
where there are only causes; when this temptation is given in to,
authority becomes just another species of reasoning, and should
be judged as such. It may work reasonably well, but will not act
as a foundation of belief, just as another type of support.[51]

Balfour's strong sense of the social rootedness of beliefs, of
the cultural foundations of belief systems, of the importance of
belief systems for defining cultures, and of the social processes
of transmission of beliefs, comes out in a remarkable passage in
the *Defence* discussing 'arguments from popular philosophy',[52]
in which he concludes that social foundations for moral or
political beliefs, such as 'general consent' or 'common sense',
can work in practice, without ever being even approximately
true. As he wrote in his later work, we therefore must resign
ourselves to error without necessarily relapsing into pessimism
or defensiveness.

> Not merely because we are ignorant of the data required for
> the solution, even of very simple problems in organic and
> social life, are we called on to acquiesce in an arrangement
> which, to be sure, we have no power to disturb; nor yet
> because these data, did we possess them, are too complex to
> be dealt with by any rational calculus we possess or are ever
> likely to acquire; but because, in addition to these difficul-
> ties, reasoning is a force most apt to divide and disintegrate;
> and though division and disintegration may often be the
> necessary preliminaries of social development, still more
> necessary are the forces that bind and stiffen, without which
> there would be no society to develop.[53]

Invasion of the liberals

Balfour was probably the most academic of all Britain's Prime
Ministers, and one of the most intellectually formidable. It

may or may not be a related fact that he was one of the least successful.

Long-term trouble for the Conservatives had been created by what seemed at first to be a disaster for the Liberals, the splitting of the party by Gladstone over the recondite (to the English) issue of Irish Home Rule during Gladstone's fleeting appearance as Prime Minister from February to July 1886. A group of unionists opposing the splitting up of the United Kingdom followed Joseph Chamberlain (1836–1914), who had been a radical social reformer and President of the Board of Trade under Gladstone in the early 1880s, out of the party.

The Liberal Unionists sat in parliament as a separate party during Salisbury's period of office, leaving the official Liberals hopelessly placed (between the general elections of November 1885 and July 1886, the Liberals lost 143 seats). The Unionists enjoyed the Empire and the flag-waving jingoism that became popular, and generally voted with the Conservatives. Chamberlain even joined the Salisbury government as Colonial Secretary.

So far so good. Not only did the defection of the Unionists split the Liberal vote, but they also brought in support for the Conservatives away from the traditional rural Tory heartland.[54] Eventually they relinquished their distinct political identity and joined the Conservatives (renamed the Conservative and Unionist Party).

This was a disaster for Balfour. The Conservatives suddenly had to absorb a large number of alien thinkers into their ranks. Liberalism is the ideology of freedom, roughly speaking.[55] All liberals (small 'l', note) value freedom. But freedom can be described in a number of ways. One distinction is between freedom to do things – the lack of restraint on one's personal choices of action – and freedom from things – being unhindered by conditions that restrict one's freedom of choice.[56] The distinction is subtle; suppose I own a factory that has a machine that creates some pollution. The former type of liberal would tend to support my freedom to use the machine (though it may be incumbent upon me to pay for the clean-up afterwards); the latter type would tend to favour legislation to restrict my use of it, to increase the general freedom of everyone else to enjoy an unpolluted environment. The former type of liberal identified with Chamberlain, and gravitated towards the Conservative Party from 1886 on, while the latter type, the high-minded Gladstonians, remained, and are the mainstays of the Liberal Democrat Party even today. Given the influx of liberals into the Conservative Party, it was inevitable that there would be tensions (often creative ones[57]).

These tensions exposed the weaknesses of Balfour's scepticism. He was convicted by commentators of the day (probably fairly) of vacillating between various camps in the party, not least between the defenders of free trade and those, like Chamberlain, who wanted a preferential tariff regime for producers in the Empire.[58] His being the author of a book called *A Defence of Philosophic Doubt* hardly helped this perception.[59] Liberal MP Sir Wilfrid Lawson wrote an insulting jingle.

> I'm not for Free Trade, and I'm not for Protection.
> I approve of them both, and to both have objection.
> In going through life I continually find
> It's a terrible business to make up one's mind.
> So in spite of all comments, reproach and predictions,
> I firmly adhere to Unsettled Convictions.[60]

In the period of Salisbury and Balfour conservatism as a creed precisely of unsettled convictions reached its heyday. But the obvious danger when arguments do flare up is drift; one can be too understanding of opposing points of view, and this is an important lesson for conservatives of all stripes.

Conservatism (small 'c') must be open-minded; but in testing conditions conservatives must be capable of taking a lead, of making stern decisions, and of building new institutions that help deal with changing circumstances; that a conservative opposes change does not – cannot – mean that conservatives can ignore change.

Other avowedly conservative Conservatives have made the

same mistake. Stanley Baldwin (1867–1947*) for example led Britain through perhaps her most difficult period, through the devastating worldwide depression and the polarisation of world politics between communists and fascists. Though as he left office he was fêted, as having in particular handled the abdication crisis well, the world system crumbled shortly after he retired, and Churchill made sure that he took a large share of the blame. He failed to see the dangers of the resurgent Germany, and, though his humanity and conciliatory skills no doubt helped to preserve Britain's social harmony during the long depression, in the end the problem was the failure of the prewar economic system, and could not be cured by a benign understanding. Radical action was needed, and Baldwin completely failed to take such action, or even conceive that it was required. Such is the danger of complacent conservatism.

Triumph of the liberals

Whether two different ideologies can co-exist within large coalitionist parties will depend on a number of factors, perhaps most notably on the nature of the forces opposing them. Through most of the 20th century, certainly since the First World War, the main opposition to the Conservatives was formed by the Labour Party, whose commitment to socialism was perhaps never quite as solid as it pretended, but which periodically declaimed that equality was the greatest political good, and that wealth should be redistributed between the classes. Within Labour ranks were also social democrats, who wished to reform capitalism to make its outcomes more equitable, and Gladstonian liberals who had fled the Liberal Party during and after its terminal decline. This opposition coalition shared a rough goal of greater equality (not necessarily total equality).

The 20th-century Conservative Party was united by opposition to Labour's brand of moderate, non-Marxist socialism.

---

* Prime Minister 1923–4, 1924–9, 1935–7.

Small 'c' conservatives opposed redistribution partly because they opposed the assumption that any society should have a goal to which it was working, partly because they worried about how such meddling in economic structures would affect social relations, partly because they thought the degree of planning involved in such a redistribution of wealth was too great, and partly because they disliked the shift in responsibility for a citizen's welfare from the citizen him- or herself to the state. Free market liberals opposed the interference with market-delivered outcomes.

Because of this happy coincidence of aims of both conservatives and liberals, it has been possible to paint the British conservative as being merely opposed to equality,[61] and the Conservative Party as being made up entirely of conservatives.[62] But this is much too simplistic a picture. At the very least, it leaves unexplained the obvious fact that the 20th century saw a good deal of argument *within* the Conservative Party about whether or not to move in a liberal, free market direction.

For instance, in 1970, Edward Heath was elected Prime Minister on a relatively free market ticket; by 1972, he had withdrawn from that position, and was pursuing policies that were very much a continuation of those of Harold Macmillan. Why, then, if both types of policy are conservative policies, did Heath get such a lot of flak from those opposed to his U-turn?

Small 'c' conservatives and liberals were able to use the Conservative Party to dominate the century, and to prevent anything more than a milk-and-water version of socialism being introduced. The conservatives delivered rural and southern seats, the liberals brought the towns, the north, and Scotland. The coalition of interests worked well. The Conservative Party felt no incongruity or inconsistency in this. Why, indeed, should it, wondered Quintin Hogg?

It was the Tory Party which took its stand in the nineteenth century against the principles of *laissez faire* liberalism of which it is now accused by its more ignorant opponents of being the sole inventor and patentee. More still, it did so on what would now be considered the orthodox Socialist ground that capitalism was an ungodly and rapacious scramble for ill-gotten gains, in the course of which the richer appeared to get richer and the poor poorer. The 'intolerable wail of serfage' of which Disraeli wrote in the forties of the nineteenth century consisted in the conditions of factory labour to which *laissez faire* had driven the workers, the condition of semi-starvation thrust upon the old craftsmen by the introduction of the new machines, and the absence of any supervision by the executive Government over the operations of the system which brought about these results. For the remedy proposed by Disraeli, embroidered in exotic and paradoxical language, and for this reason ridiculed and flouted at the time, was as entirely up to date as his analysis of the disease. The privileges of the multitude could only be safeguarded by an increase of the executive power of government which then, as now, is legally expressed in the prerogative of the crown.

...

It so happened that the despised and derided Tories, the enemies of the people, the friends of privilege, the stupid party, the party of self-interest and greed, the party that has opposed every progressive-minded prospectus of reform, had hit on the right criticism and propounded the right remedy. Odd? Or perhaps not quite so odd.

What may, more legitimately, be thought odd is that having taken this stand, Conservatives should now very largely be engaged in fighting the battle of Liberalism against the Socialists who attack *laissez faire* from almost exactly the same angle as the Conservatives in 1848. Surely this is inconsistent? Another proof of Tory hypocrisy? Or is it that this peculiar party thrives on fighting losing battles? It is, one assumes, quite beyond the bounds of possibility that these guilty men should actually turn out to be right again. Or is it? A strange Greek proverb contained the warning 'μηδὲν ἄγαν' – which being interpreted, means 'avoid extremes'. Conservatives think that the doctrinaire application of a political theory inevitably involves the statesman in extremes. In fighting Socialism in the twentieth, as they fought Liberalism in the nineteenth century, Conservatives will be found to have changed their front to meet a new danger, but not the ground they are defending.[63]

Note how the capitalisation of the term 'Conservative' allows Hogg to avoid the making of important distinctions between party and ideology.

The pleasing fact of a common enemy brought conservatives and liberals together, but some thinkers tried to develop a stronger unity between the ideologies. One of the most sophisticated was the fearsomely intellectual, and ideologically driven, Enoch Powell (1912–98). Powell was explicitly conservative, and explicitly drawn to market liberalism. As a conservative, he celebrated, often in poetic terms, the continuity of English traditions.

> Backward travels our gaze, beyond the grenadiers and the philosophers of the eighteenth century, beyond the pikemen and the preachers of the seventeenth, back through the brash adventurous days of the first Elizabeth and the hard materialism of the Tudors, and there at last we find them [the old Englishmen], or seem to find them, in many a village church, beneath the tall tracery of a perpendicular East window and the coffered ceiling of the chantry chapel. From brass and stone, from line and effigy, their eyes look out at us, and we gaze into them, as if we would win some answer from their inscrutable silence.
>
> 'Tell us what it is that binds us together; show us the clue that leads through a thousand years; whisper to us the secret of this charmed life of England, that we in our time may know how to hold it fast.'
>
> What would they say? They would speak to us in our own English tongue, the tongue made for telling truth in, tuned already to songs that haunt the hearer like the sadness of spring. They would tell us of that marvellous land, so

sweetly mixed of opposites in climate that all the seasons of the year appear there in their greatest perfection; of the fields amid which they built their halls, their cottages, their churches, and where the same blackthorn showered its petals upon them as upon us; they would tell us, surely, of the rivers, the hills, and of the island coasts of England. They would tell us too of a palace near the great city which the Romans built at a ford of the River Thames, a palace with many chambers and one lofty hall, with angel faces carved on the hammer beams, to which men resorted out of all England to speak on behalf of their fellows, a thing called 'Parliament', and from that hall went out men with fur-trimmed gowns and strange caps on their heads, to judge the same judgements, and dispense the same justice, to all the people of England.

One thing above all they assuredly would not forget, Lancastrian or Yorkist, squire or lord, priest or layman; they would point to the kingship of England, and its emblems everywhere visible. ...

For the unbroken life of the English nation over a thousand years and more is a phenomenon unique in history, the product of a specific set of circumstances like those which in biology are supposed to start by chance a new line of evolution. Institutions which elsewhere are recent and artificial creations, appear in England almost as works of nature, spontaneous and unquestioned. The deepest instinct of the Englishman – how the word 'instinct' keeps forcing itself in again and again! – is for continuity; he never acts more freely nor innovates more boldly than when he most is conscious of conserving or even of reacting.[64]

Yet Powell was also very pro-markets, so much so that his speeches on economic topics sound much more modern, to a 21st-century reader, than those of his contemporaries.

A society which runs its economic affairs on the principles of free enterprise will be a different kind of society from one where the economy is controlled and managed by the Government. The free enterprise economy is the true counterpart of democracy: it is the only system which gives everyone a say. Everyone who goes into a shop and chooses one article instead of another is casting a vote in the economic ballot box: with thousands or millions of others that choice is signalled through to production and investment and helps to mould the world just a tiny fraction nearer to people's desire. In this great and continuous general election of the free economy nobody, not even the poorest, is disenfranchised: we are all voting all the time. Socialism is designed on the opposite pattern: it is designed to prevent people getting their way, otherwise there would be no point in it. It is not by accident that on the other side of the Iron Curtain there is no choice in the shops and consumer goods are produced which the consumer does not want. In a Socialist society it is the Government which decides. Which system is the more 'humane': the one where the Government decides or the one where the people decide? I say, the one where the economy is moulded by the people as a whole, where the individual and his choice are respected and have their weight.[65]

Powell found little or no contradiction between these views.

I had lived through years in which the Government to which I belonged had been engaged in the business of attempting to create governmental control over essential prices, including the price of labour. ... I had found this profoundly repugnant, repugnant because it jarred with another Tory prejudice, the Tory prejudice that, upon the whole, things are wiser than people, that institutions are wiser than their members and that a nation is wiser than those who comprise it at any specific moment. ...

I had to reconcile [this prejudice] with the rest of my political framework, the intellectual framework within which I had been living for fifteen or sixteen years. I found

no great difficulty in doing that to my own satisfaction. ...
To my own satisfaction, I reached the conclusion that the
price mechanism is one of the means by which a society
takes certain collective decisions in a manner not necessarily ideal, but a manner which is manageable and
acceptable and broadly speaking regarded as workable, a
mechanism which cannot safely or wisely be replaced by
conscious formulation and by compulsion.[66]

Is reconciliation as easy as Powell claims? *Prima facie* evidence
for a tension can be found in his fierce reaction to mass immigration, the issue which defined 'Powellism' for a nation and
finished his career as a serious politician. Powell was convinced
that the long and continuous traditions of which he had written
depended to a large extent on a cultural and political homogeneity, a capacity to conceive of the totality of a nation.[67]
From his vantage point as an MP for Wolverhampton, with its
relatively large immigrant population, he worried about its
increasing heterogeneity, until his notorious, and deliberately
offensive, 'Rivers of Blood' speech.[68] Ideology, in the 1960s, was
much more robust, much more steak-and-Rioja, than the
steamed-chicken-and-mineral-water fare we are served nowadays. But whatever one might think of the tone of the speech,
one thing it does is repudiate the free global market for labour in
no uncertain terms.

We might even postulate that the violence of Powell's
reaction to the decline in cultural homogeneity – what is now
called the rise of multiculturalism – may well have had a cause
in the detection of inconsistency in his own thought by this
brilliant, intellectual, ideological man. How interesting it is that
Quintin Hogg found it necessary to repeat his Greek warning,
'μηδὲν ἄγαν', deliberately to Powell individually in his speech to
the 1968 Conservative Party Conference.[69]

But the attempts to meld conservatism and liberalism were
only a passing fad. By 1965, Edward Heath* had come down

* Prime Minister 1970–74.

strongly in favour of liberalism, though he retreated under political and economic pressure, famously doing a U-turn to keep Rolls-Royce solvent in 1972 (much to Powell's disgust). Blake reads the situation as Heath (and Thatcher) being 'ideologists in a sense that none of their four post-war predecessors were'.[70] In fact, the truth is rather that Heath and Thatcher were clearly liberal, whereas their predecessors were more prepared to consider conservative arguments at a time when liberal free market ideas were gaining ground, Harold Macmillan in particular being suspicious of liberal certainties.

For whatever reason, the liberals within Conservative Party ranks preferred to claim that they were the legitimate heirs to the conservative tradition. The labels clearly mattered. Enoch Powell, whose loathing for Heath was exceeded only by his loathing for Macmillan, even made a not-too-convincing effort to portray the latter as an Edwardian Whig – Superwhig, as he called him.[71] Sir Keith Joseph, Heath's Health and Social Services Secretary, underwent a noisy period of introspection following double defeats in the elections of 1974, in effect deciding that conservatism, for him, simply meant 'liberalism'.[72] Mrs Thatcher* agreed, and, though she went into government in 1979 with a manifesto not unlike Heath's in 1970, she famously did not back down when things went wrong (which they did almost immediately[73]). She persevered, and eventually triumphed.

There was certainly a grumbling in the ranks. All conservatism, according to the Joseph–Thatcher position, was a species of liberalism, and this formulation, as we shall see in the next chapter, has been accepted by most leading commentators on ideology. But on the contrary, conservatives and liberals are very different creatures, and as the distinction could not be masked, it was ultimately marked – as it would have to be marked, so clear was it – by the use of the nomenclature 'wet' (conservative) and 'dry' (liberal). In the wider field of politics, there was a tendency for the conservative element of the

* Prime Minister 1979–90.

Conservative Party to remain strong in its solid areas, such as the southern rural counties, whereas in the cities the lack of a conservative base enabled Thatcherite liberalism to get much more of a hold. (For example, with respect to development and environmental policy, there was transformation where liberal ideology was strong, and pragmatism where conservatives pulled the Thatcherite reformers back towards policy continuity.)[74] The wets complained, mightily. But they were overwhelmed. Thatcherism seemed to come at them from all angles, as Sir Ian Gilmour lamented.

> Thatcherism can be viewed as ideology, style, mood, 'I must have my own way', monarchism, 19th-century Liberalism, millenarian revivalism, right-wingery, a method of controversy, a set of moral values, statecraft, or as a combination of all of them.[75]

From 1975, the liberals were in control at the top of the Conservative Party, by 1981 solidly cemented in place. A similar battle had taken place in the Labour Party, whose founding socialists were invaded by Gladstonian liberals following the decline and collapse of the Liberal Party; the liberals won their decisive victory in that party in 1994, when Tony Blair became leader.[76]

The Liberal Party is no more; its successor, the Liberal Democrats, still only a third force (though of substantial potency). But it is the descendants of the two traditions of the 19th-century Liberals that slug it out in 21st-century politics.

CHAPTER FOUR

WHAT IS CONSERVATISM?

What conservatism is not (I)

From Socrates to Enoch Powell, we have traced a theme through human thought and political action: a certain type of scepticism, allied to a certain view of society, produces a certain type of conservatism that has often, though not always, been prominent in the thinking of the British Conservative Party. The history is interesting, but what matters with an idea at a particular moment is whether it is *alive*, whether it can be adapted to the world of that moment. In the remainder of Part One of this book, we will go beyond history and take the idea's pulse. In this chapter we will define exactly what we mean by 'conservative'; in the next, we go on to look at the extent of its current relevance.

Ideologies are defined partly by their own internal constraints, and partly by their relations with other ideologies. I propose therefore to top and tail my definition of what conservatism *is* with brief characterisations of what it *isn't*.

If we briefly assume, with the dictionaries, that conservatism involves some antagonism towards change (we will examine this assumption carefully later), then I want to rule out some specific types of conservative who immediately spring to mind.

First of all, there is the type of person who is personally unsettled by change. This is the person who doesn't like new technologies, and has complained about every innovation as it came along. He or she worried about the waltz, non-representative art, jazz, rock 'n' roll, Sputnik, hula hoops, computers, skateboards, mobile telephones, the Internet and digital television. This person is more or less satisfied with his or her life, and doesn't want the bother and difficulty of learning new behaviour, mastering more gadgets, talking to new people.

Second, there is the type of person who is doing well out of the status quo, and doesn't want any alteration to it, thank you very much. Never mind if there are deep and obvious structural reasons why the status quo is unsatisfactory; this type of person defends his or her own economic, political or social interests.

It is, of course, the right of such people to resist change. And people of these psychological types (particularly the second) do often happen to support the Conservative Party. Nevertheless, we should avoid calling these people conservatives in the ideological sense that I will define (in the same way that we should avoid calling a hedonistic layabout a 'liberal', a racist football supporter a 'nationalist', or a thief who redistributes wealth from rich people to give to the poor – i.e. himself – a 'socialist').

The reason is fairly clear: such preferences have only an incidental connection with the ideas, and they are certainly not prompted by those ideas. Those timidly afraid of change have no thought that society would be better as a result of stasis, only that their own lives would improve. Those who do well from the status quo are not really concerned with change so much as with wealth and status; if they were divested of their wealth of a sudden, then their conservatism would vanish along with their loot.

What we are looking for, in an ideology, is the existence of good *arguments*, objective *reasons* for its support. Of course, human nature is such that the ideologies we espouse are often those that will act in our interests; the poor are more often socialist than the rich; the rich are more often market liberals than the poor; you will be unlikely ever to encounter a non-Christian defending fundamentalist Christianity; those dependent on heavy industry for their livelihoods tend not to be environmentalists. So much is to be expected. But when the poor person defends socialism, the rich person market liberalism, the Christian fundamentalism, or the hippy environmentalism, you would expect the arguments to be concerned not with the personal circumstances of the arguer, but with reasons that stand alone, reasons that the interlocutor has to engage with. When hippies defend environmentalism, they do not point out their distaste for consumption and artifice; they produce evidence of imminent ecological catastrophe. When business-people reply to them, they do not produce their bank statements; they talk of the liberating power of wealth, and the importance of development. No doubt their ideological beliefs are *caused* by concern with nature or bank balances, but the reasons they produce are different from the causes, and no less valid for not being causes.

The need to articulate one's position so that it is understandable by all citizens irrespective of their preferences or ideas of the good is an imperative of *public reason*, an idea developed by the American political philosopher John Rawls.[1] If I appeal to public reason, I have to convince you, not that the ideology is in my interests – you will no doubt be happy to accept that – but instead that your interests, unbeknownst to you, are actually allied with mine. This sort of abstraction away from individual circumstances, partly to produce an ideology that is more far-reaching and applicable to others' circumstances, and partly to facilitate the persuasion of others that the ideology should be applied in real life, was one of the successful moves made by Rawls as he revitalised liberalism almost single-handedly with his classic text *A Theory of Justice*.

What Rawls did for liberalism needs to be done for conservatism; a Rawlsian turn is strongly recommended, and in this chapter I am going to try to develop a conservatism that appeals to public reason in the same way that Rawlsian liberalism (perhaps the most successful political philosophy of the last three decades) does. The two types of 'conservative' we sketched above are therefore not conservatives in the meaning of the act, because their reasons are purely self-centred. Of course one would expect those who are 'conservative' to be the ultimate beneficiaries of conservative policies; but one must also demand that the conservative be able to explain his or her reasons for conservatism in an intelligible and widely applicable way.

Not all Conservatives are conservatives, and not all conservatives are Conservatives

So, a genuine conservative, in the ideological sense, shouldn't necessarily be someone who is too rich or staid to welcome change, or someone who reveres Churchill or Mrs Thatcher, or someone who thinks that the Tories are posh and Labour coarse – sizeable though each of those constituencies are.

What about the relationship between the Conservative Party and conservatism? We have already argued that the Conservative Party is the custodian of the conservative tradition. It is time to inquire about the meaning of that statement in more detail.

As the title of this section suggests, I want to argue against assuming that what the Conservative Party does is the be-all and end-all for judging what conservatism is. I have already insisted upon making a conceptual distinction between conservatism and the Conservative Party; in this section, I now have to argue that not only is the distinction conceptual, but it also reflects reality. That involves arguing that either there are conservatives who are not Conservative, or there are Conservatives who are not conservative, or both. That in turn depends on how 'conservatism' is characterised (assuming for the minute that the notion of being a member of the Conservative Party is unproblematic, which, as for instance in the case of Enoch Powell, it is not).

Several projects came together in the 1980s under the rubric of the 'new right', which engendered a lot of interest from all sides of the political spectrum. In general, the new right were enthused by the attack on corporatism, and the promotion of supply-side economics, under totemic icon Margaret Thatcher, and iconic totem Ronald Reagan. The philosophers of the new right, armed with references to Friedman, Nozick and Hayek, developed quite an armoury of distinctive social policies, to do with the welfare state, identity and citizenship, as well as the market-driven economics that were the mainstay and chief attraction. It is fair to say that the general public never really bought the whole package, but that the resulting vast increase in consumer choice (a change which is literally unintelligible for anyone under the age of 30) was, and remains, extremely popular. For this reason if for no other, it is very unlikely that there will be a speedy return to social corporatism in the English-speaking Anglo-Saxon nations.

This project has been identified with conservatism by many, not least by some of the new rightists themselves. As political scientist Andrew Gamble put it, 'the New Right would like to be conservative but they are forced to be radicals.'[2] In other words, the world was so far from what they considered acceptable that they had to remake it in their own image. The necessary aim of the new right in the 1980s was to create the conditions that would permit a culture and set of institutions conducive to the free market to flourish. The implication, then, is that they were not therefore conservatives – for, to adapt Disraeli's rhetorical question, what did they conserve?

Was the new right ideologically coherent? To an extent, yes, at least with respect to what they opposed.[3] They opposed egalitarianism: the whole point of market-based systems is that one creates one's own wealth by exchange, and therefore the equalising of people's wealth via redistribution would negate the whole project, as this would mean that some would gain wealth without exchanging anything for it (i.e. without making any kind of contribution to the economy), while others would be prevented from keeping the proceeds of their exchanges (and therefore would have their incentives to exchange taken away). They opposed collectivism: they agreed that the unit of social analysis was the individual, and any loyalty that he or she might have to larger agglomerations, such as social class or trade union, would detract from the efficiency of the economy in exploiting capital, and therefore from the total wealth created. And they opposed identity politics, such as feminism and gay rights, though they were often libertarian enough not to be restrictive about relations between consenting adults.

But the new right was united mainly in opposition. Mike Harris picks out four distinct and inconsistent sets of positive proposals within the new right.[4]

- **Neo-liberalism**. This follows on from classical liberalism, promoting individual autonomy and property rights, and distinguishing between the public and the private sphere. Governments or the state have only limited rights to interfere in private matters. Market freedoms are the best way to promote and secure political liberties.

- **Public choice**. This is the discipline of basing a critique of the representative political processes on the techniques of economic analysis. Public choice theorists assume that all agents are self-interested and rational, and therefore, for example, claim to be able to show that large-scale bureaucracies of the type required to administer major public projects actually act against the public interest.

- **Libertarianism**. Libertarians prize freedom over everything else except property, even social order. If property rights are fundamental, underpinning exchange, contract and the freedom of society, then anything else can be allowed, they argue – hence their alternative name of anarcho-capitalists. Libertarians have little problem, for example, with those intent on drug abuse or other risky activities.

- **Neo-conservatism**. Neo-conservatives, an American breed, are concerned with three main topics: the breakdown of the family; poverty and the underclass; and the cultural crisis, where intellectuals are seen as promoting values alien to the American way.

Robert Eccleshall has argued that the new right project is actually constitutive of conservatism. But what about the conservative rhetoric about tradition and institutions?

> Clearly, conservatives have frequently vindicated the latent wisdom of existing institutions, accusing their ideological adversaries of succumbing to the illusion that politics is the science of human perfection. Does this mean that

traditionalism is the key to the conservative sanctum, providing a sort of creed which all who subscribe to the doctrine
readily profess? There are ... reasons for supposing that the
heart of conservatism lies elsewhere.[5]

Yet conservatives have always claimed that that is where their
hearts lie. The tradition outlined in the previous chapter seems
to have little in common with these new right ideas (though it
clearly shares many of their common *antagonisms*). In general,
the concerns of the British conservative, being related to our
imperfect knowledge, our imperfect moral status, and the
dangers of replacing social institutions and structures, particularly those of long standing, are orthogonal at best to those of
the new right who wish to alter society to anchor market institutions. Small 'c' conservatives are opposed to non-pragmatic
thought, whereas free marketeers can often be very evangelical;
many commentators have written of 'market fundamentalism'.[6]
Conservatives' suspicion of abstract thought seems also
inimical to the neo-liberal theorists.

This, however, is not to say that conservatism and market
economics are unlinked; far from it. Indeed, many of the social
structures that underpin free markets (property rights, a work
ethic, contract law, and respect for the law generally) are exactly
those that are valued by conservatives. Hence it is perfectly
possible for a conservative to argue that, as an economic regulator
of exchange, free markets are as good as any; while nationalised
industries (for example) distort valuable relationships within a
society.

On the other hand, a conservative is always sensible of outcomes; some pattern of exchanges might well lead to unfortunate
outcomes. The new right would reject the whole idea that an
outcome of a properly conducted exchange might be 'unfortunate' or 'fortunate'; they would argue strongly against the claim
that, if one was a property owner, one might have wider duties
to society when it came to exchanging that property.[7]

Why, then, does Eccleshall insist that conservatism is
unrelated to tradition? He gives four reasons.

The first is that conservatives do not invariably shun abstract thinking in favour of a pragmatic style of politics. …

Among the kind of free-market conservatives whom Disraeli lambasted there is ample evidence of a fondness for dogmatic certainties. Tory opponents of the New Right in the 1980s used to complain that their party had been captured by alien ideologues, as though all former conservatives had quietly practised the art of prudent statecraft without recourse to the certainties of political economy.[8]

He cites the example of the Liberty and Property Defence League, founded in 1882 by Conservatives, to prevent the government from meddling in economics. But its principal publicist, Lord Elcho (later the Earl of Wemyss), had at best an ambivalent relationship to the Party; in 1846, he became a Peelite, the faction that followed Peel during the Corn Law kerfuffle, and which in general drifted towards (and voted with) the Liberals. As it happened, Elcho rejoined the Conservatives. The main doctrinal inspiration for the LPDL was the thinker Herbert Spencer (1820–1903), not a member of any party, but a defender of libertarian principles. The LPDL contained both Liberals and Conservatives, though the latter predominated over time.[9] We have already seen that the Conservative Party was home to many people who did not share the conservative philosophy – after all, this was the intention of Disraeli's increasing the coalition of members. And if Elcho and their friends thought that the Conservative Party was itself a sufficiently reliable ideological vehicle to promote their free market ideas, then why set up the LPDL at all?[10] Indeed, Elcho was even able to accuse Lord Salisbury, perhaps the most reactionary politician of stature ever in Britain, of crypto-socialism![11]

There were many minor political figures and organisations of similar ilk, but the libertarian free market groups which proliferated at the turn of the century like flowers in the spring have a difficult relation with mainstream politics, certainly too difficult to rest much of an argument on. We have already mentioned the split in the Liberal Party between the Gladstonians and the libertarians, and the defection of the latter group to the Tories. The development of this individualist strain within the Conservative Party can be seen as simply a symptom of that historical movement; at best, Eccleshall's first argument begs the question, as historian E.H.H. Green illustrates.

> Suffice it here to say that from 1880 onwards it becomes easier and more meaningful to identify Conservative individualists. Organizations such as the Liberty and Property Defence League (LPDL) and the British Constitutional Association (BCA), and individuals like Lord Wemyss, Herbert Spencer, A.V. Dicey, Auberon Herbert, and Ernest Benn, all explicitly espoused individualist ideas and were supporters or members of the Conservative Party. Yet, in spite of their party-political affiliation, the political *philosophy* to which these 'men versus the State' were self-consciously closest was nineteenth-century Liberalism. Dicey, Herbert, and many others associated with the LPDL and BCA had no great love for Conservatism, but, when faced with the development of a Collectivist New Liberalism, saw the Conservative party as the best chance for preserving old Liberal individualism. This is not to say that *all* individualist sympathizers in the Conservative ranks were former Liberals – Lords Wemyss, Hugh Cecil, and Robert Cecil stand out as Conservatives of long standing – but there is a marked coincidence between the rise of Conservative individualist thought and the arrival in the Conservative party, at all levels, of Liberal defectors.[12]

Eccleshall's other arguments that conservatism is nothing to do with tradition and opposition to change are similarly question-begging.

> [Conservatives'] attraction to purposive politics is obscured by the right's caricature of the rationalist as a starry-eyed optimist on the ideological left, someone naïve enough to

suppose that a classless society can be delivered by application of the appropriate axioms. ... [But] the New Right was one manifestation of this sort of perfectionism. There was little evidence of distaste for doctrinal certainties in the New Right's flirtation with monetarism and other refinements of the science of political economy, of preference for gradual reform in its crusade to push back the state from the economy, of respect for a customary way of life in its assault upon the post-war settlement, or of an aversion to simplistic solutions in its portrayal of a brave new world of competitive individualism. The ideological right is as capable as the left of utopian speculation.

The third reason why conservatism cannot be equated with traditionalism is that the right is not invariably against radical change. Conservatives certainly possess a stock of arguments, inherited from the counter-revolutionary response of Burke and others to the attack on the *ancien regime*, by which they have frequently defended the established political order. The point is that these arguments have been used to oppose political programmes of which the right disapproves. On other occasions, as in the 1980s, conservatives can be as fervent as their adversaries in advocating schemes of political reconstruction.

This is so because, fourthly, conservatism is not ... a negative or 'positional' ideology which warns against tampering with the *status quo*, whatever that happens to be at a particular historical moment. Conservatism, like other ideologies, does stand for something in that its adherents have a clear conception of how society should be organised. ... [A]ll favour a society in which certain inequalities are preserved, and in condemning purposive politics their intention is to ridicule the egalitarian ideals of their opponents. ... A principal objection of the New Right to welfare capitalism was that redistributive taxation had deprived the rich of the incentive to create wealth and discouraged the poor from improving themselves.[13]

All these arguments try to make points about conservatism by exhibiting the negative example of the new right. They all beg the question, therefore, of whether the new right was conservative at all; for if it was not, then its example is strictly irrelevant.

As W.H. Greenleaf points out,[14] the Conservative Party is so old, and its net drawn so wide, that expecting all its members to espouse the same policies is wrongheaded, but it does not follow that it is wrongheaded to point out that there are deep divisions within the party. If, as Greenleaf and Eccleshall argue, there is no fundamental *ideological* distinction between the majority of Conservative politicians, then it remains a mystery why the same arguments blow up time after time. For example, Harold Macmillan testified to a cabinet split whose fault line ran directly along the historical divide.

> Meanwhile, the Chancellor of the Exchequer and I worked on a letter to be addressed to both sides of industry proposing the creation of the National Economic Development Council, drawn from trade unions, management and government who could participate in central planning advice. ... The discussion about this plan revealed 'a rather interesting and quite deep divergence of view between Ministers, really corresponding to whether they had old Whig, Liberal, *laissez-faire* traditions, or Tory opinions, paternalists and not afraid of a little *dirigisme*.'[15]

If there is no divide within the Conservatives between the paternalist and the libertarian, the wet and the dry, then there needs to be some explanation of why that sort of terminology keeps resurfacing, and why there have been perpetual arguments within the party about precisely these issues. The whole point, surely, is that the arguments between, say, Baldwin and Churchill, Macmillan and Thorneycroft, Heath and Powell, Pym and Thatcher, Major and Redwood, Hague and Portillo, are instances of a common pathology. Surely the oddest explanation for these is that they are all *sui generis* examples of individual vendettas in a uniquely fractious party. The Greenleaf/Eccleshall claim of fundamental ideological unity seems to lack explanatory power at the point at which it is most obviously needed.

So there is pretty strong evidence that not all Conservatives are conservative. What about the argument that not all conservatives are Conservative? I have already argued against Bruce Pilbeam that there is nothing *prima facie* unreasonable about assuming that Soviet generals or Iranian mullahs are conservative (though as will be clear, I do not think they are – for different reasons from Pilbeam's).[16]

In general, over the last two centuries, inequality has been decreasing. The poor have been getting generally richer, partly because of socialist reforms, partly because of the operations of the market, partly because of the impact of technology, and partly because of the social compacts made by various Conservative governments. Everyone, it is fair to say, Tory, Liberal and Labour, gets some credit. But the effect of the increase in equality is that the rich have been generally keener to halt reform, while the poor have been generally keener to accelerate it. So far, so good: as one would expect. But since 1979, and the Thatcherite market-driven reforms, inequality has been on the increase. It halted in the 1990s under John Major (though it was not reversed), and has been on the increase again under Tony Blair.[17] Hence from 1979 it has been true, as it has not been true before, that the poor might feel (possibly incorrectly) that they could benefit from a slowing-down of the pace of change, that though they do not get very much out of the status quo, it may well be the best that they can hope for. The institutions of society that were constructed in the early part of the 20th century by Gladstonian liberals, and in the third quarter by socialists, are precisely the institutions that they wish to protect from neo-liberal market-led reforms. Such a constituency might well begin to examine the conservative arguments which we will set out in this chapter rather more seriously once they can see that they can benefit from them.

For instance, an argument along these lines was sketched by political philosopher John Gray in the final years of the Major government; Gray, formerly a leading theorist of the new right, has in recent times switched dramatically to a much more hostile position.[18]

> Nowhere has Tory market corporatism been more destructive than in the National Health Service. It is worth reflecting on Tory policy on the NHS, if only as an object lesson in ideological folly. By any international standard the old, unreformed NHS was a considerable success story. ... Furthermore, and perhaps decisively, the NHS was understood and trusted by the British people. There is not, and never has been, any popular demand for its reform. In fact, there is deep public disquiet about its dismemberment. ... In imposing on the tried and familiar institutions of the old NHS a grandiose scheme of marketizing reforms, whose ultimate outcome even they could scarcely guess at, the Tories proved once again that they have lost the concern for the continuity of institutions that is their only principled *raison d'être*.
>
> There is, then, an overwhelming conservative case – to be sure, one which today's Tories cannot be expected even to understand – for restoring the old National Health Service, as the fundamental institution within which health care is provided in Britain.[19]

The first tenet of conservatism: the change principle

How, then, to describe conservatism? A very fruitful framework for understanding ideologies generally has been developed by political philosopher Michael Freeden.[20] Freeden sees ideologies as coarse versions of political philosophies, made easier to understand and communicate, less subtle but more applicable to the real world. An ideology can be described as a small cluster of basic tenets, principles or concepts. Such tenets, beyond the political group, can be disputed, and open to a number of interpretations. But within a particular group, the meaning of the principle is *decontested*, that is, it is not disputed. The tenet is taken as something that the group holds in common.

So, for example, the term 'liberty' is open to a number of interpretations. But for a particular ideological group – for example, neo-liberal free marketeers – the meaning of liberty is not argued over. Neo-liberals may argue about many things, such as the extent to which markets should determine the distribution of a society's resources, but what they do not argue about is the nature of liberty, and whether such liberty is a good. This does not mean that all neo-liberals necessarily *agree* about the nature of liberty, or about why it is desirable. But, perhaps in the face of some common opponent, they tacitly agree not to subject their basic assumptions to argument and contest within the group.

So what are the decontested ideas of conservatism? Let us begin with the desire to avoid change. Given that we hope to take a Rawlsian turn and appeal to public reason, we need to produce arguments for opposition to change that do not simply boil down to a preference for the status quo. Robert Eccleshall insists that that is not possible.

> The proposition that conservatism is rooted in a natural dislike of change is of negligible analytic value, conflating as it does ahistorical patterns of individual behaviour with the emergence – at a specific moment in Western culture and among particular social groups – of a cluster of ideas about the purposes of government and the organisation of society.[21]

Eccleshall is articulating a view of conservatism conflating many different kinds of right-wing thought, seeking to find ideological agreement where there is only a common line of attack against a commonly recognised enemy. But in the light of our investigations in the two previous chapters, that seems inadequate; an attitude to change seems central to the epistemological conservatism that we have traced from its origins in Ancient Greece.

We need to make two arguments here. First, we need to decide precisely what the content is of the conservative's attitude to change. And second, we then need an appeal to public reason that goes beyond 'natural dislike'.

Can any politician oppose change *tout court*? There are great social forces, and it seems crazy for a politician to stand in their way. Indeed, Tolstoy in the Epilogue to *War and Peace* went so far as to argue that no individual, not even Napoleon, could have any effect on history at all. That view is too extreme, but nevertheless it is fair to say that to try to prevent change utterly would be impossible. Conservative philosopher Roger Scruton suggests that much greater flexibility is desirable here.

> It is a limp definition of conservatism to describe it as the desire to conserve; for although there is in every man and woman some impulse to conserve that which is safe and familiar, it is the nature of this 'familiarity' that needs to be examined. To put it briefly, conservatism arises directly from the sense that one belongs to some continuing, and pre-existing social order, and that this fact is all-important in determining what to do.[22]

The social order, then, is the focus of conservative belief. As Scruton points out, the social order to which one is attracted will vary from person to person. He concentrates on institutions, but actually one can be linked to very nebulous groups indeed. In the Internet age, many communities are online, and conservatism can arise in the resistance of many netizens to authoritarian attempts to fix the Internet's architecture, for example, to force users to reveal their identities (the whole institutional point of many online communities is the very fluid notion of identity that the Internet affords).[23] Similarly, many young people place their loyalty in a set of fashion statements that include certain types of clothes, related genres of music and, uh, like, particular ways of talking? Y'know? Early adulthood has been shown to be uniquely open to the gain of knowledge and to the influence of memory and generational identity; patterns of fashion stay with one for a lifetime.[24] *Blue Peter*ish attempts to direct such fashions, or even to channel their energy, are doomed to fail. Communities, societies, institutions or even fashions change under their own steam; they cannot be steered from outside.

> The desire to conserve is compatible with all manner of change, provided only that change is also continuity.[25]

Scruton's point is well taken; conservatism is *not* intended to preserve the status quo against all comers. It is an ideology *concerned* with the difficulties that change provides, and is intended to manage change and to render it safe to handle. Allowable change is seen as *organic* or *natural*, in contradistinction to imposed or designed change.[26] Conservative philosopher Michael Oakeshott puts it like this.

> Changes, then, have to be suffered; and a man of conservative temperament (that is, one strongly disposed to preserve his identity) cannot be indifferent to them. In the main, he judges them by the disturbance they entail and, like everyone else, deploys his resources to meet them. The idea of innovation, on the other hand, is improvement. Nevertheless, a man of this temperament will not himself be an ardent innovator. In the first place, he is not inclined to think that nothing is happening unless great changes are afoot and therefore he is not worried by the absence of innovation: the use and enjoyment of things as they are occupies most of his attention. Further, he is aware that not all innovation is, in fact, improvement; and he will think that to innovate without improving is either designed or inadvertent folly. ... Innovating is always an equivocal enterprise, in which gain and loss (even excluding the loss of familiarity) are so closely interwoven that it is exceedingly difficult to forecast the final up-shot: there is no such

thing as an unqualified improvement. For, innovating is an activity which generates not only the 'improvement' sought, but a new and complex situation of which this is only one of the components. The total change is always more extensive than the change designed; and the whole of what is entailed can neither be foreseen nor circumscribed. Thus, whenever there is innovation there is the certainty that the change will be greater than was intended, that there will be loss as well as gain and that the loss and the gain will not be equally distributed among the people affected; there is the chance that the benefits derived will be greater than those which were designed; and there is the risk that they will be off-set by changes for the worse.[27]

Hence the answer to our first question is that the conservative privileges particular types of change – 'organic' change – and tries to avoid others.

Oakeshott begins to answer our second question too; the reason for this attitude towards change is that 'inorganic' change, innovation, may have bad effects. Existing social structures confer huge benefits, which can be easily overlooked. The fact that 60 million people share the United Kingdom and interact as often and as peacefully as they do, the fact that prosperity spreads reasonably well, if not perfectly, through the nation is in and of itself a reason for celebration. It is something to value.

Equally, it is not something to risk lightly, because we know how fragile functioning societies are. We have seen many times how peaceful, relatively prosperous populations have been prepared to throw away the advantages of peace and prosperity in favour of murderous civil war, because of wrongs, or imagined wrongs, committed centuries ago (of which many are only dimly aware). In the United Kingdom, there are still communities wavering on the brink of throwing away the benefits of stable society, preferring pointless, barely motivated conflict. In Northern Ireland, the peace process is stalled despite its obvious benefits. In some forgotten towns in the north of England racial tensions threaten the peace. It seems incredible that the disorganised racist rabble that is the British National Party could launch a sustained assault on British society, but stranger things have happened.

The benefits that society brings are often not noticed by their recipients (until they have gone), and are very fragile. Change will therefore entail a risk, and the conservative point is that that risk should be weighed very carefully. We will call this first central tenet of conservatism the **change principle**.

The case for a conservative attitude will depend to a large extent on the particular context. Small 'c' conservatism will be attractive in an attractive society. The concrete benefits of an existing society must, says the conservative, be taken more seriously than potential, abstract benefits that could be gained through applying a social theory. That does not, self-evidently, entail that one should never innovate, nor that the concrete should always be valued more highly than the abstract. It is only to say that there is an extra burden of proof on those who are willing change.

So, for example, consider Japan. Japan is a very pleasant country, prosperous, orderly – and conservative. But since the property bubble burst at the end of the 1980s, there has been a prolonged slump. Part of the problem is that the banks took on a lot of bad debt in the preceding boom, and now are reluctant to lend to further clients, which means that it is hard for investors to build up new businesses. The Anglo-Saxon, red-blooded variety of capitalism has a simple solution: let the banks go bust (Mrs Thatcher, of course, famously let much of British industry die). But the Japanese are reluctant to do this, because the social shock will be too great. Are the Japanese right or wrong?

The change principle does not determine right and wrong. From its standpoint, however, the Japanese are undoubtedly correct to value social continuity, and to try to solve their debt problem without wiping out savings, even if those savings are invested unwisely. But there must come a point at which the concrete benefits of the status quo are too small to take into consideration, particularly when the potential benefits of drastic action are large.

The effect of the change principle is not to prevent change, nor to set out the exact circumstances when change is acceptable, but *to throw the burden of proof onto the innovator*. That burden will become higher when the benefits of an existing society are high. In this way, the change principle does not direct policy, so much as indicate the proper subject matter of the important political arguments.

The change principle entails that conservatism will vary across societies. Hence, unlike liberals or Marxists, conservatives from different societies will say different things. Marxists from Liberia or Letchworth will agree on policy fundamentals; their conservative opponents will not. This is why it is so hard to lump conservatives together and treat them as a single unit. For example, an American conservative maintains that a written constitution is the guarantor of liberty; a British conservative claims that it would be the first step on the road to tyranny. They cannot agree, because each conservative values the benefits visible in his or her own society.

But the change principle also rules out the idea that conservatism can be a mere exercise in nationalistic nostalgia. Many people claim, or have claimed, to be conservative on the basis of their preference for a 'kinder, gentler age', usually a sort of *Passport to Pimlico* Britain where life was simpler, we had pounds, shillings and pence, rods, poles and perches, and you could leave your back door open all day. I adore the Ealing comedies myself. But it was a theme-park Britain even when the films were made, and was finally satirised to death in the 1960s by *The Avengers*. It is neither feasible nor desirable to recreate that society today. No one who accepts the change principle should wish a return to a golden age, even if that golden age is particularly inviting.

And this is for the obvious reason that someone turning the clock back is forcing unwelcome, inorganic change every bit as much as someone who speeds the clock forward. Each is ruled out, as conservatism, by the change principle. When the Ayatollah Khomeini set off the Iranian revolution, and returned Iran from a modernising society under the brutal Shah to a 'conservative' one where 9th-century *Sharia* law predominates, he had to change the place, and he and his successors have had to hold the development of Iranian society back, painfully and with great difficulty. The result is a deeply divided country which, despite its being a nominal theocracy, does not seem any more godly than anywhere else. The malign consequences of forcing Iranian society back several centuries were obvious to anyone who took the change principle seriously.

The roots of social order

The change principle defines a certain type of mild conservatism. It is mild because the politician is exhorted to privilege the present over future possibilities. Nevertheless, this description applies to virtually every British government, including those of Mrs Thatcher and Mr Blair. It has often been remarked how the inertia of the massive government machine prevents British governments from making wholesale changes (modernisations, they are often called). At some point, the intellectual, administrative and financial effort of throwing away the governmental infrastructure of the nation is too great even for the most determined reformers.

Many governments will happily volunteer support for the change principle. It would not, for example, be at all fanciful to factorise democratic socialism as socialism plus the change principle.[28] Something more is required, a second principle, if we are to define a conservatism that is both consistent with the sceptical conservative philosophical and political tradition, while ruling out related non-conservative ideologies.

Michael Freeden's impressive analysis of the conservative ideology supplements the change principle with an idea that cleverly incorporates the conservative acceptance of (or insistence on) human imperfection.

> The defence of a specific, 'normal' type of change [i.e. the change principle] is significantly assisted by a second core component of conservatism that underlies whatever quasi-

contingent guises its various manifestations may borrow: a belief in the extra-human origins of the social order, i.e. as independent of human will. It is undoubtedly a substantive and valorized core concept, though not always recognized as such by its practitioners. The phrase 'extra-human', rather than the more common phrase 'natural', is deliberate because it is an intriguing extension of the latter. The search for harmony, equilibrium, and order – itself a raising of the concern with change to a state of awareness – has adopted many forms. God, history, biology, and science, as understood by different generations, have served in turn as the extra-human anchor of the social order and have been harnessed to validate its practices. In the nineteenth century, conservatives saw stability as a function of the natural order or hierarchy, 'my station and my duties', with their concomitants of status and responsibility anchored in a strong sense of history. In the early part of the twentieth century, the emphasis was on identifying immutable 'psychological' principles of human nature, such as the need to provide incentives to action, or the desire to compete, which justified property-holdings as expressions of human worth and facilitators of human activity. Some contemporary conservatives still adhere to such notions of necessity, invoking the bonds of family or the natural instinct to endorse prevailing practices and institutions. In the era of welfare-state Keynesianism, as well as free-market post-Keynesianism, the appeal has been to another natural order – that of 'scientific' economic laws ostensibly endowed with universal validity.[29]

In other words, the conservative accepts that he or she has no control over the conditions that underlie the natural order. Whether those conditions involve God, free markets or something else, the job of the conservative politician, on this reading, is to ensure that humans do not try to interfere with, or impede, the 'extra-human order'. This inclusion of free markets under the rubric of 'extra-human order', incidentally, makes Freeden's argument that free market liberalism is a type of conservatism completely straightforward.[30]

Roger Scruton's very British conservatism provides an example of a conservative philosophy that Freeden's characterisation includes. We have already seen that Scruton endorses the change principle;[31] but Scruton also reveres a particular type of extra-human order. His view of conservatism is only marginally related to the free market,[32] and nothing whatsoever to do with the hostility to the state characteristic of market liberalism or American neo-conservatism.[33] The aim of the British conservative tradition as Scruton sees it is to provide the conditions in which individual freedom and security can flourish.[34] Unlike liberalism, the individual is not the starting point of political discussion, but the end.[35] Hence abstracting operations and conceptualisations, such as social justice or egalitarianism, are ruled out of court.[36] Instead, Scruton focuses on the importance of the institutions that provide security while simultaneously allowing the space within which individuals can express their individuality; he insists that such institutions should remain clear of government control.[37] The law should protect the shared values that bring the community together, not the rights of individuals, including those who wish to pull the community apart and create an environment for radical individualism.[38]

In other words, Scruton rests his idea of conservatism on an extra-human order to do with institutions, law and family relations, all of which are given (i.e. our relationships with them are not contractual, and therefore not voluntary on our part, and cannot be adjusted or redrawn as we like). His conservatism is based around allegiance and loyalty to these institutions. The change principle ensures (a) that no one should make any attempt to impose their own ideas of right, efficiency or morality on this extra-human order, and (b) continuity from generation to generation that marks out a particular type of life as British (maybe English), and confers legitimacy on the institutions as ways of regulating social and economic life.

As a characterisation of conservatism, the change principle plus the adherence to the extra-human roots of the social order has its attractions. However, there are three reasons for thinking that this is an inadequate account. The combination is too unstable to support a coherent ideology.

The first reason is to do with the communicability of the conservative message. Recall our stricture that conservatives must have public reasons underlying their commitment to the status quo and its slow, organic evolution. Merely disliking change, or wanting to be posh, is not sufficient to be counted as a conservative. We recommended that conservatism take a Rawlsian turn, that it should be prepared to base itself on as few and as uncontroversial assumptions as could bear its weight, partly to provide a stronger philosophical foundation, partly to facilitate the communication of the ideology to others.

The problem with basing conservatism on the extra-human origins of the social order is that whether one accepts conservatism will then depend on one's buying into that account of the social order. If I am asked to become a conservative because God created the world, and man in His image, etc., then the recruitment drive ends there because I do not believe that there is a God. I have a deep respect for market forces, and have few moral problems with the idea of free markets, globalisation, etc. But equally it seems perfectly reasonable to me for communities to interfere with market operation when they feel that greater issues are at stake. With Scruton and Enoch Powell I think that the English common law is an amazing creation that should be nurtured, but it can lead to injustice and we should be ruthless about preventing that. I cannot be persuaded of the merits of conservatism prior to being persuaded of the merits of the extra-human order in question.

The second reason why Freeden's account of conservatism will not do is hinted at in the above argument: the fragmentation of ideas of the social order. There are dozens and dozens of views of the foundation of the social order, and any attempt to form a conservative policy will be fraught with difficulty in the absence of a consensus on what the extra-human origins actually are. A fundamentalist Christian and a free market evangelist could agree about many things, no doubt, but at some point they will come to Christ's evicting the money-changers from the temple.

The third problem is the most serious, and it is that the idea of resting conservatism on the extra-human origins of the social order actually stands in many imaginable circumstances in complete contradiction to the change principle. To state it most baldly, if the current state of the social order was such that it concealed rather than celebrated its extra-human origins, then it would be the duty of the conservative to change the social order, possibly radically. If you have strong beliefs about the extra-human origins of the social order, then you are just as likely to want to change society radically as to preserve it; and alternatively just as likely to try to prevent organic change as to allow it to happen.

So, to revisit a previous example, the Ayatollah Khomeini's Islamic Revolution in Iran was clearly based on a particular conception of the extra-human origins of the social order, as all Islamist ideologies are. But Khomeini had to violate the change principle radically, because he found the existing social structures in 1979 Iran to be literally worthless. The present and concrete was not considered for a second to be comparable to the absent, abstract and potential. That the social and moral improvements promised by Khomeini remain absent and abstract – I think I demur at 'potential' – even now is evidence of the value of the change principle.

More germane to the British case is the point that free markets are celebrated as agents of massive and thoroughgoing change (not always for the worse, not always for the better). In the post-Thatcher world, it is almost impossible to understand the pre-Thatcher experience; to read the speeches of, say, Robert Carr or George Brown is to enter a different world. Free marketry cannot inherently be a species of conservatism because free markets deliberately flout the change principle. It is no coincidence that the arch-free-marketeer Hayek (whom we will meet below), a man with very decided views of the extra-human origins of the social order, once wrote a paper explaining 'Why I am not a conservative'.[39]

Planning and targets: a lack of knowledge

We agreed earlier that the change principle would have to be supplemented by something else, and we have seen that the 'extra-human' idea doesn't work. The history of conservatism, on the other hand, suggests that knowledge might be a key to understanding conservatism. From Socrates, to Sextus Empiricus, to Montaigne, thinkers have argued that people are simply incapable of discovering the basic facts that would justify the opinions they have, and that they are very bad at extracting the relevant information from the world. When the philosophers left off, the psychologists got hold of us and managed to prove the situation is at least as bad as the philosophers had expected; we are very irrational and biased creatures, at least as measured against the yardstick of rational decision-making.[40]

Part of the problem in running human affairs has always been the uncertainty of future events. One obvious solution to uncertainty is to plan the development of society in order to reduce uncertainty, specifically to plan the economy. The idea is that, for example, a government, armed with a suitable mandate from its electorate, could make certain decisions to reduce risk for its population. So, for example, it could fix the prices of various products that were determined to be essential; it could fix the price of labour, to ensure that posts deemed to be too important to remain unfilled were attractive to enough people; it could make it harder, or even illegal, to fire people; it could ensure the supply of various commodities; it could raise the price of some imports to make sure that home-based industry could compete on easier terms; it could prevent the purchase of certain firms by foreigners to ensure an indigenous industry; most obviously of all, it could purchase (nationalise) firms to take their demand and supply decisions out of the purview of the market altogether, and in effect fund the losses through taxation. Such policies were routinely pursued in Britain in the 60s and 70s.

Since 1989, however, they have been radically discredited by the collapse of the Soviet Union, the most ambitious planned economy the world has ever known. Other planned economies on a smaller scale, most notably North Korea and Zimbabwe at the time of writing, have also proved abject failures. On the other hand, a large enough economy can live with small planned enclaves, as long as voters/taxpayers are prepared to take up the slack by paying higher prices and losing out on opportunities for trade. Particularly egregious examples include the EU's Common Agricultural Policy, designed to enrich a small number of farmers in Europe at the expense of European food consumers (i.e. everybody), and competing farmers in the developing world (i.e. everybody else); and the airline business, where most European governments insist on a 'national champion', resulting in much higher prices in Europe than the US. But even so, any planned sector of an economy requires an unplanned penumbra that keeps the whole thing going, supplying unplanned needs (and that can sometimes dwarf the planned element in size).[41]

It is recognised by most commentators that planning an economy is simply beyond the ken of most governments. It was hoped that a government could assemble a large enough bureaucratic machine to administer the millions of demand and supply decisions through transparent rules and consistent application of regulations.[42] But the difficulty has been that, though a bureaucracy might be fairly represented as being machine-like, a society cannot be, and the actions of the one upon the other may well be harmful. Added to which, individual bureaucrats are still as prone to error as the rest of us; an enduring image in virtually every British comedy film of the 1950s is the 'men from the ministry', bureaucrats invariably dressed in pinstriped suits and bowler hats, carrying rolled umbrellas and briefcases, usually played by Richard Wattis or Eric Barker, causing more problems than they solve.

As George Eliot put it:

> Fancy what a game at chess would be if all the chessmen had passions and intellects, more or less small and cunning: if you were not only uncertain about your adversary's men, but a little uncertain about your own; if your knight could

shuffle himself on to a new square by the sly; if your bishop, in disgust at your castling, could wheedle your pawns out of their places; and if your pawns, hating you because they are pawns, could make away from their appointed posts that you might get checkmate on a sudden. You might be the longest-headed of deductive reasoners, and yet you might be beaten by your own pawns. You would be especially likely to be beaten, if you depended arrogantly on your mathematical imagination, and regarded your passionate pieces with contempt.[43]

So detailed planning is now unfashionable. But the problem with unplanned systems is that they might produce undesirable outcomes. This is difficult for a government with respect to any industry or sector that it feels is strategically important, unless it is prepared to surrender that sector to the disciplines of the market (a surrender that is becoming increasingly popular with governments of all stripes, unfortunately just when it seems to be becoming decreasingly popular with voters). It is particularly difficult when the government actually owns the assets and is responsible for the system involved (as is usually the case with health and welfare systems, for example).

How should a government produce the outcomes it wishes? It could try to govern using artfully crafted market-based incentives and property rights, but this is rather too complex. A recent innovation, championed in the UK by Chancellor Gordon Brown, is to use *targets*. The government sets out a schedule of target values for particular parameters called *performance indicators*. Bureaucrats then are given incentives (e.g. promotion, more funding, bonuses) to ensure that the performance targets are reached. The changes in incentives are important – there is nothing particularly wrong, or indeed unusual, about a government setting out the outcomes that interest it. The target culture begins when the government starts to penalise people or organisations when those outcomes are *not* achieved.

The government picks out parameters that seem to it to go with or indicate good performance. So, for instance, it wants the

National Health Service to produce a healthy population, efficient use of NHS resources, and a happy relationship with their patients. But these are too nebulous and open to interpretation to operate as targets, so the government chooses quantifiable values that theoretically can act as proxies for these desirable outcomes. They might include the number of people waiting for particular operations, the average length of time someone stays in hospital, the number of people surviving some surgical procedure for a certain length of time, and so on. Schools find themselves having to meet targets concerning the number of children who pass particular exams. Universities, to meet concerns about the education of the wider community in the 'knowledge economy', are given targets for the number of admissions of students from certain social groups. The police need to meet crime reduction targets.

Focusing public servants on the outcomes of their actions is no bad thing; too often government services make little or no attempt to consider the requirements of their clients. But the trouble is that attempts to micromanage giant organisations in this way seem not to work. The focus on quantifiable targets means that more useful goals, that may be unquantifiable, get pushed aside. For example, the Ministry of Agriculture, Fisheries and Food (MAFF), in 2002, met ten of its thirteen targets. Pretty good, no? Unfortunately one of the three targets it missed was one to prevent outbreaks of serious diseases; British agriculture was devastated in 2001 by a massive epidemic of foot and mouth disease, which even caused that year's general election to be postponed for a month.[44] In the end, the government, fed up with the long list of MAFF's failings, abolished it. National targeting can be insensitive to local conditions. For instance, sickle cell anaemia, an illness that affects particular ethnic groups, is not a very common condition in the United Kingdom, so does not feature on national targets. But because there are areas of high concentration of the affected ethnic groups, there are certain areas where sickle cell anaemia is a serious problem; nevertheless, because targets are national, hospital managers are given no incentives to tackle it in those areas.[45]

This is the sort of issue that used to be dealt with by the professionalism of the people working in the particular sector. Professional bodies can uphold and monitor ethical codes, which are intended, like the targets, to ensure that the profession serves the public in the right way; the granddaddy of these codes is the Hippocratic Oath for the nascent medical profession in Ancient Greece.[46]

However, trust has rather broken down between governments and the professions. There are three reasons for this. The first dates back most obviously to the period of Mrs Thatcher's reforms of the public services; the professions interpreted many of her reforms as illicit interference with their sphere of professional confidence, and many resisted. Mrs Thatcher in her turn interpreted this as a conservative attempt to prevent progress, and indeed she has not been alone in this view of professional intransigence in the face of government policy.[47] The second reason is that when governments decide to spend large quantities of money on a service, they will inevitably extract a political price for that *largesse*, in the form of more control.

Third, there has always been a strong suspicion that professionalisation is a cover-up for restrictive practices, concerned less with the welfare of the client base than with ensuring monopoly of supply so that the professionals can trouser large fees. For example, a report for the Office of Fair Trading in 2001[48] found restricted consumer access (e.g. at the time most clients couldn't see a barrister without a solicitor), demarcation problems (e.g. competition between barristers and solicitors was restricted, and simple solutions such as 'one stop shops' were being hindered), restrictions on competition through advertising, and the use of fee guidance to prevent competition. A similar survey found that the cost of conveyancing a freehold house of £75,000 could range between £117 and £750, a massive variation showing that competition was not working well in that field. With top tax QCs earning in excess of £2 million annually, legal representation is getting to be beyond the means of most people.[49]

We will discuss the erosion of the professional ethos in more detail in Chapter Six. For now, the interesting question is why performance targets have been relatively unsuccessful as a means to control the large public service bureaucracies.

The problem is what organisational theorist Marshall Meyer calls the *performance paradox*.[50] Performance targets will never be able to create the right sort of professional behaviour except in the short term, in circumscribed contexts. According to Meyer, the needs of management are constantly shifting, and so, though managers need lots of measures of performance, static and simple measures lose their informational content over time; they become less significant, and report less useful information back to managers the longer they are in place.

First, the world changes. Targets are crafted, often at great expense, to cope with the world as it is understood at that time. In very complex systems – particularly the giant welfare systems of the big liberal democracies – the inevitable result is that by the time the targets feed back into the management process, the world has moved on, populations will have changed, priorities will have altered, new technologies will be available. And so there is a decent chance that a performance target will be completely uninformative even before it is deployed; if not, it will become less and less informative as time goes on.

Second, not only does the world change, but the system itself changes – most notably in response to the incentives provided by the performance targets. Before a target is in place, a professional will be doing her job as she understands it. Once the target is deployed, then she suddenly has incentives to hit the target. The better-crafted the target, the more likely it is to help her achieve good performance. But when professional priorities change, she may be left with incentives to achieve what are now irrelevant targets. For instance, schoolteachers are given incentives for their pupils to pass GCSE exams. The result is that children are nursed through the exams, so pass rates have increased. This is not necessarily a good thing, since the whole purpose of an exam is as a signalling system; the point is to tell employers and others which students are better than others. If everyone gets a prize, then the signalling value is zero.

Indeed, if targets are badly crafted, or out of date, then the incentives they give become perverse – the professional is actually given incentives to perform badly. For instance, if a hospital is penalised for deaths during operations, then they may have an incentive for not performing operations on patients who are at some risk from the procedure. Or – a real example – Mr Blair's government placed a target on local authorities to collect a certain quantity of recyclable waste. Many authorities insisted that their residents should separate their household waste into that which was recyclable and that which was not, and collected them separately, and therefore met their targets, and were rewarded with more funding. But there is a national shortage of recycling depots. And the target was for *collecting* recyclable waste, not for recycling it. So some authorities then put the recyclable waste back with the rest, and buried or incinerated it all together.[51]

Third, if targets are used to get rid of poor performance, by either sacking those who fail, or – more usual – bringing every-one up to uniform standards, then they signal virtually nothing, because everyone's performance is identical. The government's Research Assessment Exercises (RAEs) are intended to justify university funding by measuring their research. At the last RAE round, every university did very well, having learned to play the system, but the pot of funding for which they were competing did not grow. Hence lots of universities made huge improve-ments, at great cost to themselves, and yet were not rewarded.

The problem is that targets need to be sophisticated, fine-grained and constantly monitored and updated to be effective (and even then they are not guaranteed to be). But to be a cheap method of enforcing discipline on public servants, they need to be relatively simple (so that public servants can understand them and react to the signals they give), coarse-grained (so that there are only a few targets to be reached, not lots of small ones), and kept stable (so that people don't have to keep learning new sets of rules and fill in new lots of forms every year). Unsurprisingly, many have concluded that targets to set outcomes will never be sufficiently flexible or useful to ensure good public services.

The moral is straightforward: planning is, at best, extremely difficult. First, planners are unlikely, given a complex and dynamic society under inevitable conditions of uncertainty, to be able to achieve their goals. Second, even if they do manage to succeed, this is likely to cause unintended side-effects or perverse outcomes. And third, even if planners do achieve their goals without too many bad side-effects, the price of their control may be the erosion of important ethical and professional codes.

Where is the knowledge? Its distribution

Does this mean that there is no knowledge that can be gained from and about an economy? Are we for ever doomed to blunder about in the half-light of ignorance?

Not quite. As individual economic agents, we have some knowledge about our own circumstances, which enables us to make our own small plans. We can plan for certain outcomes, we can substitute one set of exchanges for another. If I have five pounds in my pocket, and I see that I can buy four cans of my favourite beer for five pounds from the off-licence, or a copy of Rosebery's biography of Pitt from the bookshop next door for the same price, I can decide which of those two treats – or neither – I should buy. I do that on the basis of some self-knowledge. Someone who knows me well could also make the same choice, and indeed someone who knows me better than I know myself might be able to spend five pounds on something I would never have thought of, but which I will enjoy very much. Of course, the knowledge to which I refer is rapidly changing, and not fully certain in application. It may well be that I bought the wrong thing. But I had enough knowledge about my finances and my preferences – at that particular point in time – to make a reasonable plan.

The knowledge that is essential for economic decisions is often of this sort, as argued by one of the leading economists of the Austrian tradition, Friedrich von Hayek (1899–1992). Even when we move out of the sphere of the individual decision, it is easy to see that the knowledge required to make good economic plans is of relevance only in highly circumscribed contexts. The context of operation is central to the usefulness of knowledge.[52]

> We need to remember only how much we have to learn in any occupation after we have completed our theoretical training, how big a part of our working life we spend learning particular jobs, and how valuable an asset in all walks of life is knowledge of people, of local conditions, and of special circumstances. To know of and put to use a machine not fully employed, or somebody's skill which could be better utilized, or to be aware of a surplus stock which can be drawn upon during an interruption of supplies, is socially quite as useful as the knowledge of better alternative techniques. The shipper who earns his living from using otherwise empty or half-filled journeys of tramp-steamers, or the estate agent whose whole knowledge is almost exclusively one of temporary opportunities, or the arbitrageur who gains from local differences of commodity prices – are all performing eminently useful functions based on special knowledge of circumstances of the fleeting moment not known to others.[53]

And because the relevant economic knowledge depends on 'the circumstances of the fleeting moment', it is virtually impossible to pass that sort of knowledge up the political hierarchy, to the 'men from the ministry', in a timely or cost-effective way. Indeed, bureaucrats explicitly try *not* to deal with particulars. They abstract away from the detail, often using statistical techniques, to produce a much more stable body of knowledge. This is a perfectly legitimate way of understanding the environment, and a government or big company that did not do this would be negligent. But this does not mean that the economic detail goes away.

> Even the large and highly mechanized plant keeps going largely because of an environment upon which it can draw

for all sorts of unexpected needs: tiles for its roof, stationery for its forms, and all the thousand and one kinds of equipment in which it cannot be self-contained and which the plans for the operation of the plant require to be readily available in the market.[54]

This level of detail cannot be communicated to the large-scale economic planner, and we might therefore assume that economic decisions at that level of detail are beyond the planner's purview.

In other words, the knowledge about the economy that a planner would ideally get hold of is actually distributed around the economy, held by millions of individuals, often tacitly and unconsciously. The knowledge is about conditions that affect the transactions of now; it is more often than not out of date before it is articulated.

On Hayek's view, there is one heuristic abstraction (i.e. a distillation of the relevant information that is more likely than not to be helpful) of the sum of all the individual economic contexts affecting the demand for and supply of a particular good, and that is the *price* of that good as determined in a competitive bidding market. This theory, of course, is the basis of the neo-liberal philosophy of free market economics, which is beyond the scope of this chapter. But it is an important topic in the understanding of the meaning (if any) of conservatism in the 21st century, and we will return to Hayek and the price function in Chapter Six below.

Knowledge, wisdom, institutions, tradition

This distribution of knowledge around the economy need not always be fleetingly or otherwise contained in anyone's head. It may be that important knowledge about how to achieve social goals or realise corporate aims gets ossified in procedures within institutions and organisations. In other words, when an organisation (whether formal or informal) is used to perform some task, perhaps on a regular basis, then, even though at the outset it is people doing the work, over time the organisation will take over and actually perform the task itself.[55]

How so? One example of the sort of way this happens is when a task is relatively routine. Suppose the task can be set out as a checklist of mundane subtasks, for instance a service for a car, with the mechanic going through a checklist of tests on a form, ticking the boxes as he goes. The form might initially be intended to serve as an *aide memoire* for the service mechanic, who knows all about the cars in question. But when the firm expands, the form might be copied and distributed to apprentice workers, who can perform the tasks as structured (check tyre pressure, test windscreen wipers …), even though they lack the overall knowledge to understand the car as a unity.

The firm may expand further, and begin to employ people in specialist roles; for example there might be a person with responsibility for exhaust systems, another for ignition, and so on. Then when a car is serviced, the manager of the service process will go down the checklist, sending the car to the specialist units as appropriate. Under this system, none of the specialists need know anything about the car as a whole, only about the subsystems for which they are responsible; the checklist has become a management strategy. The person managing the servicing process need only understand the routine of going down the form, and which unit is responsible for which checkbox.

Finally, suppose the original expert mechanic now retires. In that case, the new expanded firm might actually employ nobody who possesses all the knowledge about the car as a single object. The knowledge is distributed around the firm in the specialist units. But note also that some key knowledge, the knowledge of how to perform a service, and how to co-ordinate the servicing resources most efficiently while ensuring that every part of the car is tested, is possessed by no one at all, not even by a computer. The important knowledge is contained in the servicing form, together with the instruction to the manager to go down the form, doling out the tests in order. Some of the knowledge is no longer stored in a human mind.[56]

In the wider social context, there is much knowledge – to

do with how to perform social tasks, how to manage limited resources, for example – that is spread around a wider society, between people and artefacts, in this way. Many formal processes or institutions are dramatically simplified by being grafted onto existing social practices; those practices may be as important to the outcome as the formal processes themselves. For instance, free markets are artificial, rule-based creations that sit on top of various important social structures, such as the rule of law (particularly contract law), non-arbitrary government, well-respected property rights and the Protestant work ethic.[57] When these structures are not in place, the imposition of market economics can be quite disruptive.[58]

We have seen how planning outcomes can often distort existing practices or cause unfortunate side-effects. Unplanned development of practices can, as it were, encode wisdom in tradition. If a society has 'always done it that way', there will be a reason. If the traditional practice was harmful to that society, then either the practice or the society, or both, would not tend to survive. Hence there is at least a presumption that a long-standing tradition serves some sort of useful purpose, encodes some 'folk wisdom', and stamping it out will mean that that purpose will no longer be served.

This does not mean that the traditional practice is the best system possible, only that it is likely to encode knowledge about how a purpose can be achieved by that social group. Even outmoded or otherwise inefficient traditions can do this. For example, the open field system of agriculture was no doubt inefficient in various ways, but it achieved a number of useful purposes. It ensured a relatively even distribution of the good and the bad tillage; it helped the farmers of the village interact, and therefore spread good ideas among themselves; it helped equalise the resources that each villager had access to. The ending of that system produced efficiency, at the cost of losing the benefits of the system. The system itself encoded traditional wisdom about how members of a society should get along together. Its relative inefficiency as a system of agriculture, which resulted in its falling into disrepute, has to be balanced against the social solidarity it supported, at least in assessing the part it played in medieval society.

There are many examples of traditions and practices that encode important knowledge about a community. The identity of a community through time (over generations) is often sustained by obscure (to the participants) rituals that implicitly exclude others, or practices of allowing only people with certain genealogy access to group-owned resources.[59] Religions are particularly potent identity-conferring traditions. Each new generation may alter the tradition, reinterpret it, but all they will do is to adjust the pre-existing social practices that are embedded in social order. Such flexible, organically growing traditions both help unify a society, and perform certain social tasks in such a way as not to disturb what may be a delicate social order.[60]

The British system of Common Law is perhaps the classic example of a system of transmission of wisdom via tradition through generations. Under a system of common law, people are allowed to get on with their own lives until a dispute develops. The dispute is then taken to an agreed arbitration system, which will provide a principled resolution of the dispute. In future disputes, that judgement can be reused; the parties to the future dispute have the task of showing whether their dispute resembles earlier ones, and if so, in what respects. The 'rules' are not laid down by any individual; rather they develop over time, via a series of judgements about problematic cases. With such an underlying system, when more formal rules are required they can be overlaid onto the existing system, as has happened in Britain.[61] Much of law is made by judges' decisions, not by the Houses of Parliament; at the very least, judges play a giant role in interpreting the legislation laid down by Parliament. In this way, the abstract, dry, context-free meaning of a law receives its life from the attempt by the judiciary to place the law in the context of current behaviour and past judgements.[62]

The claim, then, is this: that traditional practices and systems that have developed organically, planned not by a remote central authority, but rather over a period of trial and error by the community itself, often encode useful knowledge learned by the community over the trial period (but which might not be known consciously by any individual member of that community), in the same way as the form encodes the knowledge of how to service a car. The traditions act as the *communal memory*. Because the knowledge is not necessarily known consciously by anyone, it may well be that no one is alert to the potential disruption to the community that would be caused by rationalising or dismantling the system.

The second tenet of conservatism: the knowledge principle

To summarise the epistemological arguments of the last three sections, the knowledge that is required to co-ordinate and direct a complex, dynamic society is almost certainly beyond the ken of an individual person, or even a hierarchical bureaucratic machine. So interconnected is a modern society (indeed, probably every kind of society, but in this book I am focusing on modern democracies) that an attempt to plan its future development is likely to result in many side-effects that cannot be anticipated. The knowledge that is relevant to the planning of a society or an economy will be distributed across that society, and furthermore at least some of it will be encoded in practices, texts or rituals so that no individual can be said to possess that knowledge him- or herself. This makes up the second tenet of conservatism, which we shall call the **knowledge principle**. We have seen the knowledge principle foreshadowed through the Pyrrhonism of Sextus Empiricus, Montaigne, Browne, Hume and Balfour.

The knowledge principle links with the change principle to create an elegant but powerful conservative philosophy. If we accept the change principle, we accept that the concrete benefits of an existing society are given greater weight over the potential benefits of an abstract theory. The knowledge principle, when added to that, suggests that an abstract theory about something as complex and dynamic as a society, even a relatively rigidly structured one, will almost certainly be inadequate, that there will be unintended side-effects of major changes that will threaten those concrete benefits. Worse, the knowledge principle enjoins us to be highly sceptical that the advertised potential will ever appear.

This result backs up the instinct articulated by Oakeshott, that innovation always carries a risk. The conservative will turn away from innovation as much as he possibly can – and continue to bear in mind that innovation *includes* the dubious practice of trying to turn the clock back to restore some golden past. That sort of nostalgia is (a) an innovation, and therefore risky, and (b) based on a theory of society, and therefore probably wrong.

Compare the effect of substituting Freeden's 'extra-human' idea for the knowledge principle. We have already aired several arguments that knowledge and certainty are hard to obtain, arrogant to assume. But a thinker who is positive about the extra-human origins of the social order will *be* certain; his handicap *is* arrogance. The assumption, for example, that the world is God's creation brings with it the disastrous certitude that holy writ should steer political action. Small 'c' conservatism is premised on the avoidance, not the fostering, of fundamentalism, on the humble assumption of ignorance, not arrogant certainty.

The sceptical conservative philosophy does not contradict the idea that some complex organisations, for example very large firms, require innovation. The knowledge principle still operates in such environments, for sure. But there are import-ant disanalogies between a society and a large organisation, however complex (and there are corporations that are larger and more complex than many societies). The organisation, unlike a society, has *goals*, and the imperative to reach those goals will on many occasions rule out adherence to the change principle. If an organisation is not on course to reach its goals, then it has to change, even though – in the commercial world, *because* – that involves risk.

Does the conservative philosophy, endorsing the sum of the change principle and the knowledge principle, mean stasis, a boring, unadventurous society? No, unless that society is boring by inclination. If a society is dynamic and changes under its own steam, then it is certainly not the business of the conservative to impede that. As long as the changes are the results of people in their own spheres of influence, exploiting the small amount of economic knowledge that they possess about their own circumstances, being prepared to take risks upon themselves, then there is no problem.

Does the conservative philosophy mean inactive government, that stands by to allow injustice and economic failure? This is not at all implied by either the change principle or the knowledge principle. In the first place, the change principle depends on the concrete benefits of an existing society being tangible. In a dysfunctional society, the change principle becomes less applicable as the society provides fewer benefits for its members. Whether change is actively sought will depend on how bad the society is, what abstract benefits are in the offing from possible innovations, and the plausibility of those innovations. It is, of course, a political question, to be answered at the time, as to when potential benefits become worth exploring.

Some, like Bruce Pilbeam, have argued that this is problematic.

It is flawed because it leaves too vague the circumstances requiring conservatives' defensive efforts: for example, how long must an institution have been in existence before it is considered established? Equally, in that few conservatives have ever opposed all change, without further principled appeal the line between unacceptable 'radical' and acceptable gradual change is similarly unclear.[63]

However, the conservative ideology of course reflexively applies to itself. No conservative ideologue (with the possible exception of Enoch Powell) would wish to lay down in advance the circumstances in which innovation is allowable. The decision is a political one, and therefore to be taken in accordance with the democratic political decision-making processes operative in the society at the time. A conservative government in the early

21st century in Britain could well move in a number of policy directions; my aim in Part Two of this book is to flesh out that claim by looking at some of the policy arguments that might go on in a conservative forum.

If a conservative government did move in the direction of change, then the knowledge principle also provides some guidance. The knowledge principle says that the government will of necessity be unaware of the effects of its innovations. That suggests that managed change should be incremental, rather than thoroughgoing, and, where possible, reversible. Incrementally changing policy or institutions should mean that the effects of changes can be measured, and unfortunate side effects detected early. In practice, the difference between a conservative government and those of other ideologies is that the conservatives will be in favour only of incremental changes; their ambition will be smaller, their scepticism higher.

Does this all mean that conservatism is empty? That we should avoid change, except when it can't be avoided? The appearance of vacuity here is appearance only. No ideology can *dictate* political action in a concrete circumstance – how could it, any more than a speed limit can dictate slower driving? Liberalism says that freedom is important; a liberal government ensures freedom, except where people's freedom needs to be curbed. Socialism recommends equality; a socialist government ensures equality, except where things have to be unequal. Free market governments still collect taxes, green governments still allow industry. An ideology is but one pressure on a government. Ironically, most ideologies, being absolutist in tone, will find that difficult to explain, whereas conservatism explicitly accepts that the political context will play a massive role in determining what can and can't, what must and mustn't, be done. Like all ideologies, conservatism is a guide to action, a rallying cry for the party, a political and moral compass. These are all important functions, but a government in a complex democracy responds to much more than that.

A conservative government will be sceptical of its power to solve problems (even sceptical of its power to *diagnose* problems).

It will be conscious that institutions, practices and processes, unguided by interfering hand, are likely to be better regulators of a society, because rooted in that society, because going with the grain of that society, than clever theories imposed from outside. This is what marks out conservative governments from those of other types.

The vaccination strategy

The alert will recall that there is another reason why British Conservative Party governments have adopted change, and for reasons that chime in well with conservative doctrine. This is the strategy I described briefly in Chapter Three, and which I called the *vaccination strategy*.

The idea of this is that the conservative, who is not, of course, worried about change while he is in power, may well worry in the longer term about what the opposition might do. In a democracy, his fear, both for the country and, more prosaically, for his own political career, will be that the radical opposition will win elections. Hence the vaccination strategy: the conservative takes over the process of change, providing enough of the radicals' programme to satisfy some of its voters; thereby inoculating the future against radicalism by a small injection of the virus now. To be sure, the conservative will not do this with any great enthusiasm, but he will hope to preserve social unity, and to ensure that as many people as possible retain their loyalty to the state as it is. We saw the vaccination strategy in operation with Peel's repeal of the Corn Laws, with Disraeli's, and to a lesser extent Salisbury's, social reforms, and with the development of the Butskellite policy to manage the post-war settlement in the long period of Conservative government from 1951–64.

So prevalent has the vaccination strategy been in conservatism that Michael Freeden suggests elevating it to a third central principle.

> Here we arrive at a paradox at the heart of conservatism. It is an ideology that attains self-awareness when exposed by

its ideological opponents, rather than at its own behest, and it reacts to them in looking-glass manner. In rebuffing what appear to be universal, abstract, and systematic theories, the conservative too is impelled, in direct response, to suggest counter-interpretations to those creeds ... based on the substantive terms of reference of the latter. When conservatism perceives change as unproblematic it remains intellectually dormant, and its principles or theoretical stances are only elicited when it is forced to mirror the opponents' arguments.[64]

This follows an observation by the sociologist Karl Mannheim (1893–1947), that conservatives, being more or less happy with the status quo, are driven to theorise only under political pressure.

The conservative only thinks systematically when he is moved to reaction, perhaps because he is forced to set up a system counter to that of the progressive, or because the process has progressed to a point where he has lost touch with the present state of things, so that he is compelled to intervene actively in order to reverse the process of history.[65]

In other words, the conservative has to react against progressive pressures, and to do that he develops a specific philosophy to counter the opponent. This is not a philosophy that he would have wanted to develop in other circumstances, so the addition to conservative thought is not necessarily smooth, consistent or – to use a favourite conservative adjective – organic.

This reactive response is, I think, implicit in the change principle plus the knowledge principle, plus the conservative's desire to think beyond the five-year term of democratic office. The vaccination strategy inoculates the future against the radical virus, and since the strategy is likely to involve the conservative actually doing what he has emphatically said that he wouldn't do, some sort of ideological flim-flam is required to justify the *volte face*. It is the development of this flim-flam that Freeden, following Mannheim, has spotted.

The conservative recognises that it is vital not to allow a large constituency for change to develop. Hence it is important not to demonise the radical opposition, but rather it is sensible to make a limited number of concessions – often in the teeth of the most reactionary of conservative allies – in order to ensure that the radical element is kept small. But the result can certainly be internal strife *between* conservatives, because when to operate the vaccination strategy is a fine judgement. There was a falling-out of this very kind between Disraeli and Salisbury over the Second Reform Act in 1867; Disraeli wanted to extend the voting franchise to poorer voters using precisely the vaccination strategy, whereas Salisbury thought the result would be permanent Liberal Party government and strongly opposed him in Cabinet. In the end, Disraeli won the day and Salisbury resigned;[66] Disraeli was proved right in the end. Salisbury as Prime Minister found himself adopting the vaccination strategy in social policy.

What conservatism is not (II)

Finally, having specified at a general level what conservatism is, it might be instructive to contrast the ideology with others that have superficial similarities. To begin with, there are clear links between religiously based ideologies and conservatism. Religion is the basis for many societies, and contains, in a suite of rituals and moral precepts, much of a society's inherited wisdom, and many important aspects of a culture's identity. So conservatives can join with, say, Islamists[67] or Christian fundamentalists[68] to oppose progressive attempts to impose an instrumental reason (that is, reason directed towards the attainment of a particular ideological or material end) over and above the practical reason expressed in the institutions and practices of those religions.

That practical reason is of deep importance to many conservatives.[69] For example, Quintin Hogg wrote in 1947 that:

For myself I say quite plainly that I can see no hope for secular society unless it be based on a fundamental recognition of the spiritual nature of man and the providence of God, and in return I believe that religion owes to secular society the debt of recognizing that without the stability of the social order a full religious life becomes impossible except in the hermit's cell or in the monastery.[70]

A cleavage appears between the religious ideologies and conservatism, though, in two ways. First of all, much depends on the society. A religious society, as for example America or many of the conservative Muslim states of the Middle East, with a high level of belief and observance, might well require religious precepts to be enacted at a political level in order to respect the change principle. In that case, conservatives would at a minimum not wish to impose anti-religious policies on such a society. On the other hand, in a secular society, the imposition of religiously inspired law from a position of political authority would clearly violate the change principle, even if the perception was of a society that was formerly devout but now not. In a secular society, the conservative has no business imposing religion.

And secondly, there is a question of what religion brings to our understanding of the world. If the religion brings a certainty about the constitution of the world, about moral precepts, and about the social order – in other words, the 'extra-human' origins of the social order that Freeden describes – then it is hard to see how it can be reconciled with either the change principle or the knowledge principle. It goes without saying that the knowledge principle shows that we can never achieve such certainty about society. And anyway religiously guided politicians will find themselves either preserving a godly society and preventing its organic change and development, or actively engineering a godless society in a particular direction; in each case violating the change principle.

Religion and conservatism sit together most happily when

the religious aspect brings a deep sense of spiritual mystery, a sense that, though there is an order to things underpinned by God, that order is forever and tragically beyond our grasp. Lord Salisbury, perhaps the most religious of our conservative thinkers, was driven precisely by this sense of devout mystery, which fitted into his pessimistic conservatism from an early age. But the ideology that follows is remote from the writings of the Christian right, or the Islamist.

> 'The light is too dazzling for our weakened eyes,' [Salisbury] wrote to his sister Blanche from Cape Town about the doctrines of Original Sin and the Fall of Man; 'we must turn from it, lest it blind us. At the proper time we may logically test these doctrines, and if true accept them. But as a habit we must not think of them.' Yet for [Salisbury] there never was a proper time. He preferred to take the view that the ways of God were too unfathomable to be explicable to man, that no human experience could possibly come close enough to His to make any attempt to employ reason or logic worth while. 'God is all-powerful, and God is all-loving, and the world is what it is!' he would say to his children when they attempted to apply logic to their faith: 'How are you going to explain *that*?'[71]

There are also interesting parallels between conservatism and environmentalism; indeed Bruce Pilbeam lists no fewer than ten.[72] The common etymology of the words 'conservative' and 'conservation' is, of course, no coincidence. By rejecting accounts of instrumental reason, the conservative is open to the idea of value as something beyond mere exchange value. Many a conservative includes the landscape, and architectural beauty, as among the important aspects of a society that should be preserved. The conservative, also like the green, is opposed to the idea of individual autonomy; an individual's actions affect everyone, and politics is not simply a matter of ensuring, as neo-liberals might think, that individuals' preferences can be met by an economy.

A particularly interesting convergence between conservatism and environmentalism is their joint concern with intergenerational justice and equity. Each ideology concerns itself with people who are not currently alive. Edmund Burke, mocking the idea that one might have a superficial contractual relationship with the society into which one was born, put this clearly in a famous passage.

> Society is indeed a contract. ... It is a partnership in all science; a partnership in all art; a partnership in every virtue, and in all perfection. As the ends of such a partnership cannot be obtained in many generations, it becomes a partnership not only between those who are living, but between those who are living, those who are dead, and those who are to be born. Each contract of each particular state is but a clause in the great primaeval contract of eternal society, linking the lower with the higher natures, connecting the visible and the invisible world, according to a fixed compact sanctioned by the inviolable oath which holds all physical and all moral natures, each in their appointed place.[73]

There is much in there that the green would endorse. The main difference between the two is that the environmentalist is concerned almost exclusively with future generations, whereas the conservative looks both forward and backward; indeed, many conservatives are much more concerned with the dead than the yet-to-be-born.

Conservatives (small 'c') certainly diverge from radical environmentalists who wish to change society in order to preserve the environment. At best, such people will be seen as bossy bobble-hatted fanatics wanting to impose their own highly controversial interpretation of the good life upon everybody, and whose attempts at policing will include intolerable levels of intrusion. At worst, as with professional weirdoes like John Aspinall or James Goldsmith, the prescriptions go beyond socialistic communism and start to resemble the theories of

Pol Pot. For instance, Aspinall's musing that the ideal human population of the world is 200,000,000[74] makes one wonder not only how he arrives at that figure, not only what definition of 'ideal' he is working with, but also how the 5,800,000,000 of us that should 'ideally' make way should react. It is almost as scary when they are taken seriously by thinkers such as John Gray.[75]

But there are more philosophical differences to be discovered, upon further examination, even with moderate greens. The value of the natural environment, says the conservative, stems from its value to the society as a whole, for example by providing it with important symbols of continuity, by supporting particular ways of life that cement the link between a community and its locality, by emphasising the distinction between a community and others, and by providing a historically interpretable landscape. For the green, of course, the natural environment has a value in itself, and on its own terms.

Finally, let us briefly consider the parallels between conservatism and a temperamentally very different crew, the postmodernists.[76] The postmodernists reject the Enlightenment idea that an objective stance can be developed on the world; instead they argue that localism and diversity are the thing, that individual culture trumps any idea of an abstract 'human nature'. In these ideas, they chime in very strongly with the localism of conservatism from the tradition of Burke, and the Pyrrhonist scepticism taken from Hume.

But the postmodernists use their scepticism in a very different way. Their perpetual challenge to authority is of course highly uncongenial to conservatives. Both conservatives and postmodernists emphasise the arbitrariness of tradition and authority and the historical contingency of the particular institutions central to a society. But the postmodernists take the argument one stage further, by asserting that such traditions and institutions thereby have no hold over us. In other words, they accept the knowledge principle, but reject the change principle.

The track of the argument goes like this. The Enlightened thinker points out against the conservative that the bases of society are traditions and superstitions, and are arbitrary and irrational. Therefore they should be rebuilt in rational and purposive ways. The postmodernist attack on the Enlightenment denies the possibility of such rational rebuilding, and deduces that all ways of ordering society (or even of disordering it) are equally acceptable. In other words, the postmodernist accepts the force of the Enlightenment's 'therefore': if society is only traditional and superstitious, then any society is as good as the next, any way of life is permissible, and we should value difference and diversity. But the conservative rejects the 'therefore'. The proper response to the Enlightened person is: 'so what?' The basis, the history, the etiology of society are irrelevant; what matters is that a society exists, and that it confers benefits. So what if the conservative has no rational defence for some aspect of society (the House of Lords, perhaps)? Why should he need a *reason* at all?

We can rephrase this argument in epistemological terms. The Enlightened thinker points out against the conservative that traditional wisdom is merely localised subjective superstition, and that therefore more objective, scientific ways of discovery ought to be privileged. The postmodernist responds that no such objective viewpoint exists, there is no objective account of the world. Hence any subjective stance is as good as the next. Again, the postmodernist accepts the force of the Enlightenment argument against *particular* subjective ways of thought; he just doesn't think that an overarching objective alternative exists. The conservative refuses to accept the Enlightenment argument at all. Of course the traditional wisdom valued by the conservative is subjective; but that does *not* mean that it should not be privileged over other subjective stances, whether or not an objective stance is possible. Its value stems from its integration into a functioning society; the other subjective viewpoints which so excite the postmodernist, if they tend to fragment society, will simply be rejected by the conservative on those contingent grounds. That a point of view is subjective does not mean that it is no better than other points of view (in a particular context).

Nevertheless, it is certainly true that societies nowadays are fragmenting, that traditional ways of thought are under pressure as never before. It may well be that conservatism, as described in this chapter, has been rendered irrelevant in a fast-changing world, and that actually it is the postmodern take on things, that all subjective stances are equally good, that is winning the Darwinian battle of ideologies. In the next chapter, we will examine this proposition, and see what relevance conservatism can claim amid the uncertainties of the new century.

CHAPTER FIVE

IS CONSERVATISM DEAD?

Mad world?

There is an annual ritual in Britain. At Christmas time, there is great media interest about which pop record becomes the Christmas Number One single. This is an unofficial, yet prestigious, honour, and many pop aristocrats release a single in mid-December trying to time it to sell most in the week before Christmas. Christmas 2003 was no exception, with a hot race for the top. There were the usual old stagers, like Sir Cliff Richard; new fashionable bands with an ironic twist – step forward The Darkness, fresh from an endorsement from Tony Blair, no less; manufactured acts, like a group of contestants from the TV show *Pop Idol*; and novelties, such as perpetually bemused rocker Ozzy Osbourne and his daughter Kelly.

Yet none of these hot favourites made it to the top for Christmas (Ozzy and Kelly were there a week too soon). In the event, the Christmas Number One of 2003 was a new version of a moth-eaten piece of electronica from the 80s recorded three years previously by two blokes no one had ever heard of. It was, it can safely be said, something of a surprise.

And the significance of this? Actually, the song seemed rather to sum up many people's feelings about life, the universe and everything. Composer Michael Andrews had been working on the soundtrack to *Donnie Darko* (a movie about a giant evil rabbit, since you ask), and asked a childhood friend to record a lo-fi version of Tears for Fears' old hit 'Mad World'.[1] It was a nice idea, and a good version, but even he must have been surprised to find himself following in the footsteps of Robbie Williams, the Spice Girls, Sir Cliff, Pink Floyd and the Pet Shop Boys.*

At the end of 2003, bland was out, manufactured pop pap was out, irony was out. Andrews (using Roland Orzabal's lyrics) caught a wave of cynicism, puzzlement and darkness in the public mood.

> And I find it kinda funny
> I find it kinda sad
> The dreams in which I'm dying
> Are the best I ever had
> I find it hard to tell you
> Cos I find it hard to take
> When people run in circles
> It's a very very
> Mad world.

Maybe not great poetry, but witty and allied to a good tune; it hit the spot. It expressed a feeling – to a greater extent than when originally written – that things may look OK on the outside, but there are difficulties within. The dark thoughts are not necessarily specific; the unease may not yet be at anchor. The song expresses a feeling, a tone, a suspicion that all is not well.

Why this feeling, and why 2003? Well, there was plenty to worry about, for one thing. The world situation was looking gloomy, and for once foreign news was trickling down to the home news pages. The end of the Cold War, welcome though it was, had rid the world of two-superpower stability. International relations had become more complex, and simultaneously more ideologically fragmented, as a result. The division between capitalism and socialism turned out not to be the fundamental division after all, and, though liberal democracy briefly

---

* … and Renee and Renato and St Winifred's School Choir and Benny Hill and Little Jimmy Osmond and Mr Blobby and …

threatened to achieve hegemony (George Bush Sr's 'new world order'), religious and nationalistic loyalties, long since suppressed, sprang up with new fervour – and a new murderousness. We were out of the nuclear shadow, but around the corner the new threat was the fundamentalist with a machete or a nail bomb.

On 11 September 2001, we all watched the appalling al-Qaeda-sponsored attack on the World Trade Center in Manhattan, perhaps the most effective piece of political theatre in history. International politics came home then. A US/UK coalition overthrew the barbarous Taliban regime in Afghanistan, and the bloody dictatorship of Saddam Hussein in Iraq. Not only did this (appear to) increase the threat of terrorism at home, but it also embroiled Britain's Prime Minister Tony Blair in a major crisis when it was alleged that he misled parliament and the country about the extent of the threat that Iraq posed to world peace. Writer Alan Bennett, musing on the conduct of the British political system, called 2003 a 'shameful year'.[2]

This linked up with another set of problems. While the Cold War was on, the corresponding Us and Them situation determined the fault lines of domestic politics. People were defined by who they opposed, and how fervently. Afterwards, the absence of the big enemy allowed voters time to gaze inwards – and they did not like what they saw. Our politicians were certainly better than the dreary bureaucrats of the unlamented Soviet Union, but they weren't perfect, and they hardly came up to the high standards that they set themselves. A crisis of trust began to develop, which undermined their authority.

Indeed, distrust threatened to undo society's cohesion in all sorts of places, not just politics.[3] Our food suddenly seemed more scary, as BSE-stricken cattle and genetically modified plants had entered the food chain. Global temperature rises threatened severe climate change. Environmental damage was rife; the Aral Sea was reduced to a fraction of its former size, while out-of-control logging led to mudslides.[4] People seemed to become strangers to one another;[5] fear of crime rose much more quickly than crime itself, drugs and gangs blighted some inner city areas, and the informal links that bound people into civic society seemed to vanish. Corporate malfeasance seemed rampant, with Enron and Parmalat only the most prominent examples on each side of the Atlantic. Even if the extent of the 'crisis' was somewhat exaggerated,[6] nevertheless the constant drip of bad news and reports of failures of trust had an inevitably undermining effect.

The world's economy seemed generally in a reasonable state, though an unsustainable boom at the tail end of the 20th century caused a bumpy recession. The September 11th attacks, and then the Enron scandal, worried the stock markets still further. As globalisation spread, nations had an awkward choice. Liberalising markets, particularly labour markets (i.e. making it easier to hire and fire workers), meant that the economy felt more of the benefits, but equally increased the uncertainty of workers. In some parts of the world, the combination of free

'Could someone come into my office? I've frightened myself'

Figure 2: Fear of crime

markets, democracy and ethnic tensions between rich minorities and poor majorities led to violence.[7] Prosperity did not produce happiness.[8]

In such a world, there are good reasons for thinking that conservatism is dead, that no reasonable constituency of people would wish to develop the philosophy of scepticism outlined in Chapter Four and to focus on preservation and conservation. Surely every politician, every voter in his or her right mind will want to tear up society by the roots? Surely it is time for a bonfire of the vanities?

As we saw in Chapter Four, the change principle does not rule out the possibility that society should be changed, even radically; it only insists that the burden of proof falls upon the innovator. Many thinkers, even conservative ones, have understood that conservatism might be undermined simply by the perceived unpleasantness of the world as it stands; Michael Oakeshott points out the importance of there being something worth preserving.

> If the present is arid, offering little or nothing to be used or enjoyed, then [the conservative] inclination will be weak or absent; if the present is remarkably unsettled, it will display itself in a search for a firmer foothold and consequently in a recourse to and an exploration of the past; but it asserts itself characteristically when there is much to be enjoyed, and it will be strongest when this is combined with evident risk of loss. In short, it is a disposition appropriate to a man who is acutely aware of having something to lose which he has learned to care for; a man in some degree rich in opportunities for enjoyment, but not so rich that he can afford to be indifferent to loss. It will appear more naturally in the old man than in the young, not because the old are more sensitive to loss but because they are apt to be more fully aware of the resources of their world and therefore less likely to find them inadequate. In some people this disposition is weak merely because they are ignorant of what

their world has to offer them: the present appears to them only as a residue of inopportunities.[9]

Can conservatism flourish in a 'mad world'? In this chapter we address four arguments that say that it cannot.

The hollowing out of Tory Britain

One argument says that not only can conservatism *not* flourish, but the fact that it cannot is largely, even entirely, the fault of the Conservative Party. This was argued most forcibly and cogently by John Gray, towards the end of the period of Conservative dominance of British politics.

> [T]he conditions under which conservatism as a coherent form of political thought and practice are possible exist no longer; … conservatism has for us a Cheshire Cat quality, in that what it proposes to conserve is a spectral thing, voided of substance, partly by the policies of recent conservative governments, and partly by aspects of modern societies which such policies have reinforced; and that conservative parties and movements have in all Western countries been captured by neo-liberal ideas, more properly thought of as those of fundamentalist or classical liberalism, that in their utopian projects of world-improvement and their expectation of convergence on a universal civilization are alien to the forms of thought and practice most characteristic of a conservative outlook as that used to be understood. … In short, the subversive effects of unhampered market institutions on traditional forms of life makes free-market conservatism an inherently unstable and, over time, a self-undermining political project. For these reasons, I conclude that a genuinely conservative form of political thought and practice, the lineaments of which we can discern as at least one element in our cultural history, is no longer a real possibility for us.[10]

The charge falls, in effect, into two halves. The first is that the Conservative Party (I focus, of course, on the British context, though Gray clearly has a wider focus) has been hijacked by neo-liberals – the Thatcherites. I will not spend any time disputing this; it is certainly my view (see Chapter Three) that the Conservative Party was the ground for an ideological battle between liberals and conservatives for almost a century, though 'hijacked' is a strong term and for the most part the two ideological groups were fighting side by side in the trenches against collectivism and socialism. The neo-liberal heritage of the Conservative Party, Gray seems to say, will make its return to conservatism difficult – though the conservative nature of this argument is perhaps somewhat ironic.

So we will focus on the second half, which is that the Thatcherite neo-liberals in effect removed the institutional core of British public and political life that provided continuity with the past and was a useful source of knowledge about British social relations.

A fundamental objection to the paleo-liberal regime of incessant economic change under unfettered market institutions, then, is that in devaluing traditional knowledge it renders social and economic life ever less understandable to its human participants. In so doing, unfettered market institutions tend to deplete the cultural identities of their practitioners – upon which these institutions themselves depend. Market institutions will enhance human well-being, and will be stably renewed across the generations, when they do not go against the grain of the particular cultures that harbour them, but on the contrary assist those cultures to reproduce themselves. By imposing on people a regime of incessant change and permanent revolution, unencumbered market institutions deplete the stock of historical memory on which cultural identity depends. The common cliché that globalized markets tend to yield cultural uniformity is therefore not without an element of truth. What such cultural homogenization signifies is perhaps less obvious: a breach in historical memory which disrupts, or empties of significance, the narratives in terms of which people make sense of their lives. If, as any conservative who is also a sceptic is bound to think, the meaning of life for all of us is a local matter, this junking of local knowledge by unencumbered market processes is no small matter.[11]

And furthermore, as dislocation has been made more rapid by the economic and social changes ushered in by the liberalism of the last quarter of the 20th century, it is impossible for conservatism to keep pace.

The Old Right project of cultural fundamentalism is best understood as an ill-thought-out response to the modern dissolution of old forms of moral life that contemporary conservative policy has itself promoted or accelerated. This is not to say that all such older forms of community and moral life lacked value. On the contrary, the reactionary perception of cultural loss as a real historical phenomenon is sometimes well founded ...; but that does not mean that the old forms of life can, or even should, be reconstituted. Not only is the current conservative clamour about family breakdown dishonest in repressing the role that market-driven economic changes – sometimes occurring over several generations, but greatly accelerated since the mid 1970s, as with female participation in the workforce – have played in transforming family life, but also it is self-deceiving in imagining that older forms of family life can conceivably be revived in which modern Western demands for choice and self-fulfilment – which are in other areas elevated by conservatives to the status of fetishes – are denied. The current neo-fundamentalist clamour for a return to the traditional family is, in other words, misconceived and frivolous in the highest degree. It expresses no serious concern for the needs of people in families, nor any understanding of the diverse forms in which the institution of the family is now to be found. Such vulgar clamour is symptomatic of contemporary conservative thought in the unreality of its perception of real people and their needs.[12]

So local knowledge has been devalued and extinguished, and older forms of social interaction have been rendered irrelevant or irrecoverable by changes partly, maybe largely, brought in under the freedom facilitated by market liberalism. We cannot go back to a world in which that knowledge and those social norms obtain; it is also hard to see how a conservative could deal with a world that is inherently unstable, without continuity with past forms of life, and with a dramatically decreasing local element as globalisation continues to promote cultural homogeneity.

Conservatism as realistic social criticism

This is a tough argument; certainly the world is very different from the world in 1974 when conservatives were prominent in the Conservative Party and as commentators in the right wing press. Indeed, it is probably fair to say that a conservatism that deliberately centres on the continuity of English, or British, institutions, or of particular elements in English, or British, society, in order to emphasise continuity – in the way that, say, Stanley Baldwin used to do very successfully in the 1930s – really is in the sort of trouble that John Gray describes. The sort of conservatism espoused by Enoch Powell in his St George's Day speech quoted in Chapter Three,[13] which made great play of the almost unique thousand-year history of English institutions, or the sort described by Quintin Hogg, which made the Christian, specifically Anglican, religion central,[14] are surely doomed. Roger Scruton, who shares Powell's near-mystical view of the continuity of English social and political life, is pessimistic; his recent discussion of England was specifically cast as an elegy to the lost.[15]

On the other hand, it is an intriguing thought that the market that arguably brought about most change was the market in *labour* – a market that labours under many controls, indeed is barely free at all, but which at various times has resulted in the influx into Britain of large numbers of immigrants. This change in the character of Britain, in terms of religion and of whatever cultural unity existed previously, certainly makes the traditional form of conservatism harder, which was the burden of Powell's anti-immigration case in his more thoughtful, less contro-versialist, moments.[16] But it is hard to argue that, as swingeing immigration quotas still hold sway, and as newspapers spread scares about the hordes of Eastern Europeans about to flood into the United Kingdom from the new members of the Euro-pean Union, these changes are the result of a *free* market, or indeed of the British people's ignorance of the so-called 'dangers'.

Another key social development, highlighted by Gray, for which we can thank the labour market is the increase in the number of women in work, and the consequent changes to the structure of 'typical' family life. Once more the influence of the free market is perhaps smaller than might be assumed. Powell, among many others, always maintained that markets were gender-blind, and that the panoply of equal opportunities bodies was therefore out of place, but as all the evidence is still of women being underpaid compared with men, one can hardly argue that women are being seriously induced into the labour market.

It also has to be said that 'Britishness' never ran particularly deep, and that the British national identity, such as it is, was always deeply contested. Some, such as Linda Colley, have argued that Britishness was relatively artificial and oppositional (i.e. we're not the French).[17] To the extent that the British are driven less by ideas and principles – which certainly contrasts with the French, and Americans for that matter – and more by the business-oriented pragmatism that followed from our development as an island nation that lived on trade, that may well be true (another topic upon which Powell had much to say[18]). A recent survey pugnaciously reported that many of the distinctive symbols of Britishness are related to our not-so-good cuisine; fish and chips, and roast beef and Yorkshire pudding were voted equal first in a 'league table' of national symbols, to the mild amusement of foreigners.[19]

Though Gray's criticisms may well discomfit those whose conservatism, like Scruton's, Powell's or Hogg's, rests on a particular vision of society, they have rather less purchase on the conservatism defined in Chapter Four, a sceptical conservatism that has taken a Rawlsian turn. In other words, the conservatism I have been describing is not anchored to a particular way of life, a particular view of the good, or a particular culture or society. It is an epistemological argument that, in so far as it is persuasive at all, is persuasive for intellectual reasons and not sentimental ones.

Neither the change principle nor the knowledge principle demands particular views of society. If British society, no matter how fast-moving or multicultural it has become, is more or less satisfactory to enough people, then governmental interference with it should surely be limited to the incremental adjustment of regulation in order not to disturb what may be very delicate social balances. Indeed, if British society has become more fast-moving, then it is likely that society is more delicately balanced than ever before, and therefore the risk aversion of those who would mould society should be even greater.

Gray is understandably perturbed by the loss of institutional knowledge. But free markets also rely on the deployment of local knowledge, tacit and often untranslatable into new contexts. And the influx of new people into a society will anyway require the evolution of new institutions and ways of, for instance, managing social services. The compromises of political and bureaucratic processes are of great importance here. There is no doubt a great problem of principle about, for example, how to disburse funds intended for women or girls to a community that may well have a strong cultural bias towards keeping women subservient to men. The problem of principle may be insoluble, but the *ad hoc* methods that a local council will have to develop on the fly, offensive to somebody's principles though they will inevitably be, may be of great practical use, and will encode a great deal of social learning about the interaction between the indigenous and the immigrant culture. On the other hand, principled approaches, like the French government's ban on Muslim headscarves in schools, are rather less responsive to the changes within the indigenous culture, though undoubtedly more in line with a conservative tradition of an authoritarian kidney.

The conservatism I describe should be applicable in any society, and at any time. The 'better' the society is – and that, of course, will be very much in the eye of the beholder – the more likely conservatism is to gain support. We expect this from the change principle. The loss of important cultural knowledge, via what Gray has called the 'hollowing out' of British institutions, is no doubt to be regretted. But that does not tell against the change principle, which says that one should recognise the great risks involved in trying to engineer a society, nor against the knowledge principle, which says that societies are too complex and dynamic to be fully understood from the centre. That an important source of knowledge has been lost (viz., the institutions Gray mourns) cannot mean that sceptical conservatism is made harder, as its whole premise is the difficulty of establishing knowledge about society.

The end of tradition

A second argument that is used to suggest that conservatism is impossible nowadays is the view that tradition is dead, that we have reached the end of tradition, that we live in post-traditional times. Thinkers have long been suspicious of the concept of tradition; in the medieval period, when tradition, as we moderns see it, was ubiquitous, there was no concept of tradition.[20] It was only when the Enlightenment launched its attack on tradition and superstition in the name of rationality and humanism that it got a name.

Hence 'tradition' is something of an artificial concept in itself. And many have argued that individual traditions themselves are equally artificial, that they have generally been created and manipulated by the powers that be to prevent too much change in society, and to cement the current authority relations and the status quo. In other words, tradition is not only a resource which conservatism values greatly, but also a tool for doing the work of a selfish conservatism with.[21]

This is altogether too sinister a gloss. Of course when tradition is examined the notions of some practice or ritual 'coming down to us from time immemorial' is an idealisation. It is unsurprising that most traditions were consciously created and manipulated. It would be surprising if traditions in earlier times *weren't* created and manipulated consciously in the same way. The historical record may make it difficult to establish the facts in individual cases, but nevertheless one should surely expect those in positions of power in hierarchical medieval societies to organise traditions for short-term political reasons. The point the conservative wishes to make is that this artificiality, which is not rare and may even be the norm, does not stand in the way of tradition being an important repository of social knowledge, wisdom and memory.

The Enlightenment failed to destroy tradition; in particular, it affected public life much more than private life. But thanks to globalisation, argues sociologist Anthony Giddens, tradition now really *is* in trouble.

> Two basic changes are happening today under the impact of globalisation. In western countries, not only public institutions but also everyday life are becoming opened up from the hold of tradition. And other societies across the world that remained more traditional are becoming detraditionalised.[22]

The problem, says Giddens acutely, is that tradition is no longer being lived 'in the traditional way'. We keep many traditions going, but we are no longer in the habit of defending and promoting them in their own terms. Instead we appeal to outside principles: they're a 'bit of fun', they 'bring the community together', they 'generate tourism'. This last is one of the weakest arguments for preserving a monarchy, yet one finds it put forward perhaps more than any other.

People find themselves having to justify their peculiar beliefs and practices to others who do not share them. And then the tradition becomes rather self-conscious, something that serves a purpose, rather than something that one does for no reason at all, except that one always has. Eventually traditions are completely drained of all content and become tools of commercial development. Venerable traditions end up being carried on in name only, in performance for tourists; tradition becomes heritage. Under the gaze of tourist and TV camera, the distance from the pride and indomitability of Robert Bruce to *Donald Whaur's Yer Troosers?* kitsch can be surprisingly short.

Giddens personally has no problem with the non-traditional defence of tradition.

> Tradition can perfectly well be defended in a non-traditional way – and that should be its future. Ritual, ceremonial and repetition have an important social role, something understood and acted upon by most organisations, including governments. Traditions will continue to be sustained in so far as they can effectively be justified – not in terms of their own internal rituals, but as compared to other traditions or ways of doing things.[23]

Giddens, of course, is not concerned with conservatism. But the knowledge principle, the deep scepticism about our understanding of society, seems strongly to suggest that we can never know what value a tradition really brings (if it brings any at all), what knowledge it helps transmit from generation to generation, and what would happen if it were taken away or turned into heritage kitsch. If Giddens has genuinely detected a trend, then maybe tradition really *is* doomed, and all those important sources of local knowledge are under serious threat.

Tradition and change

But is the situation as simple as it seems? In fact, when one examines the literature, the notion of tradition is a pretty slithery one. Giddens himself remarks on the relative dearth of work on tradition,[24] and one reason for this seems to be the inherent ambiguity of the topic. For example, many thinkers see tradition as something uncomplicated, a characteristic of a simpler past, and then go on to argue that the problems of modernity are the ones deserving examination. But at the same time others think that tradition is almost too complex a notion to study.[25] The ambiguity of the notion of tradition, suggests sociologist Barbara Misztal, may mean that the end of tradition is not as worrying as first might be thought.

> At the same time, however, the assumed implicitness of the notion further contributes to the confusion surrounding the definition of tradition, with some writers referring to tradition as an object and others describing it as a process of transmission. By pointing to tradition's role in transmitting in a given community certain elements of culture from generation to generation, the latter approach does not necessarily rule out [a] generation's ability to make its own tradition. On the other hand, the former perspective's emphasis on tradition's faithfulness to forefathers limits the scope of freedom on the part of a social group to create tradition at will. Consequently, although it is frequently admitted that in everyday language the intuitive use of the concept of tradition is widespread and that probably not all traditions have disappeared, the literature is divided in terms of its evaluation of the essence and role of tradition in modern life, as well as in terms of the perceived need for the preservation or recreation of traditions in the contemporary world.[26]

In other words, it is not an open and shut case. If we see tradition as an object, made up of knowledge, beliefs, rituals, practices, texts, attitudes, morals, that we share with previous generations, then of course when we cease to share those beliefs, morals and practices (because of inevitable social change) it will look like the tradition is running out of steam. On the other hand, if we see tradition as a method for transmitting certain beliefs, sundry knowledge from generation to generation, then we will be less surprised as traditions change, because they are after all transmitting the knowledge to new people in a new context (and the knowledge will have changed as well). Some rituals will have to be dropped, because they are inappropriate; some will have to be adjusted radically. As one type of example, how many sacrificial practices, designed to transmit traditional knowledge, beliefs, morals and attitudes, have been altered to purely symbolic acts during the course of development of any number of civilisations?

One would, indeed, expect traditions to have had to change and adapt to quite dramatic social changes in the last few decades. Traditions are less localised, less concentrated, for example, in particular villages; a village with a picturesque tradition is more likely to advertise for tourists to observe it. Traditions are less likely to be transmitted orally, and more likely to become the objects of media attention. The media are also responsible for bringing traditions together, juxtaposing them. The vast migrations of the last few decades are having a similar effect. Such a world – what Marshall McLuhan pointedly called a *global village*[27] – is a very different set of ecological niches for traditions, and they will of course have to adapt to survive.

There is no reason to believe that they won't, as Giddens correctly argues. Giddens is probably also correct to say that traditions will alter their character as a result. But the alteration is unlikely to be as drastic as he claims. The creation and recreation of tradition can be equally a process of organic renewal for societies.[28] And it is organic renewal, rather than stasis, which the conservative is keen to achieve.

Change and justice

A third argument against conservatism takes issue with the idea of wanting to manage and dampen change. After all, says this argument, some changes are required in the interests of moral principles such as justice. There are many unjust practices and traditions in society. Are we to tolerate them simply because it has always been so? Surely not.

As an example, many Hebridean islands were or are owned by absentee landlords, and the crofters and others on the island had to lease their land. Some, though not all, of these landlords were neglectful of the islands, allowing properties to fall derelict. For instance, the Isle of Eigg was owned by the Clanranalds from the 15th century, being sold into the private hands of Dr Hugh Macpherson for £15,000 in 1828. By 1995, the island was sold by an unloved and eccentric millionaire to a German performance artist, who visited the island twice and seemed to have no plans to reverse its social and physical decline. In the end, a campaign by the *Guardian* and *Sunday Times*, which involved them having to win a libel battle against the millionaire, led to enough donations being given to a fund for the islanders to allow them to buy their island in 1997 for £1.5 million.[29] Surely land reform in the Hebrides is required, however contrary to the change principle, in order to establish justice.

Such change is neither inevitable, nor irreversible when it happens. But when change seems to be required by justice, how can it be denied? Furthermore, change inspired by justice requires a conscious decision to make it, and adherence to an ideology or set of principles to justify the original critique – two motors for change that the conservative eschews. How, therefore, can a conservative produce a just society?

It is certainly the case that conservatism must allow change, because holding a society back, restricting its development, is social engineering of precisely the kind it is supposed to resist. The above argument then boils down to the issue of when change should be facilitated; the conservative of course values organic change, but rejects the notion of principled change – a fatal flaw as we try to build a more principled world.

Principle and practice

We should perhaps note a distinction made by Oakeshott between two ways of making changes on principled grounds.

Now, every society which is intellectually alive is liable, from time to time, to abridge its tradition of behaviour into a scheme of abstract ideas: and on occasion political discussion will be concerned, not ... with isolated transactions, nor ... with policies and traditions of activity, but with general principles. And in this there is no harm; perhaps even some positive benefit. It is possible that the distorting mirror of an ideology will reveal important hidden passages in the tradition, as a caricature reveals the potentialities of a face; and if this is so, the intellectual enterprise of seeing what a tradition looks like when it is reduced to an ideology will be a useful part of political education. But to make use of abridgement as a technique for exploring the intimations of a political tradition, to use it, that is, as a scientist uses hypothesis, is one thing; it is something different, and something inappropriate, to understand political activity itself as the activity of amending the arrangements of a society so as to make them agree with the provisions of an ideology.[30]

In other words, by all means use principle and ideology to help spot where something, perhaps a tradition, is going wrong. But it is quite another matter to *reshape* the world using an ideology.

To go back to the example of Eigg, ideas of justice, egalitarianism and indeed environmentalism help us to realise that the situation of absentee landlordism obtaining up until 1997 on that island was clearly dysfunctional. This prompts even the conservative to support reform. This does not breach the change principle, because that only says one must take the current benefits of a situation very seriously; the critique revealed that the benefits of the pre-1997 situation were minor. This is why, incidentally, the conservative should generally remain alert to the progressive critiques that are readily available. Even though many are based on a hopeless utopianism, that does not mean that they cannot reveal important truths about social injustice; the staunchest *Torygraph* reader should dip into the *Grauniad* at least occasionally.

Land reform on Eigg does not breach the knowledge principle either, as all that says is that the potential benefits are uncertain and hard to predict, and that there are likely to be downsides to the change too. Indeed, there are still bitter arguments taking place on Eigg about land and development, even under the new regime.[31]

Hence land reform on Eigg should have been supported by conservatives, because it had been demonstrated, by a principled critique, that the present benefits of the traditional system were inadequate. But that is very different from altering land law because one's ideology claims that landlordism is wrong. If there were another Hebridean island with a similar arrangement, but where, as it happened, the relationship of the landlord and his tenants was good, the island being cared for and prosperous, then the conservative would be able to argue that the present benefits were adequate to support resistance to change.

The progressive thinker might say at this point that such an island is not possible. He may be right; the conservative does not presume to judge that others' claims about society are necessarily wrong. But if the progressive's ground is that he read it in Marx, or Gramsci's Prison Diaries, or whatever, then the conservative is perfectly entitled to be sceptical. If, on the other hand, the progressive has performed a good deal of empirical and unbiased research on the actual communities about which he presumes to speak, then the conservative is equally bound to take notice.

Both Eigg and our hypothetical second isle have a system that would be condemned by egalitarians. On ideological grounds, an egalitarian would wish to change the systems of both; he assumes that no island so constituted can be well run. The conservative makes no such sweeping claim; Eigg was indeed badly run, but a whole new argument is required to establish the same claim about the second island (and an argument, moreover, based on the actual experiences and desires of the population).

The conservative should be grateful to the egalitarian for pointing out problems, but should resist calls for wholesale change where problems are less prominent, or are offset by benefits. The conservative's point is that if change is not pursued except when it is necessary, then one can reasonably hope that society will be relatively pleasant, tolerant and beneficial for its members. The flip side of that, of course, is that change should be pursued when it *is* necessary. This approach, of pursuing change only under pressure, will inevitably lead to untidy systems of government, because there will be no overarching philosophy or ideology determining their design. But, though untidy systems offend systematic ideologues, the burden of proof is surely on such ideologues to show that untidiness is necessarily a problem.

The vision thing

A fourth argument that conservatism is in crisis is thanks to Bruce Pilbeam, who argues strongly that 'conservatives no longer possess any significant defining purpose, they have neither enemies to fight nor "big ideas" to promote'.[32] Conservatism's (small 'c') enemies are diverse and don't demand a unified response; furthermore these enemies (feminists, eco-warriors, the politically correct, for example) are much less convincing as a threat to society than the Soviet Union (though fundamentalist Islam may in time take over that role).

Indeed, it might even be argued that those progressive forces are, in some cases at least, not the causes, but rather surfing a wave of change. The position of women in society has changed radically over the years, partly as a response to feminist critiques of paternalism, partly because of increased market liberalism, partly as a result of independent economic change (most notably the move from manufacturing to services[33]) and technological developments (such as the contraceptive pill). That feminist ideology was at best only a weak driver of change can be seen by its inaccurate predictions of future patterns of gender relations. Women's social roles are changing under their own momentum, not through the pressure of ideologues, and that makes those changes especially difficult for conservatives to resist. Other social changes, such as those wrought by the development and spread of mobile phones, seem to have little or no connection with the ideologies that conservatives deplore.

All this adds up, for Pilbeam, to a deficit in what George Bush Sr used to call the 'vision thing'. Conservatism has no distinctive position, no positive ideas, it is reactive and – because of the fragmented nature of modern life – incapable of forming an attractive unified viewpoint.

Is there an Anglo-American conservative tradition?

One problem with Pilbeam's approach is that he makes too few of the important distinctions. His account is handicapped by a refusal to make a distinction between conservatives and neo-liberals (which makes him see ideological incoherence where there is only opposition) and by a robustly expressed hostility to conservatism. These failings make him underestimate the difficulties of critiquing a specifically Anglo-American conservative tradition.

The seriousness lies in the fact that, though British and American societies have common roots, and share many common lines of development (most obviously that the majority of the founders of the American nation were of British descent), the two societies *are* different. Hence when one tries to adapt the change principle and the knowledge principle to the two contexts, one ends up developing two quite different approaches to government.

The biggest difference, often highlighted, is that British society has no common governing ideological theme, unlike the US (and other countries such as France or Iran). Britain is an island trading nation, and pretty well the whole of its independent history has been devoted to ensuring that identity. America, on the other hand, was founded by a conscious revolutionary act, and is rooted in the liberal ideology, via the writings of its founding fathers, the declaration of independence, and the long years of the practice of celebrating the ideological basis for its governance, symbolised by the flag.

Hence American conservatism has very much in common with Enlightenment liberalism.[34] When the American conservative wishes to take measures to preserve what he perceives as important aspects of American society, he will tend to try to preserve the relatively progressive context of freedom and democracy interpreted narrowly through the lens of the constitution. A British conservative, on the other hand, should also defend freedom and democracy, as these are important and long-lasting British traditions too, but our liberties were developed piecemeal, and certainly have little or no underlying common character. Hence a British conservative would always find it easier to curb liberty, when necessary (for instance, during some perceived national emergency).

Incidentally, I believe this accounts for one very striking aspect of American exceptionalism: that as the country has modernised, and in many ways embraced modernity, it has *not* become more modern in the sense of becoming less religious, or more tolerant of personal morality choice (such as being gay). American development has not been as the classical sociologists would have predicted, towards a secular, instrumental, rational society. Values that a European would think incredibly old-fashioned, even bumpkinish, remain strong, and in apparent contradiction to other American liberal values and developments.[35] Figure 3 shows a representation of the values of various societies on a two-dimensional graph, developed by the World Values Survey.[36] Those societies towards the right of the graph are more liberal than those to their left, as measured by opinion surveys; those to the top of the graph are more secular, more rational, less religious than those below them. America, as can be seen, is one of the most liberal nations on Earth, yet is towards the bottom in terms of cultural modernity, roughly level with Bangladesh and Northern Ireland.

This odd mix of cultural reaction and philosophical liberalism is, I think, rather neatly explained by its being a conservative country conserving a liberal tradition. Of course America is a complex country of diverse traditions; I am clearly guilty of glibness as I generalise. Nevertheless it makes sense to suggest

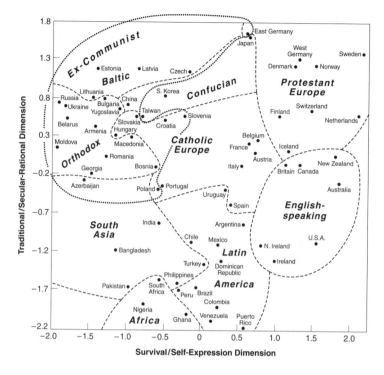

Figure 3: Locations of 65 societies on two dimensions of cross-cultural variation[37]

that a conservative society will try to preserve the cultural status quo, which in America is one where many freedoms are promoted. But someone who is predominantly a conservative will not wish to use his culturally preserved liberalism to develop *new* freedoms not sanctified by the constitution any more than he can help.

Compare this with Europe, where liberalism was *not* a founding aspect of most cultures, but actually a reaction against deeply entrenched religious, monarchical, rural and anti-democratic regimes. A conservative European will tend to see the liberal as the *enemy* who tries to change things, and indeed European liberals are much keener on change, because they have no attachment to the conservative vision of the past, no loyalty to traditional ways of doing things, at all.

Hence the response to Pilbeam, and to others, like Aughey and colleagues, who argue for a unified Anglo-American conservative tradition,[38] is 'yes and no'. There is certainly a common tradition, because conservatism has common features at the abstract level – the change principle and the knowledge principle. But when we look at *policy*, and the specific *social* and *economic* measures that conservatives promote, they can be – and are – very different indeed between Britain and America.

A distinctive conservative identity

In fact, all four of the arguments that conservatism is dead in the changing world of the 21st century lack, and require, some positive sense of what conservatism can deliver in policy terms. This will be the task of Part Two of this book. Chapter Six will look at a major fault line in right wing thought (and increasingly in left wing thought too), that of the role of free markets in determining the allocation of resources. Chapter Seven will get back to the Conservative Party's greatest embarrassment, its seemingly irrevocable association with Mrs Thatcher's widely quoted remark that there is no such thing as society. Chapter Eight looks at how conservatism might be a response to one of the biggest perceived crises in British political life, the decline of trust.

PART TWO

CONSERVATISM IN THE 21ST CENTURY

But the human character, however it may be exalted or depressed by a temporary enthusiasm, will return by degrees to its proper and natural level, and will resume those passions that seem the most adapted to its present condition.

Edward Gibbon, *Decline and Fall of the Roman Empire*

It's like the fashions. A hat may be as new-fashioned as you like, but it must stick on a woman's head.

Joyce Cary, *Herself Surprised*

CHAPTER SIX

CONSERVATISM AND MARKETS

The allocation of resources and the knowledge principle

We have argued at some length that conservatism and the free market liberalism that has become important, even fashionable on occasion, in the last couple of decades are two separate ideologies. That does not mean that a conservative has to be opposed to free markets; as we also argued in Chapter Five, conservatism is all about preserving one's culture, and if the culture to be preserved values free markets, then the conservative will wish to do that. The liberal underpinning of American political society means that, in that country, conservatives sound like free market liberals.

Britain has a long tradition of free trade and free markets. Indeed, Britain has always been a major trading nation. It developed an empire almost accidentally, on the back of the desire to secure trading outlets. Furthermore, since 1979, Britain has absorbed neo-liberal ideology to some extent, and British political culture now naturally leans towards developing market-based or market-imitating solutions for many of its central resource allocation problems. Mrs Thatcher began this trend, after the post-war years when planning and regulation were a standard solution. But neither Mr Major nor Mr Blair has seriously challenged the use of markets to allocate resources.

Hence a 21st-century conservative would certainly not think of scrapping all vestige of free market ideology. Remember the conservative's attachment to incremental change. Britain simply does not have the expertise in planning and centralised control any more; its civil service, unlike that of France where top civil servants and politicians share a common political culture and often a training from the elite Ecole Nationale d'Administration, is not properly equipped. We could not simply revert to the systems used in the 1960s, nor easily shift to new methods, without giant, risky, probably costly, disruption to government.

However, conservatives have a distinctive position with respect to free markets, because they are not wedded to them either. The charge against markets, made for example by John Gray, is that they are too disruptive to society to be compatible with conservatism. Can a conservative map out a clear position with respect to markets, one that avoids both following blindly in the neo-liberals' wake and beating an impractical retreat from them?

In addressing that question, I'm going to focus initially on the writings of two thinkers, F.A. Hayek and Enoch Powell, not because they are the most perspicuous of theorists – though each is recognised to be a brilliant analyst and propagandist – but because they have interestingly different takes on the relation between conservatism and markets.

Conservatism is the conjunction of the change principle and the knowledge principle. Hence if free market ideology is to be consistent with conservatism, then it should not contravene either of those principles. Both Hayek and Powell agree that markets are infinitely better from the point of view of the knowledge principle than any other method for allocating resources.

> Strictly speaking … there are two reasons why all controls of prices and quantities are incompatible with a free system: one is that all such controls must be arbitrary, and the other is that it is impossible to exercise them in such a manner as to allow the market to function adequately. A free system can adapt itself to almost any set of data, almost any general prohibition or regulation, so long as the adjusting mechanism itself is kept functioning. And it is mainly changes in prices that bring about the necessary adjustments.[1]

For Hayek, the arbitrariness of controls means that there is literally no sensible decision to be taken about price and production except relative to what people want, and what they want to exchange for what they want. These are the only parameters that matter, and nothing will tell you about them except the state of a free market. The more that a government interferes with the freedoms of that market, the less useful its signalling will be. Moreover, the beauty of the price system is that the knowledge that a consumer requires is actually tiny: all he or she needs to know is what he or she wants, and what he or she is prepared to pay for it. Other systems always require that someone possesses more knowledge than that, knowledge that the knowledge principle tells us is very hard to get hold of. Here is Enoch Powell campaigning for the 1964 election, excoriating the schemes of Harold Wilson and George Brown to plan the economy, putting the point in a practical context; his arguments are covertly aimed at many in his own party as well as the Labour opposition.

> I mean no disrespect to the intelligence of Mr Wilson, Mr Brown and their colleagues, when I say that to do all this, and to do it efficiently and promptly in the continuously and rapidly changing economic environment in which Britain lives, is beyond their capacity. It is beyond the capacity of any set of human beings, politicians or economists or officials, however wise, however dedicated. There is only one machine that can do the job. That machine is all of us together, every single person, using our effort, our observation, our insight and our opportunities, by means of those very 'market forces' which the Labour Party intends to banish.
>
> There is something infinitely pathetic, if it were not infinitely dangerous, in the spectacle of Mr Wilson, Mr Brown and the rest pitting their puny strength against this task – as though they were to go into an undertaking which uses the computers they are so fond of talking about and insist on 'Taking control' by doing all the sums themselves with a pencil and paper. We know what the result would be

if they attempted what they threaten: plans, like so many of the plans of our nationalized industries, lumbering along in the wake of events, years out of date, until even their own authors are forced belatedly to abandon them.

Let me just point this with a recent lesson. Two or three years ago no one, except perhaps a few scientists, even suspected that we were about to see sources of power opened up on our very door-step in the North Sea which will change the power economics not only of Britain and Europe but of the world. The influence of those events on this country's whole economy, industry and population pattern will be immense. Not being a Socialist, I do not pretend to foresee what that influence will be precisely, or indeed even in outline. But this I do know, that economic plans drawn up a year or two ago will soon be out of date from this cause alone, and that plans adumbrated now will look absurd before we are much older. The only effect of a Socialist economic plan, worked out now and imposed, as they say, 'with all the resources of government', would be to delay, to diminish or even to frustrate, the blessings which will flow from this unexpected discovery. There is only one kind of national economic plan which could be safe for Britain. That would be a plan of which no one took any notice except where it happened to coincide with what they were in any case going to do themselves.[2]

Markets and the change principle: Powell

Both Powell and Hayek were pro-markets. For Powell, markets were a conservative mechanism – it was central planning, equated by Powell with socialism, that caused change to go too quickly and too far.

It is another dangerous delusion to think that there is no harm in trying a bit more Socialism experimentally and that if after a while we do not like the consequences, we can stop and go back where we started from. As in an individual's life, so in that of a nation, with every step you take in a particular direction it becomes harder to return or to change. As in an individual's life, so in a nation's, there are some mistakes which, once made, can never be undone; some decisions, and those are often the gravest, which are irreversible. ... We are not like scientists, doing an experiment in a laboratory and able to repeat it as often as we wish with different ingredients or under different conditions.[3]

Markets are important mechanisms for telling us about the consequences of our desires and financial decisions, better than journalists, better than politicians, better than academics, better than clergymen. They do not flatter.

I hear people complaining about the high prices of building land for houses. But prices are only telling us the truth about the consequences of our own actions. The price an article will fetch in a given set of circumstances is its value in those circumstances. To rail at prices and threaten to control them is to behave like a petulant child who smashes the clock because he wishes it were a different time of day.[4]

The lessons of economics can be exported outside the economy.

As in economic life, so in social life, the wealth of knowledge and experience, the impulses to growth and change, lie with the people themselves, not with the state. The pattern of our social life, the character of our education, in school or university, the content of our family life, the physical environment of our homes – may I add, the unique texture of our medical care, in hospital or in general practice? – all these things, happily, have not been laid down or devised by the state. They are what the people themselves have chosen to make them, over the generations. Being such, they are richer and more varied by far than the state would have imagined. If from now on the state only is to decide, then the price must be an impoverishment of ideas, a pitiful narrowing of possibilities. The question is how the community can discharge the duty of care for its members without killing spontaneous development and change for all time to come.[5]

Rigging markets will skew the natural 'flow' of development in society, no matter how well-meant the attempt. For example, here is Powell dissecting the notion, in the Universal Declaration of Human Rights, that everyone has the right to housing of a standard adequate for his or her health and well-being and those of their family. This was a topic that Powell, as a former housing minister and author of the deregulating 1957 Rent Act, was always deeply interested in.

> But when we say, of something we do not actually possess, 'I have a right to that', the statement clearly means that somebody else – whether an individual or a body corporate or the community itself – ought to furnish me with it, and that if he does not do so voluntarily, he can and should be forced to do so.
>
> Since compulsion is thus involved, the question whether the statement 'I have a right to that' is true or false must, in a society that lives under the rule of law, be decided by legal process. The judge orders, at the end of the day: 'This man has a right to this; let it be taken from someone else and given to him.' …
>
> The statement is obviously incomplete in two vital respects. It does not say what is meant by a house, and it does not say on what terms, such as rent, I have a right to it. … [T]he director of Shelter … made the point for me. 'The houses,' he said, 'must be in the right place, at the right price, of the right size and of the right standard.' …
>
> Although price is only one of the specifications, it is the crucial one. In effect it contains all the rest. Where a good or a service is offered for sale at a price at which the supply and demand balance, the notion of enforceable right does not arise: between willing seller and willing buyer there is, by

definition, no room for compulsion. The question of compulsion only arises if a right is claimed to have the article at a price below that at which the seller would dispose of it voluntarily. The idea of a right to a house therefore necessarily means the right to a house (whatever its other characteristics) at a price below the market price. When that right is made universal, by saying 'everyone has a right to a house,' this is tantamount to taking housing out of the market altogether.

...

Here, in a nutshell, is the anatomy of rent restriction and subsidised housing. Rent restriction prevents maintenance and replacement and creates the slum. Subsidy enables public authorities to order and to let accommodation at prices at which it does not pay to produce it. In either case, because the price is artificially reduced, the demand must by definition always exceed the supply. And so it does. We know it as what we call 'the housing shortage'.

Thus, where everyone has a right to a house, shortage of housing is guaranteed in perpetuity.[6]

Powell takes the view that the 'impulses to growth and change' should not be hampered, because then the change will be unnatural and costly. Furthermore, in many if not all areas of society, a free market is the only mechanism that will allow this 'organic' change to happen at society's preferred pace. Anything else either holds society back, or pushes it forward in directions that it does not necessarily wish to go. Hence one function of a free market, according to Powell, is to ensure adherence to the change principle.

Markets and the change principle: Hayek

Ironically, Hayek agreed with pretty well everything that Powell says here. Hayek, like Powell, is very much in favour of free markets. The difference between them is that Powell (believes he) is a conservative, while Hayek (believes he) is not.

Hayek indeed would accept much of the stringent critique of conservatism, and right wing ideology generally, put forward by John Gray, whom we met in Chapter Five. The idea that markets can cause rapid change, possibly even going so far as to produce what we might call 'creative destruction', was part of what attracted him. An Austrian who had witnessed the rise of fascism, Hayek saw in markets the potential for people to be the masters of their own fate. When individual economic decisions were given their proper weight, dictatorship became next to impossible. If the cost of liberty was a certain chaos in public affairs, Hayek didn't mind; indeed, he wasn't even sure it was a cost, rather than a benefit, at least for those nimble enough to take advantage of opportunities as they fleetingly became available.

> As has often been acknowledged by conservative writers, one of the fundamental traits of the conservative attitude is a fear of change, a timid distrust of the new as such, while the liberal position is based on courage and confidence, on a preparedness to let change run its course even if we cannot predict where it will lead. There would not be much to object to if the conservatives merely disliked too rapid change in institutions and public policy; here the case for caution and slow progress is indeed strong. But the conservatives are inclined to use the powers of government to prevent change or to limit its rate to whatever appeals to the more timid mind. In looking forward, they lack the faith in the spontaneous forces of adjustment which makes the liberal accept changes without apprehension, even though he does not know how the necessary adaptations will be brought about.[7]

Aside from an understandable contrast in loaded vocabulary – 'fear', 'timid', 'courage', 'confidence' – Hayek welcomes markets as potential agents for great change, and agrees with Powell that they liberate the consumer. But Powell also values the continuity that conservatism hopes to protect.

> All government rests … upon habit, upon being exercised in the same way or a similar way to that in which the governed remember or believe that it was exercised before. Brute force can break with habit; but as soon as brute force begins to turn into government, it does so by starting to observe habitual modes of behaviour. Habitual forms or institutions for counsel and consent are thus of the essence of government.
>
> These institutions and forms persist while all other realities are changing around them.[8]

The problem for conservatives, as Gray and Hayek point out, is that free markets are highly disruptive of settled forms of social interaction, including government. It is unrealistic to suggest that far-reaching social and economic changes will not affect the continuity of government that Powell values so highly. The alteration of a law to admit more market exchanges will always produce unintended and unpredictable alterations correspondingly in social arrangements. This is not to say that these unintended alterations will always be bad – far from it. It is only to state the corollary of the change principle that, if society is in a happy state prior to the change (even if obviously not optimal), then the risk of change needs to be taken very seriously.

Let me illustrate this with a couple of examples. First consider the 1986 Building Society Act, which allowed the mutually owned building societies to convert themselves into limited companies; this was an ideologically driven idea from Mrs Thatcher's government, designed to inject competition into financial markets. Through the 1980s, the building societies had complained that restrictions upon their activities – their lending could only be for the mortgage of freehold and leasehold property in the UK – were preventing them from competing with the banks. They wished to emulate their American equivalents, the Savings and Loans institutions (which in fact were running into financial difficulties as a result of their premature expansions).

Once allowed to convert, building societies tended to compensate their members with free shares; these 'windfalls' were very tempting. The artificial shortage of stock in the new banks that this created pushed prices up in the short term as the big institutions scrambled to get their share. The building society sector was decimated thanks to these windfall gains; so-called 'carpetbaggers' would open accounts in order to be able to vote for conversion and get free shares. There are still champions of mutuality – the Nationwide is the biggest of the 63 remaining building societies now – but the sector's decline was far swifter than anyone expected. No one could call the new financial regime a disaster, but the actions of the market – the individual savers – were completely unpredictable, and led to dramatic institutional change. Furthermore, the changes have left savers and borrowers rather worse off.[9] Surely a conservative would never have brought in the 1986 Building Society Act.

Or let us move from the economic sphere to our private life. Britain has always been a nation of relatively uncouth beer drinkers (I am one myself, so I am not being snooty here). Mr Blair's New Labour government, in its early days of 'rebranding Britain' as 'cool Britannia', wished to change the ingrained habit of pub drinking, with its predominantly male ethos, uncool beery denizens, lack of atmosphere and lousy food. The preferred model was the continental bar, the café culture of Europe.

It was thought that the problem was the restrictive licensing laws, which encouraged bingeing and threw everyone onto the streets at closing time: a recipe for disaster. So it seemed in 1998.

> Britain's killjoy laws are over 30 years old. The 1964 Licensing Act forces most bars and pubs to stop serving at 11 p.m. To open later, a bar first needs an entertainment licence from the local authority, requiring it to offer music, dancing and food. Then it has to apply to magistrates for a special hours certificate, which can extend opening hours in central London to 3 a.m., and to 2 a.m. elsewhere. New licences and certificates are granted rarely. So most of the few late-night bars can charge hefty membership or admission fees.

Criticism of the current system is growing. Ian Corfield, former research director of the Fabian Society, a leftish think-tank, complains that today's laws mean that only the rich can drink late. John Grogan, a new Labour MP, thinks more flexible licensing laws should reflect more flexible life-styles. And the government's own Better Regulation Task-force has just finished consultation about licensing reform.[10]

The Labour government wished to develop Euro-style licences, to encourage Euro-style drinking. In fact, Britons did not drink a particularly large amount compared with their European cousins, but they did tend to cram it all into short periods. By 2000, the government was seriously worried by the problem of bingeing, but wasn't about to change tack. Though Alcohol Concern reckoned that in any particular year the cost to the nation of boozing was £3.3 *billion*, and 33,000 deaths,[11] liber-ating the licensing laws remained a priority.

Last month Jack Straw, the home secretary, announced that he plans to change Britain's licensing laws. He argued that the current regime of uniform opening hours for pubs and bars results in 'lots of people hitting the streets, and sometimes each other, at the same time.' The theory is that closing pubs at 11pm encourages people to drink faster. Mr Straw wants pubs and clubs to be able to apply for licences to serve alcohol up to 24 hours a day, and for the police to have new powers to punish rowdy drinkers and licensees who behave irresponsibly. In southern Europe, which has more flexible regulations, the link between crime and drink is less clear. But it may take more than a change in the licens-ing laws to alter the British fondness for getting pissed.[12]

The café culture never arrived.

The cafes are open during the day, and the clubs stay open until two or three in the morning most nights. In this respect, Romford is typical of contemporary Britain. In the late 1980s, the centres of many towns and cities went into decline as retailers, and particularly supermarkets, moved to new big, out-of-town shopping centres. So in the early 1990s, many local councils, in league with local businesses, re-developed their increasingly desolate town centres into 'leisure zones'. They looked to continental Europe for the inspiration to create modern 24-hour environments, mixing cafes, bars and clubs to keep people in the centres spending money for as long as possible.

This change coincided with the increasing prosperity of the 1990s, and the growing popularity of clubbing, to create compact leisure centres such as South Street. There are six clubs within a few hundred yards of each other in Romford town centre, some taking as many as 1,800 customers each. In the 'Bigg Market' area of Newcastle, there are enough pubs and clubs to accommodate 70,000 drinkers within one square mile. The cities of Leeds, Glasgow and Manchester have all converted run-down commercial areas into leisure zones.

… Advocates of 24-hour cities argue that they have improved the quality of life in Romford. That may be true of the daytime. But it is at dusk that the problems start.

For by night, South Street turns into a very different place. The street becomes a mass of 18–26-year-olds, drinking as much as they can. For anyone else, the place becomes almost a no-go area. Gillian Balfe, the council's town-centre manager and a strong supporter of the 'leisuring' of South Street, concedes that the crowds become uncontrollable, and the atmosphere quickly turns 'hostile and threatening'. Buses are now barred from going down South Street after 9.30pm: there are too many drunken people milling about.

In a survey for the local council done last year, 49% of the residents of the surrounding borough of Havering confessed that they did not want to come to the city centre any more for fear of crime. The local police concede that they are virtually overwhelmed. Violence is commonplace. There has only been one consequent fatality in the area in the past couple of years, but the police say that this is mainly thanks to the merciful proximity of the local hospital.[13]

As a conservative would have argued in advance, the change was unstoppable once it had occurred. Even the perceived awfulness of the night-time revelries could not be used as a reason for returning to the previous regime.

> For all the problems, however, Romford's local authority thinks that the idea of a 24-hour-city is already too profitable to be stopped. Local authorities think that new repressive legislation, or even a decision not to reform the licensing laws, would be unworkable. So instead of trying to pack everyone back off to bed, Romford is trying to reclaim the town centre for a broader mix of people, and so to fulfil the original ambitions of the 24-hour-city dreamers.[14]

The end result by 2004?

> How do you turn a nation of sots into responsible drinkers? Five years ago, the answer seemed obvious: sweep away the archaic licensing laws, which encouraged rapid 'drinking up' and filled the streets with legless punters at eleven o'clock. Once liberated from the tyranny of last orders, it was thought, people would calm down and grow up. A childish, candy-store attitude to alcohol would gradually lose out to continental hauteur.
>
> That convivial notion led to the relaxation of licensing codes and then to the Licensing Act, which comes into force this year. But police and politicians are already starting to get a morning-after feeling. This week, the prime minister's Strategy Unit acknowledged a growing drinking problem that costs the nation £20 billion a year, and outlined some stern measures to discipline drunks and the pubs that serve them.[15]

If Mr Blair ever thought that his strategy of rebranding Britain as a 24/7 happening place would lead to our youngsters donning berets and discussing the relative merits of Sartre and Camus over a chilled calvados at a pavement café as the sun set over South Street, Romford, he has presumably long since been disabused of that notion.

The market reforms, the liberalising of the licensing laws, brought with them dramatic changes in society, in the use and function of our city centres, and in our health. There have also been dramatic changes in our institutions as a result: the police, overwhelmed by the demands on them in city centres at night, have had to delegate a large amount of security patrolling to private outfits – bouncers, in other words – creating a severe shortage at the reputable end of *that* market. None of these changes was foreseen; all were produced by people voluntarily doing what they were legally entitled to do. Hayek's 'spontaneous forces of adjustment' do not necessarily produce results that all would welcome.

The price signal and the knowledge principle

What should the conservative say about markets and knowledge? Let us continue Hayek's argument quoted on page 178.

> In looking forward, [conservatives] lack the faith in the spontaneous forces of adjustment which makes the liberal accept changes without apprehension, even though he does not know how the necessary adaptations will be brought about. It is, indeed, part of the liberal attitude to assume that, especially in the economic field, the self-regulating forces of the market will somehow bring about the required adjustments to new conditions, although no one can foretell how they will do this in a particular instance. There is perhaps no single factor contributing so much to people's frequent reluctance to let the market work as their inability to conceive how some necessary balance, between demand and supply, between exports and imports, or the like, will be brought about without deliberate control. The conservative

feels safe and content only if he is assured that some higher wisdom watches and supervises change, only if he knows that some authority is charged with keeping the change 'orderly.'[16]

This quote is very true. In general, conservatives lack faith; faith is a bad predictor of events. It is true that, under certain assumptions, markets distribute resources in the most efficient way. But this is, as economist Kenneth Arrow has pointed out, more of a theorem than a fact.[17] It may well be true by definition that markets will reach a balance inevitably; there is still surely a question about the desirability of the balance reached. A balance was achieved in Romford between the drunken revellers and the havering people of Havering by in effect terrifying the latter from entering the town centre.

Let us consider a more serious example: rational use of carbon-based fuels, particularly in the USA, is leading to climate change, and a general global warming. Of course the entire system – that is, the world and the world's economy conceived over a period of decades – will reach some sort of equilibrium no doubt. That equilibrium may include the loss of many square miles of land surface, the alteration in character of a number of fascinating wilderness environments, the Arctic perhaps most prominent among them, massive alterations in patterns of disease and agriculture, and the expenditure of many billions of dollars by our descendants in order to preserve various cities or other centres of population. All well and good. But that might not be an equilibrium in which one would want to live; more to the point, it might be an equilibrium that one would wish to avoid if possible.

The liberal adherence to free markets appears to respect the knowledge principle while covertly contravening it. The liberal assumption that the most efficient allocation of resources is equivalent to the best outcome is exactly the type of theoretical fiat that is *ruled out* by the knowledge principle. The world is a complex place, says the knowledge principle, and knowledge of its operations is almost certainly impossible to get (or impossible to recognise when, by chance, it is achieved). To assume that the price system will automatically produce the best outcome is to place too much faith in the theory of free markets.

Markets are no doubt very sensible guides to resource allocation; they will no doubt enrich more people most of the time. And once examined in depth, the idea that there might be some 'deserved' price or wage – that a nurse, for example, should receive more than David Beckham because he or she does more 'good' – is surprisingly hard to make out, as Enoch Powell argued.

> There is no virtue in productivity in itself: what matters is *what* is produced. It is better to produce inefficiently a small output of what people happen to want than a large output efficiently of what they do not. Price, and everything which stems from it, such as profits, are the way people say what they want, and which things they want more badly than others. That is what price is all about – not merit or efficiency or quality or anything else, but just what people want in relation to what there is to be had: in short, supply and demand.
>
> There is an obvious corollary which I must state, although for some reason it seems to cause intense discomfort to some people. This is that price will not work, and people consequently will be prevented from getting what they want, unless the seller, be it of goods or labour or enterprise, is trying to get the best return he can. Of course, when I say, get the best return, I do not mean get it by deceit or by violence or by conspiracy. One only needs to imagine what would be the result if everyone was trying to get the lowest possible return, or indeed anything other than what seems to him the best. It would be … an economic bedlam, where everybody's intentions would be frustrated by everybody else.[18]

But there is more to social life – more even to economic life – than this. Powell may well be right that the price system tells us more than other systems. Nevertheless, that does not mean that the price system tells us everything we want to know; nor does it mean that, *pace* Hayek, we should be meekly accepting of whatever outcomes free markets produce.

For example, free markets, fine as they are in principle, bring with them a number of connotations – some of which may be unfair – which are unfortunate for any society in which prosperity is not the only yardstick of success. Most obviously, markets can lead to outcomes that may simply not be felt to be desirable: inegalitarian outcomes; outcomes where freedom is paradoxically reduced; outcomes where morality is outraged.[19]

These have been important criticisms of markets ever since they have been seriously theorised. Even so, it is worth saying a little bit about them. Inequality is not, in itself, bad. Indeed, one common effect of freeing a market is to increase inequality while actually making everyone, or virtually everyone, better off in an absolute sense. Hence it is certainly not enough, as an egalitarian socialist would obviously wish to do, to point at the increase in inequality as if it automatically made the case against markets. But a free market economy can produce pockets of severe poverty in which some people simply cannot raise the capital (human or financial) to escape. It can produce quite spectacular disparities between rich and poor, which we may wish to condemn on moral grounds alone. And it happens to be a fact of human nature, shown in a number of empirical investigations, that within limits people are more bothered by inequality than poverty.[20]

Again, free markets allow people to exchange what they like for what they like; in this respect, as Hayek correctly emphasised, they are important guarantors of freedom. However, this freedom of action may well be somewhat illusory. Clearly, someone with little to exchange will have remarkably little freedom. From the wider perspective, merely having a free choice need not necessarily be very exciting if that choice is from a set of unexciting things.

Third, the prevailing moral climate of a society may be outraged by free markets. Things may be made into commodities that many people do not want to be turned into commodities; these may include babies with certain genetic characteristics chosen by the parents, or sexual services, or local football teams, or medical treatment. Or free market proselytisers may go too far in making a virtue of selfishness. It makes a lot of sense to plan for people's selfishness, because people often are selfish and a society based on altruism would collapse within days. Furthermore, as Adam Smith pointed out, everyone's individual selfishness produces very good net benefits. But the vista of a small number of greedy and unpleasant people enriching themselves almost without limit in the greed-is-good 80s was a repellent spectacle, and set back the cause of free markets in many societies by many years.

Fourth, economic decisions are rarely as autonomous as is assumed. Some goods impose costs on others, the prime example of such a cost being pollution. The 'polluter pays' idea, that those who cause pollution should pay the costs of clearing up, is no doubt very sensible, but in practice fiendishly hard to enforce. Even if we exclude deliberate law-breaking, the crafting of property rights and cost allocations so that someone pays all and only the cost of his polluting is deeply tricky. What *exactly* is the contribution to global warming that my car makes – and indeed what *exactly* is the total cost of global warming of which I should pay my share?

Markets have their limitations like any system, and the conservative will have to agree with Hayek, *contra* Powell, that if they operate unchecked there is little control over outcomes. To assume that outcomes can be left to look after themselves is to assume that markets will always work – a faith in theory that the knowledge principle simply will not allow. As Oakeshott is said to have said about Hayek's philosophy, 'I suppose a plan not to have a plan is better than most plans.' Salisbury, for example, was a keen promoter of free market policies, and in fact for pretty much the same reasons as Powell, but when he detected unfortunate outcomes he was prepared to turn to, in Andrew Roberts' phrase, 'enlightened quasi-public bodies' to reverse them subsidised by government.[21] There is a big difference between being a free market liberal, and being in favour of free markets except when they do not work; a conservative can clearly be the latter.

Add to that the possibility that an unchecked market is likely to contravene the change principle as well, and it is clear that conservatism is a distinct ideology from market liberalism. Given the definition of conservatism that we painstakingly produced in Chapter Four, free market liberalism, in its pure form, actually contravenes *both* governing principles of conservatism.

Important though this result is, it is *not* to say that conservatives are always, or even often, opposed to the free operation of markets. Much will depend on the market orientation of the traditions of the society in which the conservative lives. And much will depend on the outcomes of the markets themselves. In Britain, we have a highly developed market tradition, and a British conservative will take notice of that. Indeed, the Thatcherite revolution has altered the centre ground of British politics, so that, even with a left wing government run by Tony Blair, market solutions for many resource allocation problems are unquestioned (they may be criticised, but few if any practicable alternatives are on the table). A British conservative might well rely on market mechanisms more often than not; but this reliance *cannot* be uncritical, or based solely on ideology.

So how will this difference in emphasis pan out in practice? That will be the subject of the investigations of the second half of this chapter.

Autonomy as a good

One particular aspect of neo-liberal free market philosophy that should draw the attention of the conservative is that of the autonomy of the individual. This means, in effect, that society should not interfere with the legitimate decisions made by an individual, at least as long as that individual does not propose to interfere with anyone else's. A man with a five pound note should be able to buy an improving book, make a charitable donation, get a packet of cigarettes, invest it in a building society account or place it on a horse as he sees fit; he no doubt has preferences as to which of these and other options are superior, as far as he is concerned and at this particular moment, and those preferences should be sovereign here. It may be that others have opinions about what this gentleman's interests are (and therefore what his preferences should ideally be). It may be that such persons would wish to try to persuade, cajole or even force him to pursue his 'correct' interests, as opposed to the interests he believes he has. But if the observer is committed to regarding the consumer as autonomous, then he must eschew any temptation to interfere with the consumer's choice.

The notion that consumers can be completely autonomous is one that conservatives should view with a little suspicion. One might, with Lord Salisbury, assume that governments, or experts, will in most if not all circumstances be less than capable (often laughably incapable) of estimating when consumer choices should be interfered with. Or one might, with Enoch Powell, believe that such interference is in most if not all cases an unwarranted infringement of liberty. But the conservative, with his or her sensitivity to the outcome of market exchanges in the actual contexts of real communities, will always be prepared to step in to prevent a market operating completely freely; furthermore, he or she will try to avoid rapid liberalis-ation of a currently controlled sector, allowing change to be incremental as conservatives would prefer. The conservative should wonder precisely what the *conditions* of autonomy are for the consumer, who is after all not an abstract entity, the matrix of preferences and resources of neo-liberal theory; any individual, any consumer is a *person* existing in some social milieu.

This means that the conservative is immediately suspicious of the market liberal's distinction between the autonomous indi-vidual, with a settled identity, able to calculate, make decisions and rank preferences adequately, and the non-autonomous person, whose identity is imposed and who relies on the judgements of others when it comes to making decisions. The conservative, sensitive to the immersion of a person within a

190

society, sees this as a false contrast; these are rather the end points of a continuum, with no real person ever occupying the extremes. In fact our identities are functions of many influences; our preferences are sometimes, but not always, determined by ourselves.

To focus only on autonomy, says the conservative, is to risk an unhealthy preoccupation with the narcissistic sides of ourselves. Pressure is placed on people to be the creators of their own identities, to be the authors of their own values, and the effect is to disconnect them from the values of their own societies and cultures. Cultural conformity appears to be a failure of individuality. The result, in Britain at least, is a peculiar obsession with celebrity, exhibitionism and hedonism; everyone wants to be 'doing it' on the telly.

Cultural commentator Mark Lawson even made the extraordinarily weird claim that Maxine Carr's forced anonymity, after death threats made to her because of her relationship with child murderer Ian Huntley (for whom she perjured herself, even though she played no part in, and was unaware of, Huntley's crimes), would be a stern punishment in itself, because she will for ever be prevented from appearing in reality TV shows. One doubts whether the vigilantes who wish to promote their own vile brand of self-imposed justice (and whose willingness to go beyond the law is another symptom of social individualism and narcissism) will be very persuaded by this argument.[22]

But the bizarre twist is that, with less support from the rich nexus of cultural and social values that help determine identity and preference, autonomy is arguably being *undermined*. Young men have always found beer and sex deeply enjoyable no doubt, but we live in an age where, for some reason, they *all* seem to prefer Jordan to anyone else. Young women, given much greater freedom than at almost any other time, appear not to have chosen very many different ways of exploring that freedom – to the extent, it seems, that every girl between the ages of fifteen and thirty has an identical tattoo on the small of her back.

That we have turned out a generation of FCUKwits is

probably not so terrible. But the growth in respect for individual autonomy has not led to a growth in autonomy itself.[23] And so the neo-liberal's claim that people's preferences ought to be respected wherever possible does start to look shaky when it seems that people's actual choices seem to be imposed from without even when the interference is minimal.

This argument provides one foothold for a conservative assault on the adverse consequences of markets, when detected, such as the contention by Oliver Letwin that household debt is reaching unsupportable and dangerous levels. The neo-liberal view is that people, autonomous individuals all, should make their own decisions about their financial arrangements. Whether they spend all they have, spend less than they have, or spend more than they have, is up to them. They need to judge based on their understanding of their financial position, their current commitments and their future expectations. If they miscalculate, and borrow more than they can pay back, then they will lose some of their possessions, if the loans are secured. There will be, as Hayek would point out, a reckoning. If people have been unwise, even in large numbers, then that is their affair.

But Letwin argued in speeches in 2003 and 2004 that such an outcome is unacceptable, not really for wider economic reasons, but because people were making unwise decisions and they should be protected from the consequences of those decisions (or, rather, they should be prevented or dissuaded from making those decisions in the first place). His call for a revival of the British savings culture, whatever else it may be, is certainly not respectful of people's autonomy in the financial markets.[24] His arguments that debt levels were reaching socially unacceptable levels cut across the Hayekian idea that a good society should be 'means-connected, not ends-connected', that society has 'no common purpose'.[25]

The worry about the social unacceptability of debt is a conservative worry, because for the strict neo-liberal such as Hayek, nothing – nothing economic at least – is socially unacceptable. People want to borrow, that's their business. Indeed, a decade ago, when free marketry enjoyed hegemony in the Conservative

Party, even strong defences of the importance of community would take the Hayekian line.[26]

But Mr Letwin now juggles the two ideological wings of the Conservative Party, as he also looks for measures that will not distort the market. This is a particularly hard nut to crack. He can recommend all sorts of stuff, support for the indebted, more funding for citizens' advice bureaux, publicity campaigns, he can urge creditors to be more understanding, or allow people to back out of loan agreements after signing. But most people surely already understand that interest rates can rise as well as fall. Most people are already aware that their main source of wealth, their house, will fluctuate dramatically in value, and in particular will not continue to rise for ever (memories of the slowdown in the housing market that ruined the reputation of Nigel Lawson cannot all have dissipated in the intervening decade). And, at a deeper level of common sense, most people surely realise that they cannot continue to spend money that they do not have indefinitely without their coming up with the cash from their own labours at some point. Nevertheless, they continue to borrow, and will do as long as the market for money remains undistorted and house prices continue to rise.

If you are worried about the consequences of a market's operations, then you should distort the market. If you believe that market distortions are always wrong or unwise, then you should not complain about the consequences. It is a rather stark dilemma, and goes to the heart of the Conservative Party's dual hosting of the conservative and neo-liberal ideologies. As the green shoots of conservative ideology are beginning to force their way once more through the concrete pavements, senior conservatives like Letwin are having to find nuanced formulations for problems and solutions that leave open as many ideological questions as possible.

Autonomy and authority

Autonomy undermines authority.[27] Sometimes this is good, sometimes bad, depending on the authority it is undermining.

But conservatism has had a long association with authoritarianism, and so the underlying tension between authority and individual autonomy can be troubling for the conservative.

It is not immediately clear why this is so. There is nothing necessarily harmful to authority in respecting an individual's autonomy. If it is to be assumed that an individual should not be constrained by anything other than his or her reason, will or conscience – which is what his or her autonomy consists in – then that is not to say that he or she will not defer to authorities. And there is nothing necessarily to connect conservatism with authoritarianism. Conservatism (small 'c') is an attitude towards change and towards knowledge of society; there is no commitment to particular forms of authority (and much destructive change, of course, is brought in by legitimate authorities).

However, the assumption of autonomy has created a tendency for the individual to construct him- or herself anew, with all the fragmentation, instability and fragility that implies. People are very unwilling to be constrained at all; authority figures are particularly unlikely to be trusted even when they are talking sense.[28]

Furthermore, many stable societies are based on the delegation of authority to certain people or social roles. In such cases, the undermining of authority can be damaging. If we have a functioning society, then various processes within that society will be carried out by public servants of differing types (from the Queen down to the park-keeper).

The balance between what we do for ourselves, what society does for us, and how much the government contributes is a delicate one, and much of what makes a society distinctive is contained in the ways in which these boundaries are drawn. Dramatic shifts upset expectations in very many ways, inherently unpredictably. The increase in individual autonomy ushered in by free market ideologies has redrawn the boundaries in two different ways. First, we as individuals have taken control of many aspects of life; for example, our patterns of consumption and our personal morality. And second, where the control of an area of society by the government has brought with it responsibilities for the individual, we are refusing to take those responsibilities seriously; for example, Britain's voters are very reluctant to pay taxes, even though they want improved services. One does not have to be a natural authoritarian to worry about the effects of a sudden release from constraint.[29]

Markets and public services

So far, I have been focusing on political authority. But there are other kinds of authority too, notably epistemological authority, or *expertise*. Small 'c' conservatives, from Lord Salisbury downwards, have always had something of a problem with experts, but in a complex society it seems sensible to outsource some decision-making to experts (doctors, mechanics, scientists, etc). The authority of expertise has also been undermined in recent years by the advance of the market.

In a fascinating study, economist and social scientist Julian Le Grand has traced the history of governments' understanding of public service during the half century of the welfare state.[30] In particular he looks at the different views of the motivations of the providers of public services, and of the capabilities of the recipients. He argues that, roughly speaking, the view of the entire structure of the welfare state has gone from a social democratic view at its beginning, to a neo-liberal view now. Even post-Thatcher, the general focus of policy has been neo-liberal.[31]

What has this meant in practice? Le Grand shows that it has had two effects on governmental perceptions. First, with respect to the service providers, the civil servants, doctors and other professionals, the view has changed, in Le Grand's terminology, from seeing them as 'knights' to seeing them as 'knaves'. In other words, the social democratic view of the founders of the welfare state was that public service providers were focused on getting services out to the people that needed them. Producing a good service was what they wanted to do. They were, to some extent, altruistic, with the interests of their clients at heart. The modern, neo-liberal view is that they are self-interested, requiring incentives to work in the interests of their clients. This, it is worth adding, applies only to individual providers; when it came to representative professional organisations (e.g. the British Medical Association as representing the interests of doctors) and trade unions, even the social democrats assumed that they were acting solely in the interests of their members, even though, once on the job, the individuals would be altruistically concerned with the interests of their clients.

Similarly, the understanding of the recipients of welfare has changed. The social democratic founders of the welfare state looked upon them as 'pawns', as passive receivers of help in standardised form. Today's neo-liberals see them as 'queens', actively seeking the best services tailored for their own purposes.

Hence there has been a dramatic change in policy formulation for the welfare state which has, of course, been much remarked upon. Le Grand's analysis shows why the change has taken place as governments' assumptions have changed.

If you take the social democratic view, that service providers are knights, and that clients are essentially passive pawns, then the system that makes sense is a trust system. You may wish to set budget limits, which may be more or less flexible, for the welfare services, but after that you should allow the providers to disburse funds as they see fit. Because they are not self-interested, they won't be concerned with using the funds for their own benefit. Their judgements, as they are professionals, will be more or less sound as to where the money will best be spent. And because the recipients are pawns, they won't complain or demand a different pattern of outlay.

On the other hand, if you assume that the providers are self-interested knaves, and that recipients are active seekers of services, then a market system looks best able to regulate the field, to ensure that money gets allocated efficiently and that the complex nexus of everyone's self-interest is harnessed to the greater good. Hence the increased marketisation of welfare services.

The problem with this from the conservative point of view is that it is patently obvious that service providers actually have many knightly characteristics, and that they are not always self-interested knaves.[32] Indeed, their view of their job differs dramatically from that of comparable people in the private sector. As a result, the market structures will undermine that knightliness. Indeed, when a system actively rewards self-interest and penalises altruism, as market systems do, the results can be far-reaching and by no means benign.[33] The profession-alism of our professions has always carried a large quantity of weight in the system. But the professional ethos is in distinct danger of being rendered obsolete.

On the other hand, it is no trivial matter simply to switch from neo-liberal marketisation back to social democratic trust, even if it were known for a fact (which it is not) that all welfare service providers are knights. From the conservative point of view, there are three reasons for this.

First, the market culture has been imbued into the welfare services for a good while now, at least since 1979. If that has meant an increase in the pursuit of self-interest within the system since then, then any trust-based system will be seriously compromised, because trust systems do not work well with self-interested persons. This is an application of the change principle, in fact; a culture that has been in place for 25 years cannot be replaced as a trivial operation without all sorts of unintended consequences.

Second, whether or not the welfare service providers are knights or knaves, it is very clear that recipients have moved from being pawns to queens. Trust of the expert, and deference to his or her expertise, has diminished dramatically.[34] The idea that patients might sit in militaristic wards snatching sleep where possible and eating horrible food to a timetable set largely for the benefit of the ward's ancillary staff seems quaintly old-fashioned now. I may err in thinking that all significant social developments from the mid-50s to the mid-70s are chronicled by the *Carry On* films, but nevertheless if one compares *Carry On Nurse*, made in late 1958, where the patients are kept regimented in Colditz-style accommodation, *Carry On Doctor* from 1967, where the patients revolt and attack surgeon Kenneth Williams to get him to change the regime, and *Carry On Again, Doctor* from 1969, where the patients (fat ladies) are demanding particular treatments and willing to pay good money for them, one cannot help but detect a pattern. This decline in trust makes it unlikely that the social democratic system could satisfy the new more active clientele (I hesitate to use Le Grand's terminology of 'active queens' here to avoid a *Carry On*-style *double entendre*).

Third, conservatives do not share the social democrats' faith in expertise, for the epistemological reasons outlined in Chapter Four. The knowledge principle suggests that putting experts in charge of the disbursal of funds is risky; indeed, though Le Grand assembles an impressive weight of evidence that many if not all public servants are knights at least much of the time, it is noticeable how few of them admit to any commitment to the financial health of the welfare system.[35] To put it crudely, that they are admirably public-spirited does not mean that they know what they are doing.

Le Grand himself endorses the view that we should be planning for a knight/queen system, and that finding the right set of incentives and funding structures is very complex. His recommendation of 'quasi-markets', where the government provides the funding, but individual service recipients are empowered, seems plausible in this context.[36]

Perhaps the best move would be towards schemes that are essentially voucher schemes; providing funding for the recipient to 'buy' services, under advice from experts. This has several advantages for the conservative, most notably meeting the three objections to trust-based systems, and – as Le Grand argues – many of the objections to market systems. It also respects the current position of the political centre, as such schemes would fit into the post-Blair landscape easily. And it does not involve a wholesale alteration of the political culture of the welfare system. The Conservative Party is toying with ideas of this sort, as for example with their Pupil and Patient Passport schemes.[37]

Markets in their context

We have talked so far about getting a distinctive conservative position on free markets in terms of increasing the distance from neo-liberalism's uncritical Hayekian support for markets. We have quite properly drawn attention to the damage that the assumption of and respect for individual autonomy can do to communities, and to authority, and to the provision and delivery of public services.

However, the story is not all negative. In fact, given that the Conservative Party's imperative at the moment is to distance itself from ideologically driven free marketeering (if for no other reason than the pragmatic one that it is not very popular), without repudiating the legacy of Mrs Thatcher's period of office which is of course totemically important for them, the story is not bad at all.

The advantage for the conservative is that the free market sits rather well in British society, with its traditionally 'hands off' approach to its citizens, its relative lack of social solidarity and its trading outlook. David Willetts has promoted this view in a number of books and speeches.

> First here is a question which tests whether or not you are an optimist about British society and social mobility. If you take a child aged 7, which is the better predictor of the eventual occupational status of the child: his or her performance in a simple aptitude test at the age of 7, or the occupational status of the child's father? The answer is that performance in the aptitude test is the better predictor. *Britain is an open, mobile society.* I do not think that many Labour politicians would feel comfortable with that fact. They are driven by a different view of this country, one in which they have to spend billions of pounds on the New Deal to overcome what they see as a structural social disadvantage.
>
> ...
>
> So it is not the case that Britain had the Industrial Revolution and then became a market society. It is the other way round – it is because we were a market society that we were the place where the Industrial Revolution started. *Britain has always been far more of a market economy than the*

Continent. So when we talk of the cash economy, the rise of the market or individualism, we are not speaking of some extraordinary alien import from America that arrived in 1963. We are talking about a fundamental feature of English society. And the importance of this market culture is that it ties in with the individualistic mobile society we described above. Again, can you imagine a Labour MP, even Tony Blair, speaking in praise of Britain as the world's first market economy and praising the fact that we historically have been a far more individualistic culture than the continent? They still cannot do it and yet it is true.[38]

The slide from 'Britain' to 'England' implies that the point is not so clear cut as Willetts makes it seem. But he is right that market economics sits on top of a particular world view, which is prevalent in British society: the emphasis on hard work, and on the rewards of that work going to the worker; the uncomplicated view of social mobility and the acceptance of self-made men in the higher echelons of society; the robust individualism; the impatience with the finer things of life, philosophy, history, art, literature, music, especially when their instrumental value is small.

These may not all be attractive traits. But Britain has not been a slouch in the arts, ironically, even with her market ideas. We have no Mozart, no Beethoven, but Elgar, Vaughan Williams, Purcell or Britten could string a note or two together. Again, few of our visual artists are of the first rank, but Turner and Constable would grace any nation. Our great philosophers – Hobbes, Locke, Hume, Russell – are not only of the first rank, but also laid a foundation for the characteristic British focus on unsystematic analytic philosophy, exploration of detail rather than system, which continues to this day (ironically, one of the exceptions to this rule is conservative philosopher Michael Oakeshott, who began his career as a follower of arch-systematiser Hegel). It is perhaps unsurprising that the area where Britain has had, and continues to have, most aesthetic success is the one most strongly connected to the commercial world, the artistic medium where talent is most easily converted to money: literature. The same goes for popular culture (though our cuisine, however …). And surely it goes without saying that when markets generate wealth, that at least will finance the leisure time required for some people to produce pleasant or exciting things without immediate instrumental value.

The British context lends itself quite readily to market systems of exchange, Willetts continues. There is much to fear from rampant individualism, but equally much to savour about individualism in an individualistic country. I, like many, live in horror of the man next to me on the train starting a conversation.

> If one turns to normal people's everyday experience, those fears about the destructive forces unloosed by free markets seem absurd and hysterical. The British suburb is not a place of rootless, miserable apathy. People, admittedly, do pursue their material aspirations – to own their house, to pay off the mortgage, to be able to afford a good holiday – but these are not immoral or shameful. And at the same time the latest sociological researchers confirm what one may anyway have suspected: that suburbs comprise rich networks of voluntary association, from Rotary Club to British Legion, from the rota for driving the children to school to the firm's social club. Even that urge to home ownership, satisfied more successfully in the 1980s than in any other decade, has given people new and stronger ties to their neighbourhood. Ownership and belonging go together. Our civic culture is under greatest strain not in the suburbs but in the inner cities from where so many businesses have fled. It is the absence of a modern capitalist economy which brings the real problems, not its success.[39]

One can overstate the case – I am as horrified by the Rotary Club as by the garrulous train passenger, and would always prefer to go bowling alone. But *chacun à son goût*.

Joking aside, Willetts' point here is well made. Nonetheless, as John Gray correctly predicted in the final days of Mr Major's government, it was that suburban lifestyle that was threatened by the liberalism of the day, and it was those usually Conservative voters who fled to New Labour.[40] As Willetts himself has pointed out, the rural rump – which during the 1840s and 1850s, remember, pretty well constituted the initial Conservative Party – is what remains; the Tory urban workers, imported by Joseph Chamberlain, the supposed chief beneficiaries of market economics, are the ones that have been lost.[41] Many communities are getting along nicely without well-meaning 'help' from government, but there are pockets which are not. What follows from this?

Communities are trumps

Markets can sit very successfully on top of British society. But if this is to continue, and if they are to increase their spread, then it is essential that they do not appear too threatening; the creative destruction that is their forte should not be overdone. If people's jobs are perceived as being perpetually under threat, then that will obviate the security that people need. Gray argues that that would adversely affect the viability of conservatism itself; Chapter Five argued that that was too strong a conclusion. But there is no doubt that the settled nature of British life would be – and indeed, in many sectors of the economy, has been – undermined by the Hayekian flux.

There is no doubt that a properly functioning competitive bidding market will allocate capital more efficiently, and make those in the market, in the aggregate, richer. Such wealth as would be created is particularly valuable to future generations – an important point for conservatives, recalling Burke. Furthermore, it should also be understood, as Salisbury and Powell among others argued very forcibly, that standing in the way of great economic forces is something that only masochists should do for any period of time. And finally the policy of keeping obviously failing businesses going indefinitely, the rescuing of 'lame ducks', is not any kind of long-term solution for industrial or social problems.

But bearing these important points, accepted by most if not all conservatives, in mind, it still does not follow that free markets should be adopted as methods of allocating resources unconditionally. Quite apart from the unconservative overtones of providing ideological reasons for a policy, the conservative should be defending incremental change, and he or she should be doing this with an eye on the outcomes that changes cause. Issues such as security matter, especially for a conservative, as they are strongly connected to the sorts of behaviour that conservatives endorse: planning for the future, working for one's community, defending existing practices.

If someone believed that his or her job was completely safe under any circumstances, then his or her planning for the future would be seriously distorted under the moral hazard that 'someone else will provide'. But equally, conservatism values stable conditions, and the idea of *closure*, the idea that one can stop striving and settle down to live the same way for a period of years, is very important. Many people, though certainly not all, are temperamentally opposed to the continuous climbing of the greasy pole; they aim to achieve a particular standard of living or social status, and then they wish to enjoy that as a reward. Indeed, since it is everyone's striving for themselves and their families that drives the economy, and since many people wish to enter the rat race only if there is a decent prospect of winning it, even moderate market liberals should think in terms of platforms and safety nets. Markets provide massive disincentives to the idea of closure, and a conservative should be wary of this.

Harold Macmillan and Reginald Maudling's experiments with micro-managing economic activity are unlikely to be repeated soon, not even by the Labour Party. The ideological warfare that followed the introduction of Macmillanite policies lasted over 30 years on and off and was bruising; no Conservative is likely to try to unite the party around that sort of policy.[42]

On the other hand, the mood music is important. Small 'c' conservatism is based around a preference for the actual over the abstract, the concrete over the potential. Any conservative message should therefore stress the actual advantages of stable and contented communities over and above the abstract advantages of dynamic market-based economies. Even Margaret Thatcher and Enoch Powell were known to make that case in their milder moments.[43]

Markets are good, at least in the British context. But the conservative has to believe that, even if only *in extremis*, communities trump markets.

The Conservative Party and markets: tactics and summary

Small 'c' conservatives have more of a suspicion of free markets than neo-liberals. That does not mean that they are against markets, because – in the right place – they are not. It does mean that they do not take it as read that free markets should be introduced. They also are prepared to intervene when markets are delivering outcomes that are, in some political or social way, unfortunate. How should a conservative explain that position, which, whatever its merits, is less clear than the alternatives of liberalism or socialism?

Let us note first of all that free markets are not very popular. In 1998, for example, an Angus Reid/*Economist* values poll found a reasonably large majority in favour of protection against free trade.[44] Many people wish the state to take a larger role in our economic life; perhaps the most commonly argued-for example of this is that many people want to see Britain's hopeless privatised railways re-nationalised (73 per cent in 1999[45]).

Now it is certainly true that many of these anti-market feelings are based on rather unrealistic views of what is possible and on unduly negative views of the effects of free markets. David Willetts, for example, vented his frustration at four particular fallacies: free markets mean every man for himself and the devil take the hindmost; if you are rich, then others must be poor; there is no real competition in big business; and markets are immoral because everything has a price.[46] But even after correction for these fallacies, there is little appetite for the extension of economic liberalism.

Furthermore, the Tories are of course remarkably badly placed here, because they are irrevocably associated with free market philosophy following the Thatcher years. Even though a post-Blair Labour Party would hardly be likely to roll back economic liberalism very far, they are perceived as much less sympathetic to it. Free markets are likely, in Britain at least, to be a staple of post-Blair politics, but Labour's ability to be seen as the reluctant marketisers ironically works in their favour.

On the other hand, neo-liberalism is not the only ideology available to the Conservatives; on pragmatic grounds alone, there is a strong case for soft-pedalling on the liberal messages and pushing conservative ones. Needless to say, ideology is only one driver of policy within a political party, but ideological signals and window-dressing do get taken very seriously by commentators and voters. Other interest groups within the Conservative coalition have little commitment to free markets; for example, the business community is certainly interested in increasing markets and reducing regulation, but it is also not averse to subsidies, regional policies and protectionism. So it should not be impossible to find voices within the Conservative Party prepared to shift the focus of policy away from market-oriented solutions, and towards solutions that emphasise local control, a decline in respect for autonomy in certain circumstances, and a reinvigoration of the professional ethic and the ethos of public service.

As we have argued above, this need not entail any kind of retreat from free markets that are currently in place and operating well. Nor, because of the strong associations between British social norms and market systems of exchange, should this entail a repudiation of the Thatcher years. But conservatism refuses to allow the Hayekian acceptance that the price mechanism tells you all that it is possible to know about an economy, and refuses to allow markets to function unchecked when they promise rapid change.

A conservative can always introduce a free market, or remove economic controls. But he or she must have a reason. And that reason cannot be: on ideological grounds a market is the best system. Instead the reason must be that some aspect of the current imperfect market is not functioning well, and that the current set of economic controls either has no purpose, or is doing demonstrable harm. The support for the removal of controls must be rooted in the relevant circumstances; the argument cannot be abstract.

Chapter Seven

Conservatism and societies

'There is no such thing as society'

The magazine *Woman's Own* has rarely been the centre of major political controversy in its 70-odd years of existence. But in 1987, an interview with Mrs Thatcher included a passage that has caused immense embarrassment to the Tories ever since. The key section is very well known and oft-quoted – it goes as follows.

> We've been through a period where too many people have been given to understand that if they have a problem, it's the government's job to cope with it. 'I have a problem, I'll get a grant.' 'I'm homeless, the government must house me.' They're casting their problems on society. And you know, there's no such thing as society. There are individual men and women, there are families. And no government can do anything except through people, and people must look after themselves first. It's our duty to look after ourselves and then, also, to look after our neighbours.[1]

Doubtless the hoo-hah came as some surprise to Mrs Thatcher's team. The expression of the sentiments is very carefully crafted, attempting to do three things at once. First, the interview was published shortly after Mrs Thatcher's third election victory, and rallies the gut supporters while simultaneously giving her opponents apoplexy. In other words, good knockabout politics. And second, it clearly sends a straightforward neo-liberal individualist message with a hint of Samuel Smiles-style self-help.

Nevertheless, the quote isn't incompatible with conservatism either, and the third thing it does is to lay stress on personal responsibility. It claims that 'society' is not some great abstract agent, but rather is made up of people each of whom has to make decisions for him- or herself. It is a perennial worry for the conservative that 'society' will, as it were, take over. The conservative certainly thinks society is important, and that policies that damage society, or change it too rapidly and artificially, are very risky and should only be contemplated *in extremis*. But the conservative is also aware of the importance of individual liberty, so that we can avoid regimenting everyone, making people do things 'for the good of society'.

Mrs Thatcher's perception is that some people have ceased to address their own problems, but try to involve the state as the first resort. The so-called dependency trap enmeshes people who do not think it worth their while to work, to plan their own lives, or to try to be independent. Though the state offers a very low standard of living as its safety net, nevertheless many people, sometimes on the basis of calculation, sometimes merely because they lack the skills to forge their own independent existence, prefer to stay in the net rather than striking out on their own. This moral hazard is worrying for conservatives, and the *Woman's Own* interview is unobjectionable from that point of view.

Nevertheless, carefully crafted or not, one sentence has become immortal – 'there's no such thing as society.' That single clause seems to encapsulate the 'I'm all right Jack' individualism of the 1980s that so many voters found, and still find, so distasteful. Taken thus, Mrs Thatcher seems to be saying that people can divest themselves of their moral responsibility for their fellows, and legitimately pursue their own interests instead.

Mrs Thatcher herself believed that the furore was caused by the success of her government, and the unstoppable spread of liberal free marketry across the globe as socialism ceased to be an intellectually serious alternative.

The surge of prosperity – most of it soundly based but some of it unsustainable – which occurred from 1986 to 1989 had one paradoxical effect. Deprived for the moment at least of the opportunity to chastise the Government and blame free enterprise capitalism for failing to create jobs and raise living standards, the Left turned their attention to non-economic issues. The idea that the state was the engine of economic progress was discredited – and ever more so as the failures of communism became more widely known. But was the price of capitalist prosperity too high? Was it not resulting in a gross and offensive materialism, traffic congestion and pollution? Were not the attitudes required to get on in Thatcher's Britain causing the weak to be marginalized, homelessness to grow, communities to break down? In short, was not the 'quality of life' being threatened?

I found all this misguided and hypocritical. If socialism had produced economic success those same critics would have been celebrating in the streets. But socialism had failed. And it was the poorer, weaker members of society who had suffered worst as a result of that failure. More than that, however, socialism, in spite of all the high-minded rhetoric in which its arguments were framed, had played on the worst aspects of human nature. It had literally demoralized communities and families, offering dependency in place of independence as well as subjecting traditional values to sustained derision. It was a cynical ploy for the Left to start talking as if they were old-fashioned Tories, fighting to preserve decency amid social disintegration.[2]

Mrs Thatcher thought that she had, as the left had not, a way of re-forming those demoralised communities: personal responsibility needed to be revitalised. Hence the *Woman's Own* interview.

My meaning, clear at the time but subsequently distorted beyond recognition, was that society was not an abstraction, separate from the men and women who composed it, but a living structure of individuals, families, neighbours and voluntary associations. I expected great things from society in this sense because I believed that as economic wealth grew, individuals and voluntary groups should assume more responsibility for their neighbours' misfortunes. The error to which I was objecting was the confusion of society with the state as the helper of first resort. Whenever I heard people complain that 'society' should not permit some particular misfortune, I would retort, 'And what are you doing about it, then?' Society for me was not an excuse, it was a source of obligation.[3]

However that may be, the quote was disastrous for the image of the Tories, and they have been living it down ever since. Mr Major was clearly a Tory of a different kidney from Mrs Thatcher, but early on in his period of office, the 'no such thing' argument received rather more scholarly flesh than *Woman's Own* might have been able to support. David Willetts:

Reading the full text of the 1987 interview, it is clear that all she meant was that we could not evade personal responsibility for our actions by saying everything we did wrong was really society's fault. And if we want 'government' or 'society' to do something, that means putting a duty on other people and collecting taxes from them. But Mrs Thatcher did not mean that we had no responsibilities to others, or could lead any meaningful existence outside society. Indeed, one of her preoccupations was with reconciling the world of economic calculation with our moral obligations to our fellow-citizens. For her that reconciliation was achieved through her strong sense of religious obligation.[4]

By 1997, disabusing the British people of the idea that Tories believed that there was no such thing as society was rapidly becoming imperative. In a book brought out for the general election of that year, David Willetts called one chapter 'Is there such a thing as society?', and answered his own question with a paragraph consisting of a single word: 'Yes'.[5] He went on explicitly to distance Mr Major's Tories from the (popular perception of the) Thatcherites.

> The truth is that the Conservative stands between the two errors of socialist collectivism and libertarian individualism and, indeed, recognizes that they are mutually dependent. Big government undermines community and leaves us just as atomized individuals expecting the welfare state to do everything. Rampant individualism without ties of duty, loyalty and affiliation is only checked by powerful and intrusive government.[6]

Even as late as 2002, Iain Duncan Smith was feeling the after-effects of the *Woman's Own* fallout. The expression of his personal credo dispensed with Willetts' interrogative, and merely asserted that there *was* such a thing as society.[7] Incredibly, fifteen years after the original unfortunate remark, intellectual heavy hitters – this time Oliver Letwin – were still being brought in to try to explain the misunderstanding.

> Mrs Thatcher was attacking the Left's unthinking call for 'society' to rush in and solve every ill. And when the Left say 'society' – then and still today – they inevitably mean the state. In the part of the quotation that the Left never repeat, Mrs Thatcher points to a more enduring vision of society – a society composed of active citizens and strong families.[8]

It is extraordinary that one backfiring remark in a popular ladies' magazine could still dog the Tories today, but it does. Partly this may be because the quote has now been rather over-interpreted, with the various glosses on it being none too consistent with each other. But more importantly, there is a sense that Mrs Thatcher made a sort of Freudian slip, that the 'no such thing' slogan, though it is not what she meant to say, does rather sum up the vision of society as being made up of nothing above and beyond the individualistic interests of its members. Society is not, therefore, something that you can destroy, break down or otherwise harm.

The struggle for Tories such as Willetts and Letwin, who are after all trying to reconcile two different ideological traditions, is that the British conservative simply does not believe this to be true, though the neo-liberal might.

But is the only alternative that society 'takes over', perhaps in the blundering form of the state, perhaps in a prevailing puritan climate of fervour and moral coercion? The business of this chapter is to sketch some of the problem areas for which the Conservative Party is perceived (not necessarily fairly) to be lacking in answers, and to show how a conservatism based on the epistemological principles outlined in Part One can be the basis of a humane, socially responsible philosophy, or set of policies, that nevertheless gives sufficient scope for individual expression.

Society is a sprawling concept, and this chapter is therefore a bit of a ragbag. We begin with personal life, looking at morality, the services that individuals require from the state, and the obligations on people in return for those services. Moving on to more formal social structures, we will then look at the constitution. And finally we will look at the relationship between our society and others. In all these areas, the Conservative Party is a step or two behind Mr Blair's Labour government; I hope to show that a revived conservatism might well provide the basis for a viable policy platform in post-Blair Britain, and help the Tories to rid themselves of the reputation, in Theresa May's famous phrase, of being the 'nasty party'.

Personal morality

One issue that has dogged the Conservative Party for a number of years is that of personal morality: when should we respect, and when should we not respect, the personal autonomy of individuals in areas of behaviour that affect no one else? Much personal behaviour, of course, offends those with strong moral tastes. Furthermore, the broadly liberal direction in which society is moving means that those of a conservative disposition will be ranged against increasing *freedom*.

The charges against the Conservative Party when it takes a reactionary stand against changes in personal morality are threefold. The first is that, because by definition the actions being criticised by Tories affect no one other than the individual involved (and other consenting adults), nothing tangible is gained by any prohibition, and much is lost, including personal liberty and the resources of policing authorities who have to track down unfairly criminalised people. The second is that, by making something against the law, the wherewithal for an illegal supply industry, attracting juicy price premiums, will have been created. And third, moral rectitude can attract charges of hypocrisy if members of one's own party are caught out indulging.

Let's look briefly at a couple of such activities, how they have affected the Conservative Party, and how conservatives should react. We'll look initially at the issue of homosexuality, and then move on to the more complex case of drug abuse.

Homosexuality is condemned by the Bible quite explicitly. If you take your Bible without layers of interpretation, you should be against it. This is the basis for the traditional conservative rejection of homosexuality, which meant that the activity was criminalised for a long period in Britain, being legalised only in the 1960s. All well and good. This is not a sufficient rationale, however. In the first place, many perfectly innocuous activities are explicitly condemned by the Bible, and few if any people argue that they all should be criminalised. And secondly, we have recommended that conservatism should take a Rawlsian turn: that is, it should not rest its arguments on disputed views of society, or particular moral or cultural perspectives that may not be shared. That homosexuality is condemned in the Bible is of course sufficient for some – by no means all – Christians, but the rest of us who are not Christian are unlikely to be swayed if the argument does not go beyond that into a more public realm of reason.

The taboo surrounding homosexuality is disappearing from British society. Gay couples live together quite openly without condemnation. Even if one were not a liberal, and refused to agree that in the personal sphere the individual should be sovereign, one might still accept homosexuality because it is so obviously harmless to its practitioners, and to everyone else. The major problems with gay behaviour stem from the social stigma attached, which could be and is being dispelled to some extent by the equalisation of treatment by the authorities (and anyway is hardly gay people's *fault*), and, in the British context, the greater risk compared with heterosexual couples of contracting AIDS, which is a function of promiscuity rather than homosexuality *per se*. In short, discrimination against gay people is unjust pure and simple.

Let us make a further point here. Conservatives (small 'c') need to deal with society as it is, whether or not they are happy with it. Even if conservatives are opposed to homosexual behaviour, this is not sufficient reason to try to prevent it. Gay relationships are clearly common in society, are frowned upon by few, do no one any serious harm and make a lot of people very happy. Surely the change principle must weigh against trying to engineer society to discourage the practice.

All this then makes the Tories' past support for various anti-gay initiatives – in particular the notorious, if largely symbolic, Section 28 of the 1988 Local Government Act, which forbade local authorities from promoting homosexuality within schools – rather unfortunate. And indeed, the only Tory leader ever to be elected by party members, Iain Duncan Smith, traditional right winger though he was, openly toyed with the withdrawal of support for the measure as a prominent part of his campaign, as for example with this high-profile interview with the Tory Party's house newsletter, the *Daily Telegraph*.

'What about Clause 28?' I ask. (This is the legislation that prohibits the promotion of homosexuality by local authorities.)

His response surprises me. Suddenly, it could be Michael

Portillo speaking. 'I'm not going to come out in favour of gay marriage, Gyles, but I do have to recognise that we as a party have become identified with what we dislike and hate rather than the things we like. Clause 28, I accept, has about it a totem which is about saying to a group in the community, "We actually rather dislike you."

'That is a problem and a party like ours has to recognise the problem and think, how do we resolve that? It is important to protect children from influences that are malign or manipulative, but, at the same time, I want to get rid of the concept that it's all about one community. So, yes, I'd look at it again.'[9]

Not perfect: there is an implication at the end that homosexuals are perhaps more likely to be malign or manipulative towards children, a proposition for which there exists no evidence whatever (though of course children should be protected from the sexually predatory no matter what their sexual orientation). But the points IDS makes here are sound. They are twofold. First, the party badly needs to sever the link between itself and repressive legislation against homosexuality. And second, a wider issue is that the Tories are in danger of defining themselves against a series of lifestyles that they do not like. In an increasingly liberal society, this sort of stance does not respect the organic changes which are occurring. Even if the conservative privately deplores them, that cannot be used as an excuse for legislation.

One should therefore applaud the initiative of Michael Howard and Charles Hendry in holding a 'gay summit' in Westminster in 2004, planned so that Tories could hear first-hand accounts of anti-gay discrimination.[10] The initiative was a mixed success: only five MPs turned up.[11] Furthermore, it was strongly criticised by Ann Widdecombe. Nevertheless, it was no disaster. There was oodles of press coverage – and as presumably the point of the jamboree was to try to create an image of the Tories as no longer an anti-gay party, rather than actually being of any use in itself as a 'listening exercise', that doubtless served the purpose. And upon further examination, Miss Widdecombe's criticisms, though strongly influenced of course by her robust religious views on the family, were more about the marginality of the issue than anything else. This is exactly wrong: with the Tories needing to move towards the centre the issue is not at all marginal.

The recreational use of drugs is a much more complex case for the conservative (as for any politician of any ideology). The issue has caused a great deal of difficulty for the Tories in their years of opposition, most notably at the party conference of 2000, when Shadow Home Secretary Widdecombe outlined a zero tolerance strategy, only to be sandbagged as seven of her Shadow Cabinet colleagues admitted to taking recreational drugs in the past and the Police Federation condemned the policy as unworkable.[12]

Few ideologies are so specific that they determine a right and a wrong drug policy (except for libertarianism, which recommends legalisation of course). Conservatives (small 'c') are not naturally drawn to the liberating properties of drugs, nor to the artificial and chaotic lifestyle of the user; why should a conservative wish to cleanse the doors of perception? But on the other hand, the conservative has always prided him- or herself on being able to look at the facts with an unsentimental eye. What sort of arguments should he or she take seriously?

Some arguments are irrelevant. First of all, the personal liberty argument, that recreational drug users are being prevented from pursuing their own idea of the good life, is not, in itself, interesting to the conservative. Assuming drug users do no harm, the conservative's instinct should be to respect personal liberty. But whether drug users do harm is precisely the issue; they can be responsible for crime, and they also require a criminal infrastructure to supply the needs of their habit. So until that issue is resolved favourably, the infringement of liberty argument does not feature on the conservative's radar.

Second, there is an argument that some drugs, such as cannabis or ecstasy, are notably less harmful to society, and their users, than other drugs that are legal, most obviously tobacco and alcohol. All that is true, but the conservative is unimpressed. Admittedly, to make drug laws consistent with alcohol and tobacco laws it is necessary to either legalise soft drugs or make alcohol and tobacco illegal. But who said that laws need to be consistent as long as they are clear? Granted that, all things being equal, it is good for laws to be consistent, it does not follow that where laws are adequate yet inconsistent they should be altered to make them consistent. For that may stop them being adequate.

There are plenty of arguments for keeping drug laws as they stand. One would invoke the change principle on the need to avoid change. A second, related argument goes beyond the law and looks at how the law interacts with society; laws do not exist in the abstract, and one cannot gauge the effect of a law merely by analysing its content. The combined effect of the law being as it is, policing policy being as it is (i.e. cracking down much harder on hard drugs such as heroin), and social mores being as they are, is that the recreational use of cannabis and ecstasy is relatively less risky for users. Indeed, anyone worried about illegality can fairly easily make their way to places, such as Amsterdam, where the practice is tolerated. As a matter of fact, goes this second argument, cannabis or ecstasy users are barely impinged on, while heroin and cocaine users are given a much harder time, which is more or less commensurate with the effects of the drugs. Hence, as *the system as a whole* is much more punitive towards hard drugs, there is no need to change things round. Any liberalisation, on the other hand, would send quite the wrong signals.

A third argument is that drugs undermine human dignity, and erode community relationships; such an argument clearly resonates with conservatives.[13] Heroin is severely addictive and leads users very easily into crime; crack cocaine can turn abusers into one-man crime waves. Crime patterns vary with patterns of drug abuse.[14] And the attraction of any kind of tolerant zone for criminal activity means that criminality will tend to spread anyway to other members of the community beyond the drug-using element. It is essential to prevent drugs getting a hold of society, and similarly essential for governments to give out strong anti-drugs messages.

The arguments for decriminalisation fall into two types. The first type recognises that drug use is widespread and tolerated by many people; as with the arguments about homosexuality, this view says that conservatives need to recognise that society is tolerant, and that the change principle entails that that tolerance should be respected. Again, Iain Duncan Smith nodded in the direction of such arguments during his leadership election campaign.[15]

The second type of decriminalisation argument accepts the challenge of the change principle by insisting that the current situation is completely unsatisfactory, and that therefore change, if only incremental change, is legitimate in this case; any harm done is likely to be less harmful than the law as it stands. For example, the so-called war on drugs has done little other than create astonishingly lucrative networks of organised crime, notably in South America (cocaine) and the Middle East (opium), by creating the conditions for the generation of astonishing quantities of money by undertaking the small risks of supply to meet the giant demand for drugs in America and Europe. The American prohibition of alcohol that fostered the gangsters of the 1920s is but a tamer example of the same phenomenon.

Or it might be said that current drugs policies are not keeping vulnerable people from drugs at all; a medically based strategy of intervention, rehabilitation and support might be a better policy. Or, given the large number of young people who take ecstasy of a Friday night while clubbing, a conservative might reasonably worry about the effects on millions of youngsters' respect for the rule of law of making criminals of themselves with impunity on a weekly basis.

None of these arguments, either for or against the current system, is decisive. But we can at least see how the conservative will expect to argue and be argued against. Arguments addressing the health of the community should be regarded as over and above arguments about personal liberty. Arguments should take the facts as they stand, public attitudes as they are, over and above any preferences about how society should be run. Justice should count for more than making laws consistent or 'modern'.

Education

Education is a social issue that, like personal morality, divides groups; indeed, so complex an issue is it that it is hard to frame obviously fair and sensible policies. There will always be awkward cases which threaten to fall between various stools; sweeping statements or wide-ranging laws will always be embarrassed eventually.

In this section, I want to adumbrate four lines of thought along conservative principles to show what a conservative critique of the current system would look like. I do not suggest that these four criticisms are the only ones that a conservative would want to make, nor that only conservatives would make them. I will round off with a discussion of some of the positive suggestions that a conservative might wish to endorse.

The first criticism is perhaps the most obvious: there is no need for a comprehensive system, or a national curriculum. Education officials cannot know, even in broad outline, what type of education is better for everyone. Children have wildly varying needs. Neighbourhoods have important requirements too: a leafy suburb might well want an education that prepares its offspring for university, while an inner city estate would actually benefit from prioritising good behaviour and social awareness, and an area with a large proportion of recent immigrants might focus on language (if it is then argued that the suburban children are thereby getting an unfairly better start in life, the rejoinder has to be that the education they receive is a symptom of that, not its cause). And different localities have requirements, for example preserving local customs or knowledge of local industries (even dying ones), such as the heritage of the pottery industry in Stoke-on-Trent, or of the influence of the sea in Portsmouth.

Hence a conservative will work towards a system with as fine a grain as is feasible. As much control as possible should be ceded to as local a level as possible. In short, education is currently looking like too much of a commodity, needlessly so, with children becoming exam fodder and teachers being given very perverse incentives and targets by the system. But this can be changed. To use the terminology of Julian Le Grand introduced in the previous chapter,[16] most teachers and officials are more knight than knave, and the education system should exploit this to ensure as individual an education as possible for the child. It is only performance evaluation systems that make teachers treat children as exam fodder, and education as a process of peristalsis; without them they would be able to focus much more on the individual child's needs.

A second criticism goes to the heart of what education is. The problem is this: there is actually remarkably little agreement about the purpose of education. Is it supposed to impart the values and heritage of a particular culture? To create the citizens of the future? To equip youngsters for the future? To make youngsters independent and able to pursue their own ideas of the good life? To make youngsters willing and able to contribute to the community? To impart currently understood knowledge across a range of subjects? To give youngsters the skills they need to be economically successful? To produce an educated, knowledge-rich workforce to increase the future wealth of the nation? To instil discipline? Should children be seen and not heard? Or should we encourage them to explore their own values, make their own decisions and have confidence in their own independently reached ideas?

Given the lack of consensus, and corresponding lack of direction from central government, it is hardly surprising that comprehensive education has flaws, or that the national curriculum is overloaded and complex. Furthermore, many think that the value of an education is easily measurable, that good education consists in good teaching methods, or exam results, or whatever (even if we disagree about the purposes to which these are put). Quite the contrary: education is a highly complex interaction between children, teachers, families, institutions (i.e. schools) and communities, and it affects the basic make-up of all five.[17] Education is not something that you plonk down on top of a society; education remakes society in various ways that are hard to measure, hard to spot and next to impossible to reverse.

The knowledge principle tells us that no one can decide what education system is best for a society, for a culture, or for all its citizens. The question is too ill-defined, and too open-ended. So we might raise a cheer when the Chief Inspector of Schools David Bell argues that the education system works only for pupils of a certain type, and is failing the rest. But when he says that vocational education is 'about putting forward something that will meet the needs of the British economy' one has to sigh, partly at the rebarbative managementspeak, but mainly at the idea that the purpose of education is to create square pegs for the square holes in the economy (even if we assume, which we most assuredly should not, that the Chief Inspector of Schools has any competence to recognise what pegs the economy needs).[18] Anyway, the idea that education *per se* can produce economic growth is hardly convincing.[19]

A third conservative criticism of the education system as it stands is that standards are being neglected. Much of this goes back to performance targets; government (once more, of all stripes) spends giant sums on education, and so it feels it has to prove that that is money well spent. So why not use test results to show that pupils are improving? Net result: everyone is above average.

Furthermore there is an unfortunate move to make education more 'relevant' to today's young people. In 2002, for instance, John Harwood, chief executive of the Learning and Skills Council, argued that there are two reasons that so many young people in Britain are in neither education, work nor training (9 per cent of sixteen to eighteen year olds): first they are eagerly imbibing a culture of unlearning, and second there is a failure to make learning seem relevant.[20] This attitude has tended to shift the focus of education away from 'hard' topics and towards ones that interest the children.[21] Hmm. Given that educational achievement is a major predictor of wealth, health and social status, how relevant do you want it to be?

Moves to tailor standards to the desires, rather than the needs, of children actually hurt the children of the poorer and less educated classes more. In such systems no one gets taught the skills that seem too hard or too boring. In which case, preference in later life goes to those who imbibed them at their parents' knees. Faced with a large number of graduates, and also with grade inflation, employers are actually finding that those old stand-bys 'literacy, numeracy and the right attitude' are more useful predictors of who will be a good employee.[22] Put another way, given that the examination system is sending out fewer signals of any use, employers look for a nice smile, nice suit, politeness, appropriate behaviour and language, willingness to please, well-spokenness – all that stuff that nice middle-class gels and boys do so well. Developing an education system with the express aim of giving a helping hand to those born with fewer natural advantages – a worthy aim, and one which I certainly won't criticise – has produced a system that favours those with more natural advantages. The knowledge principle would have told them that society is never as simple as it looks.

The fourth conservative criticism is of the helter-skelter expansion of universities during the Blair years. In 1979, 12.4 per cent of school leavers went on to higher education; the aim is to get that figure up to 50 per cent by 2010 (and, unlike many government initiatives, this one is on target). No doubt it is a good thing to receive a higher education. But, as the conservative would remind the government, the unintended consequences of this dramatic expansion will soon outweigh the intended ones (if the latter ever happen at all).

For example, the two universities in Leeds, in 1993, together catered for under 40,000 students. In 2003, this number was up to 73,000. But while numbers have expanded, the residential capacity of the universities has not expanded so quickly; most of these new students have been left to find flats in the city. And patterns of residency have dramatically altered as long-term residents move away from the noise and disruption that large numbers of students cause.[23]

Furthermore, many of the people going to university really rather wouldn't. Commentators have written of the increase of an alcoholic, yobbish culture among some students that has turned university into 'uni', a rite of passage that happily puts off the boring tedium of getting a job for three more precious years.[24] No doubt that label applies to a minority of students, and even less doubt attaches to the observation that the opportunity will be grasped greedily with both hands by the wise. But equally, the question of whether, even if it contributed to growth, money should be spent on the target of cramming 50 per cent of people into university, when something like 20 per cent of the population appears to be functionally illiterate, seems not to have been raised.

Finally, as university lecturers get relatively small amounts of credit for teaching compared to research, and relatively few resources to cope with the expansion of universities, the standards of teaching at universities have inevitably fallen.

Four negative criticisms; what are the positives? Two important themes have emerged from the conservative critique of the state of education. First, central involvement in education should be reduced; decisions need to be made locally, with the involvement of the child (sometimes), parents, teachers and local education officials – and not on the basis of ideology, either. Second, independent and firm standards are also a benefit. The Tories' hints at making exam bodies independent of government control should be welcomed in this context.

It may well be that market mechanisms could be introduced into the education system, giving parents choices over which schools their children were sent to; voucher systems have many things going for them, if only making schools and education authorities responsive to the people they serve. So, for instance, above we listed a series of reasons why you might want an education system. If schools were encouraged to differentiate between themselves, and compete for pupils, then different schools might try to cater for the different aims, and parents could choose between them.

Any major change like this would of course need to be monitored very carefully: one would not want the poor to be condemned automatically to worse education; one would want the variety of schools increased; one would want teachers to feel that the job was moving back towards a vocation; one would want bureaucracy and paperwork reduced. But on the other hand there is no doubt that centrally directed education works against all four of these important aims.

Funding, naturally, will be all-important; hence something like a voucher system would be required to ensure that the good education did not all go to the rich. This in itself, of course, ensures that a proper market system could not work here, because schools could not realistically compete on price. The system would have to be a quasi-market, in the terminology of Julian Le Grand.[25]

The university system can compete on price rather more easily, partly because graduates tend to become richer than others (and therefore will have funds available in later life to repay fees), and partly because university education, being less politically fraught, is more amenable to experimentation. Messrs Howard and Duncan Smith should therefore stand in the corner for criticising Mr Blair's mild moves in the direction of allowing top-up fees for universities. As a bribe for the middle classes, and as a short-term method for discomfiting Mr Blair, opposition to top-up fees is comprehensible, but not as a method for improving our universities.

The public services

Education is something of a special case, on the assumption (not usually examined deeply) that it is responsible for transmitting cultural values across generations. Space precludes us from examining every public service in equivalent detail, but we can make a few notes on what a conservative policy on public services would look like.

First of all, public services remain popular, on the twin grounds that people like to know that there is a recognised supplier not after commercial advantage, and they like to think that the poor will not be disadvantaged by being unable to meet the costs. People seem prepared to be tolerant of a less than efficient service. And they tell pollsters that they are prepared to pay more tax to receive one (though they may be lying when they say that).

The split between what the public sector provides and what the private sector provides is very defining for the identity of any polity. What you get as an entitlement, what you get at cheap rates, and what you pay market rates for seems terribly important, and yet it is trivial to go abroad to discover different ways of paying for the same thing.

It isn't terribly easy to order states according to what they provide. The USA provides generally much less for its citizens, but then it is a much more deeply religious country than anywhere in Europe, and has a long tradition of charitable provision and generous philanthropy. Across Europe, the position is one of overlaps – a service provided by one state is paid for in another, which itself provides stuff free of charge that you would have to pay for in the first state.

And so when the Conservatives under Iain Duncan Smith wished to drum up support for reforms to the National Health Service (NHS), including greater use of private sector resources, it was relatively straightforward to discover plenty of European countries with impeccable social democratic credentials using local financing, contracting out services, payment for certain services, and so on.[26] Combined with a four-point critique of Labour's handling of the NHS produced at around the same time,[27] the implicit message was clear: that many other health services, whose performance was often better than the NHS on a number of indicators, used impeccably *Thatcherite* principles to disburse care and attract funding. Interestingly, a conservative reply to this argument was made by Matthew Taylor, the Shadow Chancellor of the impeccably *radical* Liberal Democrats, in a budget resolution in Parliament![28]

There are three major problems with the Tories' desire to reform public services, understandable though this desire is. First, the balance between public and private provision is, as I say, less a matter of quantity than of distribution; the type of services people expect from a government depends on the piecemeal way that public service provision has developed over the decades. Such untidy provision reflects what people of that country are prepared to pay, what they are prepared to pay for, and what has not been provided traditionally in an affordable and reliable form by charities or the private sector. No doubt reforms are always desirable to some extent, and no doubt the British like nothing more than a good grumble about their public services, but the central importance of those services to people's expectations of society entails, on the change principle, that reform should be patient, quiet and incremental.

Second, the Labour government from 1997 has indulged in quite a quantity of reform itself, under self-consciously prudent Chancellor Gordon Brown. No doubt much of that reform has had the unfortunate side-effects that the change principle and the knowledge principle would predict, but equally statistics are trickling out to show that Labour's reforms have been successful in many areas. To take the NHS once more, reports are finding many positive developments among the false starts,[29] and, even if it takes a while for public perceptions to catch up with administrative progress, insisting on further reforms may well be several steps too far. The conservative principles, though of course allowing organic and incremental change, also imply that, once reform is carried out, it should be given time to work. This means that (a) it is possible to check that changes are really a result of the reforms, rather than some other temporary or otherwise unpredicted cause, and (b) a little more knowledge can be gained about the system by seeing what the effects of particular reforms are.

Third, public servants are under a great deal of pressure.

Placing performance targets on the public services often warps their work patterns, gives them perverse incentives, and deters many of their most altruistic instincts. We must also not forget the vast quantity of change – usually entailing dramatic increases in paperwork – that public servants have had to endure since 1979. One's work is an important part of one's identity, and when it ceases to be a vocation, and becomes an endless round of form-filling, that is very undermining of morale.

Different services will require different levels of change, reform and attention; it is hard to generalise across defence, policing, health, energy, transport and so on. But the above reflections suggest a potential line of conservative policy. Labour has carried out many reforms. It has, indeed, often responded, when reforms don't seem to have worked immediately, with further rounds of reforms. Reforms built on reforms, a hyperactive government; the public sector is in flux.

The Conservative Party has already pledged, were it to win the General Election expected in 2005, to protect a number of Labour's spending plans. A conservative extension of this policy would be to freeze the process of reform. This would have a number of effects. First, Labour's reforms could be properly evaluated. Second, it would provide a conservative initiative to make the politics of public services less oppositional and confrontational. Third, it would demonstrate the conservative's anti-ideological preference for making things work.

And fourth, most happily, it would provide a much-needed respite for public servants to ensure that the latest sets of reform bed down, and to not have to learn a whole new set of time-consuming paperwork, because though paperwork is a terrible chronovore, what *really* eats time is having to ascend the learning curve yet again on a new system. Once it is routine, then it has to some extent been tamed, but Labour's hyperactivity is preventing the new systems from *becoming* routine.

Such a policy might actually produce the novelty of delivering substantial numbers of public sector votes for the Tories! Even if not, ordinary voters will certainly see the sense in the policy. It would be a strategy borrowed from Disraeli, against Gladstone's incessant interfering, for the 1874 election: its time may have come again.

Tax

This takes us to the sensitive area of tax. Since Mrs Thatcher demonstrated the reluctance of the British to pay tax (shown perhaps most graphically after her departure when Chris Patten's 'double whammy' campaign was so successful against Shadow Chancellor John Smith's shadow budget of 1992), the political parties in Britain have vied with each other to be tax cutters. This has generally meant, of course, sneakier tax raisers, who would never on any pretext raise income tax, the fairest method of taxing, because it is that that features in the news headlines. In Britain we are supposedly opposed to stealth taxes, yet when a tax is relatively transparent – as, for example, the council tax – we complain loudly at having to pay it, even when the sums are relatively small – as, for example, with the council tax. And parties who wish to promote a 'sensible debate' on tax – as, for example, the Liberal Democrats – end up attacking the transparent taxes they in theory are in favour of – as, for example, the council tax, which the Liberal Democrats are committed to abolishing.

The government, in effect, has three sources of money: taxing, borrowing it or printing it. Any government will try to seek the sensible balance between the three. Borrowing pushes up interest rates and depresses the economy; printing money is inflationary. Hence it is inevitable that if public spending has to rise for any unforeseen reason – say, for instance, a giant war and reconstruction effort in a large country thousands of miles away – there will be some pressure on taxes to rise. The two likely parties of government are currently locked in an embrace of mutually assured destruction, where neither of them in government dares raise taxes (i.e. income tax) because the opposition will be down on them like a ton of bricks, which means that when the opposition party makes it to Downing

Street it is hamstrung, having made lots of manifesto promises it cannot fund.

This is ridiculous. A conservative approach to taxes should never preclude tax rises, because sometimes tax rises are needed, and better than borrowing or printing more money. Income tax and straightforward consumption taxes between them are fairer than any alternatives, because they will be so much less distorting of the economy. That is not to say that conservatives *want* to raise taxes; far from it. As we have seen, conservatives are not very confident that government activity will be fruitful, and all things being equal a conservative government would be much less active than a socialist one, say, or the Gladstonian liberal one we have now. Nevertheless, the conservative, unlike the neo-liberal, is quite happy for the government to do some things, particularly things which it always has done, or which its voters wish it to do, and doing things costs money, and money has to be raised somehow.

This has to act in the Tories' interests. In the first place, perpetuating the myth that tax-raising has become impossible since 1979 benefits Labour more than the Tories, as Labour is much readier to put up taxes. When taxes do go up – all governments must put up taxes on occasion – they go up stealthily, and the political arguments become messy and inconclusive as a result. Furthermore, the Tories have a well-established brand as enemies of tax, which they should exploit. Even if the Tories put taxes up for whatever reason, very few people actually think that taxes will be lower under Labour. There is, to reiterate, nothing wrong with reducing public spending. But equally there is no 'correct' level of public spending – society, and *a fortiori* the economy, does not have a 'best' form, to which it should be moulded if it does not conform.

The constitution

If we move from the sphere of concern of the private individual to the construction of an arena for public life, we are drawn inexorably to the constitution, where Mr Blair has been very active in his period of office. It is, after all, a cheap way of being radical. As well as introducing a Freedom of Information Act, and bringing the European Convention on Human Rights into British law for the first time, he devolved power to Scotland, Wales, London and Northern Ireland. Unfortunately, these made his life trickier than he anticipated.

In Scotland, his respected nominee Donald Dewar died suddenly, and now the Scottish Parliament is embroiled in an unseemly argument about the building which will house it: an initial estimate for the costs of £40 million looks like being a tiny fraction of the actual cost, which may reach £400 million, maybe more. The reception desk alone will cost £88,000, while the windows will sting the MSPs for a cool £11.8 million.[30] Personally, I have no problem with these costs. Indeed, a conservative, sensitive as ever to the importance of symbolism and myth, should support the use of imposing and grand buildings for government – and they do not come cheap. Equally the conservative, in the tradition of Lord Salisbury, wouldn't have believed the estimate in the first place.

Wales and London provided different problems for Mr Blair. An inveterate centraliser, he was loath to devolve power unless he knew how it was going to be used (which isn't devolving power at all). Things began badly when his preferred choice of Welsh leader, under some emotional strain, was tempted into a damaging indiscretion. But then cack-handed attempts to impose placemen, the bland Alun Michael and the bluff Frank Dobson for Wales and London respectively, backfired: Mr Michael was forced out of office and replaced by the off-message (but perfectly sensible) Rhodri Morgan, while Mr Dobson was humiliatingly beaten by Ken Livingstone in the election, and is currently gaining some small but doubtless sweet revenge by turning against Mr Blair in Parliament. Mr Blair has since eaten some humble pie and brought Mr Livingstone back into the Labour fold.

In Northern Ireland, the problems were different again. Lack of trust hobbled the whole enterprise, and in the end the discovery that the IRA had been exploiting Sinn Fein's presence in the Northern Irish Assembly to amass information that might have been of value in perpetrating future acts of violence kicked the whole thing into the long grass. But the criticisms here should be more muted: the peace process has obviously improved many aspects of life in Northern Ireland, and Mr Blair made some bold steps towards it (Mrs Thatcher's and Mr Major's contributions should not be forgotten either, as well as those of various Dublin governments).

Finally, a number of elected mayors have appeared in some cities and towns, of which the most well known seem to be in the north-east – a tough policeman known as Robocop and a man in Hartlepool previously known for dressing – professionally, mind – as a monkey. The evidence as to their effectiveness is mixed.

The conservative will, of course, smile smugly at the confusion, with an 'I told you so' expression on his or her face. The constitution is always in a state of delicate balance. All politicians and officials work to try to increase their responsibility, and their budgets; they oppose each other in subtle ways that have usually grown out of long experience. The baroque structure that is the constitution therefore encodes a huge amount of practical wisdom from centuries of lawmaking, legislating and protecting the rights of the citizen. Hence mucking about with it will cause problems. If you devolve power, for example, you don't have it any more. Goes without saying.

Nonetheless, it has happened. Any conservative has to make the system work, assuming he gets the opportunity, and so one can welcome Michael Howard's clear commitment to supporting, not repealing, the constitutional changes.[31] Indeed, it was the introduction of the Scottish Parliament, opposed by the Tories for good conservative reasons, and then the use of proportional representation for the Parliament, also opposed by the Tories, that gave the Tories eighteen MSPs, and therefore some decent representation north of the border. The requirement to appear a national party gives the Tories plenty of non-ideological incentive to make devolution work.

The worst area of Blairite indecision, of radicalism combined with a fatal lack of bravado, is of course in the reform of the House of Lords. Many a conservative voice, Enoch Powell's perhaps the loudest, has counselled against reform over the years. The executive, the Commons, the judiciary, the Lords, all these have various powers and a certain amount of legitimacy, and though no one would set up a system like this, the British system has grown so that those without the legitimacy of a democratic mandate have limited powers to restrict those who have. The balance is crucial.

In the most egregious example of muddled reform, Mr Blair decided to get rid of the office of Lord Chancellor. This role combines three distinct positions, quite contrary to the American doctrine of separation of powers (though the role is older than the doctrine by some seven centuries). The Lord Chancellor is head of the judiciary, the speaker of the House of Lords and a member of the Cabinet. As a member of the executive, the legislature and the judiciary, he therefore is charged with keeping an eye on himself to make sure he does not abuse his own powers.

Faced with arguments such as that, many non-conservatives have argued for the abolition of the post. Which Mr Blair did during a reshuffle forced by a surprise resignation. This was an error.

New Labour is a somewhat puritanical organisation, so the reshuffle was no doubt not jotted down on the preferred stationery for un-thought-through measures, the back of the fag packet or the beer mat. But it might as well have been. Having announced that Lord Falconer would be the Secretary for Constitutional Affairs, but not Lord Chancellor or speaker of the Lords, it was then discovered that the House of Lords, as currently constituted, could not sit without the Lord Chancellor. A turf war between Home Secretary David Blunkett and the retiring Lord Chancellor Lord Irvine contributed to the confusion. As it is, in 2004 the Lords are being somewhat awkward about the bill.

The hereditary peers, of course, are on their way out. Again, no one would set up such a system. But such a system we had, and it worked reasonably well (compared, say, with the impeccably democratic American system which often silts up with bi-partisan brinkmanship and tit-for-tat vetoes). There is still, unbelievably, little indication of what will replace the hereditaries. When Labour was elected in 1997, its radical rhetoric led most people to assume that there would be a wholly elected chamber. But Mr Blair does not now wish this to happen – an elected chamber, he believes, would challenge the primacy of the Commons.

Well, no doubt it would. That's what happens if you hope to set up a chamber to monitor and act as a check on the Commons and give it sufficient power so to do. The trick is to produce a system where the monitors have just enough power to restrain the Commons yet not enough to usurp its functions. The slow evolution of the British system over time achieved that. A completely new system designed from scratch is a much harder proposition.

The difficulty of reorganising a system that has grown up, higgledy-piggledy, over a thousand years is obvious with hindsight (as it was beforehand, actually). The Lords had certain powers consistent with their legitimacy; they occupied a place in the landscape (for example, as Lord Salisbury argued, they were well placed to represent the 'permanent as opposed to the passing feelings of the English nation'[32]). Replacing them is not simply a matter of getting rid of all these blokes and replacing them with a load of other blokes. How do you do that while retaining the exact amount of legitimacy that the first lot of blokes had? And if you fail to do that, then how can you avoid having to alter the amount of power they have?

The House of Lords had evolved – and is constantly evolving – to occupy particular ecological niches in the British system, political, social, economic. As the Lords stopped being military and became landowners primarily, as they stopped being rich, as they stopped being fascinating to the public, and as the Commons became more democratic, and more ideological, the Lords retrenched, and the system altered a bit every so often, with the result that it worked. You wouldn't – couldn't – have designed it that way, but it worked. Nothing wrong with replacing it, of course, particularly as Mr Blair could reasonably claim a mandate for doing it.

But no conservative will be surprised at the trouble he is having.

Europe

Finally, having looked all too briefly at the personal and the formal aspects of British society, we should look at the relationship between British society and others. To begin with, we should grasp what has been a stinging nettle indeed for the Tories: Europe.

The history of British policy towards the European Union and its predecessors is fairly simple to tell. There was an initial phase of benign condescension from the British, steering our more temperamental continental friends towards sharing industry and sovereignty to put an end to their incessant warfare; this view saw Europe's politics as being characterised by a state of tension between France and Germany, leading to an extended war of 1870–1945. Next, it was thought that the British economy was underperforming relative to our European competitors, and that joining the EEC, as it then was, would give us access to this major market and drag the economy back up to where it should be. In this phase, we made three applications to join, the third being successful and endorsed by referendum in 1975. In the third phase the single market got implemented, and the EU, as it now was, began to dispense little bits of liberal ideology (which was actually quite handy for the more collectivist governments of continental Europe, which could justify essential but painful reforms by blaming them on Brussels).

But the single market proved to be the undoing of the eurosceptics. The project was initially driven by Mrs Thatcher's neo-liberalism, but the eurosceptics were finessed by the eurocrats' argument that for the single market to be genuinely competitive, there would have to be strong convergence, in economy and law, between the various nations. In particular, monetary union was proposed (actually it had been on the table for decades). The resulting strains on the Tories, who had previously managed to paper over most cracks between euro-enthusiasts and eurosceptics, were too great, and Mr Major's small majority meant that swivel-eyed anti-Europeans could do enough damage to bring their party down, which they did after a failed attempt in 1995 to snatch the party leadership.

Out of power since 1997, the Tories have been able to reach a kind of *modus vivendi*, wherein a moderate but firm euro-scepticism prevails.[33] William Hague set the tone with his slogan (rather admired, incidentally, by New Labour) 'In Europe but not run by Europe'. Things calmed down. But Mr Hague made a serious mistake by focusing his election campaign on Europe in 2001; the voters are much less interested in the subject than the Tories.

Europe had two further post-election bites out of the Tories. First, their most capable potential leader, Kenneth Clarke, was beaten in the leadership election of 2001 (as in 1997) by what could only have been suspicions held by party members about his vociferous pro-Europeanism. And second, when the leadership of Iain Duncan Smith was under serious pressure, his own record as a very disloyal backbencher in Mr Major's government during the debates on the Maastricht Treaty made it impossible for him to command loyalty himself when he needed it. If a conscience was OK for IDS in the 90s, then it was surely OK for his opponents in 2003.

There are two big decisions which may have to be made about Europe in the near future: one on the EU constitution, the other on whether Britain joins the euro. If it comes to it, it looks very much as if both of these decisions will be made by referendum. One imagines the constitution referendum would come first, and that its result would have a strong effect on the other issue; a 'yes' vote would strongly imply Britain voting to join the euro, and a 'no' vote would kill the euro issue stone dead.

However that may be, we needn't spend a great deal of time over a conservative attitude to these European questions. Quite obviously a conservative in Britain at this time should be a eurosceptic. It is hard to imagine a less conservative course of action than changing the currency and putting its control in the hands of bankers over whom one has no control at all. Granted that Gordon Brown gave formal independence to the Bank of England in monetary matters. A small 'c' conservative would have opposed that at the time, though now the system seems to be operating rather well, he or she should oppose changing the system back (U-turns should be endemic with genuine conservatives – if someone else's experiments come off, then they should be willing to learn from them). But more to the point, if the Chancellor wished to take back control over monetary policy, all he or she would have to do is to legislate to do it. Regaining control over the currency once we were in the euro would be a very different proposition indeed.

We should, as ever, include the caveat that the economy is not being shown to suffer from being out of the euro. At present, it is not; our localised interest rates are helping boost the economy. On the other hand, foreign direct investment into Britain has fallen since the introduction of the euro, from $120 billion in 2000 to $14.5 billion in 2003 (similar falls, from lower levels, have been seen in Britain's fellow euro absentees Sweden and Denmark).[34] The conservative must measure tangible gains against tangible losses, and then factor in the dramatically large risk of change.

The constitution question is rather less straightforward, in that much of what the constitution does is to pull together treaties to which we are already signatories. But of course some of it does not, and the aim of Giscard d'Estaing was more or less explicitly to provide the EU with the inspiring equivalent of the American constitution (though why, therefore, he produced insufferable quantities of managementspeak is unclear). And the ultimate aim of those pushing ahead with the European project is to provide enough unity in Europe to act as the counterweight to the USA. This is enough of a change, in conditions of enough uncertainty, for a conservative to be very worried indeed. Small 'c' conservatism and euroscepticism go together pretty naturally.

Note two points, though. Britain has been in the EU for some 30 years now; it affects our financial governance, our political governance, our diplomacy, our employment patterns and our law. The effects have been enormous. Withdrawal from the EU altogether is not a conservative option (even if it were a feasible option). So, for instance, it is worrying that Mr Howard is succumbing to the temptation to be sucked into a rejectionist position by the antics of the populist UKIP (United Kingdom Independence Party), no matter how enticing its parade of deep-thinking celebrities like Robert Kilroy-Silk, Joan Collins and, er, that's it. Better that he is disciplining euro-obsessives from his own party who voice their support for UKIP.[35]

Following on from that, it is essential that the conservative takes systems as he or she finds them and makes them work. Britain is in Europe, and when the next Tory Prime Minister poses for photographs on the doorstep of Number 10, it is not inconceivable that we will have signed up to both the constitution and the euro. That fact alone puts pretty strong limits on the extent and virulence of the euroscepticism that a conservative is allowed. It cannot be so powerful that the conservative is forced into a corner by pre-election rhetoric. It has to be moderate, in favour of as loose a conglomeration of nation states as possible. As this is more or less Tory policy at the moment, it should not be a cause for worry, but for example much of Mr Hague's rhetoric, certainly post-1999, was too strong to allow him, had he won in 2001, much leeway with his fellows around the table of the European Council.

Race, immigration and asylum

The politics of race are fraught for conservatives. The reason is obvious. New entrants to a country, from markedly different cultures, will threaten to alter the indigenous culture. The change principle looks as if it will be violated. The problem with this is that the negative position will skirt very close to racism. And even if it were possible to mark out a distinctively conservative position that was just, respected human rights and could be shown to be non-racist, in our multicultural country it could still be electorally disastrous.

Marking out conservative non-racist territory in this region is very hard. Salisbury, for example, argued along these lines, and was on occasion explicitly and unacceptably racist even by the not terribly enlightened standards of the late 19th century.[36] But the most notorious campaign against immigration was that of Enoch Powell, an extraordinary *tour de force* of political philosophy. Powell's baseline was the importance of political (not racial) homogeneity in the British context.

> The concept, therefore, of a nation which talked and could be talked to and was governable as this nation was governable, depended upon this characteristic – that its members would so identify themselves with one another that the non-existence of a Conservative vote in County Durham or the non-existence of a Labour vote in Hampshire would not render Durham or Hampshire ungovernable as part of the United Kingdom by Labour or Conservative governments. I looked for a word and I did not find a satisfactory word. The only word which I found for working purposes was 'homogeneous', homogeneous in that defined sense, politically homogeneous, capable of perceiving the totality of a nation in such a way as to submit to the will of the totality, given that the totality's will could be altered, influenced and manipulated through the nation's parliamentary institutions. …
>
> Meanwhile, there had been a 'little local difficulty' over the homogeneity of the population of the United Kingdom, the question whether changes in that population did not threaten the eventual survival of political homogeneity. Were there limits of tolerance beyond which homogeneity could not be sacrificed without the whole system, the whole assumption becoming untenable?[37]

But Powell had other fish to fry as well. He had clear ambitions to lead the Conservative Party. And he had always been brilliant

– perhaps the best ever in British politics – at communicating complex concepts to mass audiences. His anti-immigration philosophy turned populist very easily, and so effectively that for some years he was Britain's best-known politician. We will probably never know how much of his famous campaign was driven by the desire for power, and how much by his incredible conviction. But what we do know is that the anti-immigration 'Rivers of Blood' speech of 1968, the 'little local difficulty' he referred to, for which he was sacked by Edward Heath from the Shadow Cabinet, crossed so many bounds of taste, decency, plausibility and acceptability that no civilised political establishment could accept him before a repudiation.

> It almost passes belief that at this moment 20 or 30 additional immigrant children are arriving from overseas in Wolverhampton alone every week – and that means 15 or 20 additional families a decade or two hence. Those whom the gods wish to destroy, they first make mad. We must be mad, literally mad, as a nation to be permitting the annual inflow of some 50,000 dependants, who are for the most part the material of the future growth of the immigrant-descended population. It is like watching a nation busily engaged in heaping up its own funeral pyre.[38]

The Rivers of Blood speech contains no racist sentiments explicitly endorsed by its author – but Powell allows himself many overtly racist quotes from unattributed sources. It is a stunning speech, brilliantly composed, and shocking in its cavalier disregard for the norms of political communication. Watching the amateurish black-and-white footage of Powell reading the above passage, one is amazed by the venom and intensity with which he spits out the words. Before Powell, racism was the prerogative of buffoonish right wingers like Sir Gerald Nabarro; Powell showed how it could be defended intellectually. It was not long before, in his speeches, talk of 'immigration' had elided into talk of 'coloured immigration';[39] many argued that this was a naked attempt to position himself for a leadership bid once Edward Heath lost the 1970 election (which in the event he didn't).[40]

If conservatism on the topic of immigration led automatically to Powellism, then it would not be an acceptable philosophy. The whole point of our enquiry is to discover whether an ideology consistent with both the traditions of the Conservative Party, and the political instincts of the people who gave New Labour its impressive landslide victories, is possible. If that ideology produces Powellism, then it certainly fails on the latter count, and probably on the former.

In his Rivers of Blood speech, Powell – who always claimed that the problem was a matter of numbers – suggested (on forgivably imprecise data) that the likely immigrant-descended population in 2000 would be 'in the region of five to seven million, approximately one-tenth of the whole population, and approaching that of Greater London'.[41] These numbers, Powell always thought, would be disastrous. He did not seek to blame immigrants for coming here; he did not seek to excoriate the indigenous population for being inhospitable. He always felt he was pointing out the inevitable consequence of the unhindered movement of large numbers of people into Britain. In a documentary filmed after the close of his full-time political career in 1987, Powell stunned a bemused Nick Ross by predicting 'appalling' civil war along racial lines.[42]

Powell's numbers are not too off beam, though overstated. The census of 2001 recorded 58,789,194 souls in the United Kingdom. Of these, the ethnic composition was: 92.1 per cent white; 2.0 per cent black (1.0 per cent of Caribbean origin, and 0.8 per cent African); 1.8 per cent Indian; 1.3 per cent Pakistani; 0.5 per cent Bangladeshi; 0.4 per cent Chinese; 1.9 per cent other and not stated. Depending how the 1.9 per cent are composed, that is a percentage of ethnic minorities of between 6 and 7.9 per cent (probably nearer to the high estimate than the lower), somewhat less than Powell thought. In terms of numbers, that is between 3.5 million and 4.5 million (most likely at the high end of that range). The recorded population of Greater London was 7,172,036, so the total is not quite approaching that.[43]

Nevertheless, these figures are certainly of the order that Powell would have found alarming.

Some comfort, then, that despite simmering tensions in a few places, civil war seems a long way away. What we see in Britain is a pattern of racial prejudice that is *inversely* proportional to the number of people from the ethnic minorities settled in a region or city. Britain's most ethnically diverse city, London, over a quarter of whose population are from an ethnic minority background, is also the most tolerant. Where the racist British National Party have had successes, you won't find many black people about at all. Their biggest triumph, a near-50 per cent share of the vote in a by-election, came in Broxbourne, Herts, a whiter-than-white sort of place. Even Burnley, where the BNP have a number of councillors and one in ten voters, actually has only a 7 per cent ethnic minority population – less than the national average.[44] Ignorance, poverty and dissatisfaction with the mainstream parties are much more plausibly the causes of a high BNP vote, not the large number of people of minority ethnic origin.

All of this, of course, is accepted by mainstream Tory politicians; indeed, by either ironic chance or clever engineering, the Conservative Parliamentary candidate for Enoch's old constituency of Wolverhampton South West at the time of writing is a businesswoman of Punjabi origin, Sandip Verma. But if Powell's apocalyptic predictions have been demonstrably incorrect, where does this leave the argument for conservatism?

We must first point out that Britain undoubtedly *is* a multicultural country. Some cities have very large populations from the ethnic minorities, and as a whole 4.5 million people obviously make a giant contribution to British culture. It is the job of the conservative to meet society as it is, not as he or she would wish it to be; indeed, unlike other ideologues, the *whole point* of the conservative's philosophy is that his or her wishes about how society be governed and constituted are explicitly understood to be irrelevant. The conservative imposes as little as possible on his or her fellow citizens.

A change in the constitution of the population has occurred, and it is the conservative's business to *manage* that change, not to prevent it, nor to reverse it. We are currently living through a period of giant migrations, which our immigration laws are designed to prevent (or, rather, to deflect elsewhere). As Lord Salisbury would no doubt have reminded us, this is irresistibly reminiscent of King Cnut trying to hold back the tide, especially at a time when short-term labour shortages and the long-term aging of the population mean an *increase* in demand for immigrant labour both short-term and long-term. It is futile to stand in the way of great social changes.

The result of our being silly Cnuts has been obvious. Some of those who wish to emigrate legally to the United Kingdom have been put off, and continue to live less productive lives in less productive parts of the world (rather than being able to send remittances back to their country of origin – and remittances from émigrés, at $100 *billion* annually on official figures alone, dwarf development aid[45]).

But many pay large sums of money to illegal people smugglers, and incidentally put their lives at risk, as several tragic incidents have recently demonstrated.* It is not at all clear why people prepared to pay large sums of money to come to the United Kingdom, and prepared to work very hard, are not simply allowed to do so in somewhat greater numbers. Indeed, given that illegal people smugglers can charge large fees, why can't the authorities undercut the gangs' source of profits by charging a somewhat lower, but still substantial, fee for immigration? And if immigration and working in Britain was made easier, then immigrants would feel less obliged to stay for long periods if they felt that they could come and go somewhat more freely, thereby – if there indeed are pressures on population and culture – reducing those pressures. The attempt to restrict immigration, as with drugs, has created all sorts of criminal

---

* It was ever thus. An Academy Award nominated short film, *Forbidden Passage*, a 1941 entry (directed by Fred Zinneman) in MGM's *Crime Does Not Pay* series, told precisely the same tale of exorbitant fees and the risk of grisly death for those who would be smuggled into the United States.

opportunities. That is not to say that the existence of criminality should lead automatically to deregulation; far from it. But when considering the situation from the point of view of the change principle and the knowledge principle, it is still an important datum.

Another route into Britain is of course by abuse of the asylum system. Unlike with immigration, we are obliged by various treaties to consider the claims of asylum seekers. If people claim asylum, then they have to be investigated, and the investigation will only conclude that the claim is bogus after a long enough time for the would-be immigrant to disappear into the shadows. The attempt to prevent people emigrating to the United Kingdom and elsewhere has distorted a system designed for essential humanitarian purposes.

It is also relevant that the tradition of provision of asylum from persecution elsewhere in the world has been an important British myth. Crackdowns on asylum threaten that tradition, which it might well be argued is a change much more devastating than the increase in the ethnic minority population. That is not to say that asylum seekers should not be investigated thoroughly, and indeed deported to a suitable country if their claim is discovered to be bogus (and not to say that a Conservative opposition should not harry the government when it fails to run the system effectively). But equally it is worth recognising that people who could move in and out of Britain reasonably easily, finding work where it was available, would have little or no incentive to apply for asylum if they were not at risk of persecution at home. If the asylum system is being abused – as it patently is – then one of the reasons for that is the vain attempt to prevent people in this country who wish to employ cheap labour from employing more than a handful of the very large number of people who are prepared to work here cheaply.

Removing this anomaly, and therefore allowing the asylum system to move towards its intended function, is arguably a much more conservative programme than opposing immigration *tout court*.

Iraq

Finally, writing in 2004 one cannot really avoid brief mention of the crisis in Iraq. Britain remained a close ally of the USA throughout the whole *imbroglio*, which at least demonstrated a very conservative understanding of the nature of political power and its relation to the ability to apply force. Compare the British stance with that of France, which almost seemed determined to provoke the Americans into an illegal invasion (had President Chirac wanted that result, it is not clear what, in the run up to the invasion, he would have done differently). France's long-term aim of establishing a counterweight to American hegemony (a counterweight dominated by France, natch) may have been served, though the aim remains long-term. The Germans, on the other hand, seem to have had a rather more sincere, though correspondingly more naïve, belief in the ability of multilateral organisations to referee international conflict.

The Americans themselves were principally driven, in the aftermath of the attack of 11 September 2001, by the neo-conservative analysis of people such as Paul Wolfowitz, Richard Perle and William Kristol. These commentators and politicians had a particular view of the Middle East, and argued for a reversal of traditional US policy in the region of garnering support by making friendly gestures towards Arab regimes, most notably Saudi Arabia – key to American energy requirements – and Egypt, the latter in return for its more compliant stance towards Israel. The neo-cons (as they have become known) argued that, given that all Arab regimes are undemocratic, and most of them corrupt, this policy, while it may have short-term benefits, is disastrous long-term, because ultimately most Arabs see their own governments, rightly, as major obstacles to their freedom and prosperity. Hence cutting deals with unsavoury Arab regimes merely fuels future anti-American terrorism.

On the neo-con analysis, then, the smart thing to do would be to remodel the Arab world in democratic fashion. Since democracy inhibits (though is obviously not sufficient to stamp out) corruption, helps spread prosperity, and is a guarantee (if not cast-iron) of freedom, Arabs would gain. And of course they would be sharing in a fundamental American value, which would provide some common ground between the two peoples. It is a fundamental assumption of American political culture that its values, based on the rights of man, are universal in a way that other sets of values are not. Add to that the peculiar circumstance of the American President being the son of another President who famously had 'unfinished business' in Iraq, and the fact that there were two or three arguably legitimate reasons for an invasion (though it was patently irrelevant to the War on Terror), and in retrospect Saddam Hussein's days of power were numbered.

I argued in Chapter Four that there was a world of difference between US neo-conservatism and British conservatism, and Iraq is a stark illustration of that fact. The invasion of Afghanistan is one thing. Afghanistan had perhaps the worst government in the world,[46] and had been strikingly misgoverned for decades – indeed its people, with their tendency to relapse into warlordism, are possibly ungovernable in the modern sense. The Taliban had been fomenting problems not just for America (by providing a headquarters for al-Qaeda), but also for Afghanistan's neighbours, quite apart from their appalling brutality to the people they purported to govern. The chief premise of the change principle, that a functioning society is in and of itself valuable, clearly did not apply to Afghanistan – it was a society that was not functioning at all.

Iraq is a different kettle of fish. The most stunning fact about the whole debacle is that the Americans seem to have gone into Iraq, after months (if Washington insiders are to be believed, years) of military and diplomatic preparation, without a single clear idea of what they would do when they won the war (and, extrapolating counterfactually, presumably what they would do if they lost). It seems that barely a single one of the famously superintelligent Republican wonks in the Washington Beltway gave any thought to reconstructing a complex society of 25 million people, or even anticipated much difficulty. Even given the natural (though in the event false) assumption that American liberators would be welcomed with open arms, putting together a democracy in a country known for authoritarian misrule was unlikely ever to be straightforward.

No conservative of the sceptical tradition would have made this elementary mistake. No sceptical conservative would have missed the potential for a power vacuum developing upon Saddam Hussein's removal; *all* attempts to reconfigure power structures leave vacuums. That Iraq is a complex place, with millions of people, including three different, often antagonistic, ethnic/religious groups, and a set of traditions distinctly uncongenial to democracy and market systems of exchange, makes the problem even harder.

That is not to say that, in the 21st century, the sort of hard realism about international affairs that has characterised many conservative thinkers is always going to be possible. Canadian cultural commentator Michael Ignatieff, in a brilliant essay, has drawn attention to the massive changes in international relations that the phenomenon of the nightly TV news has wrought.

> Television is also the instrument of a new kind of politics. Since 1945, affluence and idealism have made possible the emergence of a host of nongovernmental private charities and pressure groups – Amnesty International, Care, Save the Children, Christian Aid, Oxfam, Médecins sans Frontières, and others – that use television as a central part of their campaigns to mobilize conscience and money on behalf of endangered humans and their habitats around the world. It is a politics that takes the world rather than the nation as its political space and that takes the human species itself rather than specific citizenship, racial, religious or ethnic groups as its object. It is a 'species politics' striving to save the human species from itself, as Greenpeace and World Wildlife are striving to protect natural and animal species from the predator man. These organizations seek to circumvent the bilateral governmental relations between

peoples and institute direct political contacts between, for example, Amnesty sponsors and particular prisoners, or American families and Latin American foster children, or field service volunteers and their peasant clients. It is a politics that has tried to construct a world public opinion to keep watch over the rights of those who lack the means to protect themselves. Using the medium of television, many of these international organizations have managed to force governments to pay some degree of attention to the public-relations costs of their exercises in domestic repression.[47]

In such a world, where images of suffering, often yanked horrendously out of context, are placed on TV screens in the rich world, there are only two possible reactions for the viewer. The first is to assume that 'nothing can be done', a feeling of impotence that democratic politicians have no interest in fostering. The second is to exhort elected politicians to 'stop talking and *do* something about it'. Perhaps for the first time ever, voters in powerful countries actively want their representatives to intervene in famines, civil wars, repression; a far cry, this, from the often negative public reaction to Gladstone's hyperactive moral conscience about international injustices.

A conservative therefore no longer necessarily has the luxury of letting repression and suffering happen, even though there is generally little or nothing he or she could usefully do about it, and even though species politics, as Ignatieff demonstrates, is riddled with contradiction and groundless optimism. Hence even a conservative might well find him- or herself saddled with an imperative to intervene in other countries' affairs. But no conservative of the Pyrrhonist tradition would dream of considering him- or herself capable of creating a democratic polity in a country that had no tradition of democracy, save by taking small steps to put in place the particular relationships between people, property and the law that seem to be important.

It beggars belief – particularly after the difficult, though not uniformly unsuccessful experience of post-communist Eastern Europe – that the Americans thought that Iraq would be a breeze. Societies are not prone, like the lion from whose paw Androcles removed the thorn, to gratitude, to a long-term view of their own best interests, to having their problems sorted for them by professionalised outsiders.

Societies, as the conservative argues so forcefully, bite back.

Political science vs. political engineering

As per the warning at the outset, this chapter has been something of a ragbag, treating many topics, not one with the depth it deserves. It has been a series of sketches. But all of them have illustrated the claim in the previous paragraph: societies bite back. Our final task is to bring together some of the threads to give us a take-home message about societies and what a conservative should recommend with respect to them.

As an image for the difference between conservatism and its ideological rivals, consider the distinction between science and engineering. Science is glamorous, it is the creation of knowledge, the discovery of the eternal truths about mankind's environment, about the universe, about the Earth, about all living things. Engineering is rather a second-class thing to want to do. The engineer doesn't worry about great truths, he or she worries about getting a thing to work. Design matters to the engineer. Things aren't abstract, or isolated, or theoretical: they are typically part of some wider system with which they have to interact, and the engineer's job is to worry not about the eternal, but about the immediate and contingent trade-offs. If I make this aero engine more powerful, that will make it heavier, which will reduce passenger capacity. If I design this lift to carry twelve people, then we will need to widen the counterweight shaft at the rear. Engineering's truths are not eternal. The systems engineers design are as robust as possible, and they have to be monitored constantly to ensure that they remain robust as the context changes.

Most ideologies try to produce some version of what we might call a political science. Conservatism (small 'c'), on the other hand, is political *engineering*. There may be ideals about how people should relate to each other, but those ideals bear a very tenuous relation to real life. Real societies have to work. They have to be pleasant environments for their populations; they have to interact reasonably well with other societies. All this takes place in a world constantly changing, where the context can never be taken for granted.

The political scientist *par excellence* was Gladstone, whose idealistic pursuit of the greater good of mankind drove both Disraeli and Salisbury towards their often cynical positions. There is an interesting monograph to be written one day about Gladstone's influence on the peculiar character of British conservatism; in its perverse way it is every bit as great as that of Burke. 'There is no other statesman near him, or in sight,' said Salisbury, 'who could effect a tenth part of the evil which will be caused by a few of his phrases of gorgeous, reckless optimism.'[48]

Mr Blair certainly has tried to cast himself in the Gladstonian mould. When he is convinced of the moral rectitude of what he is doing – and I do not for an instant want to suggest that Mr Blair is not a man of great moral seriousness and sophistication – he is tireless and virtually unstoppable. I say 'virtually unstoppable' because reality often intervenes.

It is not credible that Mr Blair's vision of regime change in Iraq was as naïve as that of the neo-cons surrounding Mr Bush, but nevertheless the period following the successful toppling of Saddam has been difficult for Mr Blair in a way that he could never have expected, from the drama of Dr Kelly and the PR disaster of the Hutton report, to the increased ferocity of the uprising against the occupying forces in 2004 that demonstrated beyond doubt that rebellion was not confined to a few zealous foreigners and old regime loyalists.

And back in Blighty, the attempt to create 'Cool Britannia' has not worked, as our public services remain poor, our transport systems threadbare, our population under-educated and unproductive. The impression is sometimes left (particularly when one has encountered a large group of Brits abroad) of Mr Blair as a denim-shirted Prospero governing a crumbling island of Calibans.

Where Mr Blair has succeeded – and the problem for the Tories is that his record is comparatively good for a British Prime Minister – is in the areas where his ministers have rolled up their sleeves and done the serious, painstaking, unglamorous work of examining services, testing and evaluating improvements objectively, finding the money, and – not least – not burdening the system with Prime Ministerial expectations. This is all political engineering in the conservative tradition.

The Conservative Party's secret weapon may be that this is not what Mr Blair wants to be remembered for.

CHAPTER EIGHT

CONSERVATISM AND TRUST

The crisis of trust: the official story

In the new politics of the 21st century, 'trust' is the watchword. Like 'inflation' and 'unemployment' in the 20th, the 'T' word is the key to understanding a remarkable proportion of the things that politicians in the mature democracies do. The official story is that politicians have overused their authority and power, and that there is a huge disconnection between them and the voters; the latter are confused and bored by the new politics. Politicians seem strangely powerless to do anything about the great globalising forces that batter the country and the economy. Bizarre regulations are passed down from unaccountable officials in Brussels independently of our wishes. The concerns of the public are ignored by politicians, who focus instead on the needs of business; British interests are all too often trumped by American interests. A sense of *ennui* has settled over the democratic process. No wonder that voters are disengaged.

This change is reflected in ideological changes, though whether ideological change has caused, is caused by, or has a common cause with the decline in trust is a moot point. The 60s, 70s and to an extent the 80s were characterised by ideologies emphasising various types of social *solidarity*. Not only conservatism on the right, but also socialism on the left and the Gladstonian kind of liberalism in the centre were premised on the pooling of one's interests with others. The argument for politicians of the post-war period was how far one should sublimate one's own preferences for the greater good, and which social groups one should see one's own wider interests resting with.

251

Nowadays the ideological universe is completely different. On the right, neo-liberalism still rules. The radical left takes a postmodernist line (in the early days of postmodernism, it was often argued that it was inherently conservative,[1] but it doesn't take much study of the scene nowadays to realise that, despite superficial similarities to conservatism, the anti-authoritarian power of postmodernist creativity is being exploited by the oppositional left). In the centre, egalitarian liberalism still holds sway, but in the adaptation developed by John Rawls[2] which lays stress on the liberal's attempt to ensure that people are as free as possible to pursue their own individual idea of the good. The difference is that today's ideologies place a great deal of importance on people's individuality and autonomy.

The modern scene is almost unique in the widespread rejection of social hierarchies. Many commentators have detected a decline of trust well beyond the world of politics. We no longer trust scientists' claims about, for example, vaccines or GM foods in the wake of the BSE crisis. We do not trust businesspeople after Enron and Parmalat. According to many surveys, we do not even trust our fellow human beings very much at all; one widely quoted work worries aloud about our decreasing tendency to form social groups.[3]

This is a difficult world for politicians, and indeed anyone who wishes to do good or to be effective in the world. Trust is an essential underpinning of all social relationships; it is even possible, if not finally convincing, to argue that those societies that are most trusting are the most successful.[4] Certainly it is important to be able to export trust from the *local* context, of family, friends and villagers, to make it *global* so that we can effortlessly trust strangers;[5] that is a real motor for economic growth and socially rich communities.[6]

So the crisis of trust has the potential to be something of a disaster. It threatens to undermine Western society exactly at the point at which some perceive it as being under threat from more vigorous traditions. Is there a role for conservatism here? Is it possible that conservatism has anything interesting to say that the new individualistic ideologies cannot?

Crisis?

The official version of the crisis of trust actually can be made to pack quite an anti-authoritarian message. At its most pungent, it says, in a nutshell, that the powers that be have been inadequate for various reasons (sometimes incompetence, sometimes venality), and that, as people have valued their individuality and autonomy more, they have ceased to be the supine citizens they were in the 1950s, say, and now are complaining and questioning more. We probably should be somewhat suspicious of such a glib reading of events. Certainly when we examine particular domains where trust is an issue, such as the Internet, business, science or politics,[7] the picture is much less clear.

The pattern we tend to find in such domains is somewhat more complex. We certainly find iffy expert performance; often less to do with experts making dangerous mistakes, and more to do with their overconfidence either in the quality of their results, or in their ability to localise particular effects. Either way, experts often ignore the knowledge principle. But what we also find is that anti-establishment critiques of supposedly untrustworthy performance can overstate official errors; it is often the case that experts work under conditions of great uncertainty and that many critiques rely more on hindsight than on a demonstration of poor expert performance.

We should be wary of the claims made by people who describe themselves as non-trusting. As philosopher Onora O'Neill puts it:

> Growing mistrust would be a reasonable response to grow-ing untrustworthiness; but the evidence that people or institutions are less trustworthy is elusive.
>
> In fact I think there isn't even very good evidence that we trust less. There *is* good evidence that we *say* we trust less: we tell the pollsters, they tell the media, and the news that we say we do not trust is then put into circulation. But say-ing repeatedly that we don't trust no more shows that we

trust less, than an echo shows the truth of the echoed words; still less does it show that others are less trustworthy.

Could our actions provide better evidence than our words and show that we do indeed trust less than we used to? Curiously I think that our action often provides evidence that we still trust. We may *say* we don't trust hospital consultants, and yet apparently we want operations – and we are pretty cross if they get delayed. We may *say* that we don't trust the police, but then we call them when trouble threatens. We may *say* that we don't trust scientists and engineers, but then we rely on hi-tech clinical tests and medical devices. The supposed 'crisis of trust' may be more a matter of what we tell inquisitive pollsters than of any active refusal of trust, let alone of conclusive evidence of reduced trustworthiness. The supposed 'crisis of trust' is, I think, first and foremost a culture of suspicion.[8]

There is much to this passage. Note that O'Neill does not deny that there is a crisis; but instead she says that the crisis is one where people are needlessly, almost cynically, critical of professionals, public servants and others.[9]

Interestingly, even the novelty of the crisis may also be overstated. A remarkably similar analysis of the political scene appeared as a particular dilemma for the Tories *prior to the 1979 election*.

That aspect of the problem of trust in government and responsibility on the part of officeholders that deserves to be stressed is the extent to which political institutions and officeholders are the victims of changes in attitudes and values in society. Even though it is held that trust in those holding office in government is sustained by their conduct, it has to be remembered that we are talking about two-way relationships. Whilst the ability of contemporary politicians to maintain an independent judgement of what is right and prudent to recommend may have been eroded by the gradual breakdown of a well-defined social elite sensitive to its political functions, equally they are exposed to pressures from a society in which the ties of habit have been loosened and agreement on what is appropriate conduct dissolved. The censure of public opinion remains, but it has become more capricious and is formed all too often by dis-appointment over the non-fulfilment of material expecta-tions which it may not be within the power of the politician to satisfy. Correspondingly public opinion focuses less often on the manner in which politicians have behaved and on the degree to which they have adhered to certain procedures and standards of conduct.[10]

Granted, many politicians actively inflate expectations for electoral purposes. Higher public spending without raising taxes, sir? Certainly. We'll just cut red tape and eliminate bureaucratic waste. Such politicians should not be surprised when they are rejected when shown to be hypocrites, too cowardly to tell the electorate the truth.

But cowards make bullies, and the danger is that public expectations about what is possible become completely discon-nected from the real world. In Germany, for example, voters have for a long while accepted that economic reforms are essential to improve the performance of their sclerotic economy – but howl down any *actual* reforms that get proposed. France, thanks to a large extent to often shameless electioneering by President Chirac, is caught in a vicious circle of promised increases in spending going hand in hand with tax cuts; most French elections in the 21st century so far have been excuses to give incumbent politicians a bit of a kicking.[11]

As voters we have responsibilities, to find out what is going on and to understand why policies have been suggested in the form that they have. It is easy to be cynical about politicians, but then why elect them? It is easy to expect politicians to solve all one's problems, and easy to blame them when they don't, but do we therefore gain much worth having?[12]

Election turnouts in Britain are on the decline; this is one of the key exhibits for the 'crisis of trust'. But it surely is unsurprising that turnouts are low. We are expected to vote for bodies such as local councils and the European Parliament, with limited powers, which get minimal media coverage even on news programmes, and which are hardly likely to fire the imaginations of the vast majority of people who do not really care very much for politics. Then when politicians behave cynically to embarrass their opponents – stand up Michael Howard, who opposed Labour's plans for university top-up fees; Tony Blair, who made a glaring U-turn and proposed a referendum on the EU constitution to spike Tory eurosceptic guns; and Charles Kennedy, supposed pro-European who tried to turn the 2004 European Parliamentary election into a referendum on the Iraq War – that isn't going to help.[13] Then add the ideological dilution of recent politics: as psephology improves, political parties are competing for ever-smaller numbers of swing voters ('Basildon Man', 'Worcester Woman' and various other suburban homunculi). So parties' messages are targeted at ever-smaller numbers of key voters, ignoring the rest of us; no wonder we lose interest. Then factor in woeful ignorance and wilful cynicism on the part of many of us, to give us the net result of pipsqueak turnouts and the occasional brief flourish of silly populist parties such as the UK Independence Party.

And finally, let us note that trust actually affects voting patterns surprisingly little; we do not often prefer the politicians we trust. Polls abound saying how little trusted, in the wake of the Iraq War, Mr Blair is, yet even with this handicap, even with persistent rumours of left wing plots to unseat him, his job looks relatively safe (that is not a prediction of the outcome of the 2005 election, in advance of which I write; merely the point that, if trust ratings in opinion polls were informative, he would have virtually no chance of winning). In fact, Mr Blair, master of spin, has *never* been trusted by voters, and his two spectacular electoral successes measure up nicely to the records of other distrusted Prime Ministers, such as Harold Wilson (four general election victories out of five) and Margaret Thatcher (three out of three).[14] On the other hand, more trusted leaders have failed dismally: Michael Foot, John Major, Edward Heath. This is a pattern repeated across the mature democracies; we do not seem to value a leader's trustworthiness particularly highly, certainly not compared with his or her effectiveness and ability to embody the *Zeitgeist*.[15]

Given all that, there are four obvious questions the conservative needs to ask about trust. First, given that trust has a fairly tenuous connection with voting behaviour, should the conservative bother with the problem at all? Second, if the answer to the first question is 'yes', then what policies should he or she endorse to arrest the decline? Third, how do the answers to these questions affect the problems of the Conservative Party, and what lessons might there be to be learned from other political parties? And fourth, is it possible that the revival of conservatism as a realistic ideology in the 21st century would itself help address the problem of trust? We will answer the first two questions in the next section of this chapter, and the third in the section following that. The remainder of the chapter will be given over to answering the fourth question.

A conservative attitude to the crisis of trust

The answer to the first question is pretty straightforward: yes. Granted that the public is not very trusting of politicians. An optimistic explanation of that is that they are properly understanding of the need for dissembling, even outright mendacity, in order to get things done in a complex world of constantly changing interests. A pessimistic one is that they are needlessly cynical. But either way, the conservative should be interested in fostering trust.

It is an axiom of conservative politics that a society as currently constituted is inherently valuable. Society, at least sometimes and for at least some purposes, should come before the preferences of individuals. But trust is exceedingly important for that conception. After all, if citizens are going to (be asked to) defer or even eschew certain anticipated gratifications for a common good, then those making sacrifices must be confident that others will play their part as well; few are willing to make a sacrifice for a social good alone. In particular, those in positions of power must be perceived to have clean hands, for it is they who formulate the choices that people must make, and who, in effect, suggest the sacrifices that must be made.

Hence trust throughout society, and trust in the political class in particular, is essential if people are going to be prepared, generally, to put the interests of society before their own. Note that this is to a surprisingly large extent an issue of *perception*: what is important is not so much that politicians are *trustworthy* (most of them are, pretty well), but that voters and citizens *think* they are. The task of any politician who wishes the interests of society to be felt to be more important than the interests of the individual is to foster the networks of trust that allow individuals to feel confident enough to put their interests to one side.

So moving to our second question: how should a conservative go about arresting the decline in trust? Politicians, perhaps more than most people, want to be loved, and if they think they are not, they are likely to act. Politicians worry about low turnouts and poor opinion poll ratings, however temporary these may be (or alternatively, however consistent with other social phenomena they may be), and are often tempted to tinker with voting methods, or representational forms, in order to boost popularity. These changes, small as they usually are, can have far-reaching effects on the constitution. For instance, recent attempts in Britain to provide different methods of voting alongside the traditional polling booth – or indeed as replacements for the polling booth – will inevitably alter the profile of the constituency. Votes by post or mobile phone will be cast at varying times during the course of an election campaign, rather than, as now, at the climax of it. These changes may have negligible effect, or positive effect, or negative effect – there is no way of telling. They will tend to accentuate the divorce between people and their locality, merely by removing the requirement to stroll to the church or the town hall or whatever every so often. Combined with other electoral developments, like the introduction of the faceless proportional party list system in some elections, the result is to reward disengagement in politics. Is that a good thing or a bad thing? It is hard to tell, but the knowledge principle says that the constitutional meddlers do not know, and the change principle says that the risks are therefore too great to endure.

Conservatives (small 'c') should therefore resist constitutional change. But changes in political *behaviour* are a different matter. They should trust their opponents to be trying to do their best for society, even if they don't think that the policies being suggested actually will help. They should trust voters. And they should not be afraid to give credit where it is due to ideological opponents; as we have had cause to note before, conservatives should be prepared to make U-turns when risky policies they have opposed turn out to have good effects. Conservatism is a humble ideology; not only does it not claim to have all the answers, it specifically claims that it does not. Others may have some answers, and if they have a mandate to experiment in some directions, the conservative, though he or she may warn of the potential consequences, should not try to stand in the way.

It has long been an assumption among commentators that trust is a matter of transparency; make your calculations clear, and voters will trust you. Michael Howard certainly subscribes to this view,[16] as he has set out in great detail a timetable for all his actions once he wins the 2005 election.[17] And the Tories have been quick to deride the Labour culture of spin,[18] though it was arguably Margaret Thatcher who first demonstrated the power of news management.

Actually, this is not necessarily the best way to create trust. If people don't like what you are going to do (or don't like your reputation), then they won't like your timetables. Added to which, such a strategy can hardly *create* trust, as it requires trust to be already in place. 'Trust me, I am going to put in place such and such a policy.' 'So? You can't afford it as you've already said you won't put taxes up.' 'Ah, that's OK. Because I've costed it all. My bean counters tell me it can be done while eliminating waste from the civil service.' 'So what? Why should I trust your bean counters any more than you, or your opponent's bean counters?' Transparency cannot be used to break out of this vicious circle.

And anyway, such a firm commitment to certain actions will be bought only at the price of the flexibility necessary to govern in uncertain times. New Labour committed themselves to reducing hospital waiting lists; and had to do that even when it became clear that that was not the best use of scarce NHS resources. They committed themselves to low taxes. This means that (a) when they *do* raise taxes, as they do a lot, they must do it in such a way as not to be reported prominently, even though the headline-dominating income tax is much the fairest, and (b) they had to go by the assumption that public spending would remain in accordance with previous forecasts, even as they picked an expensive fight with Saddam Hussein. If transparency is bought at the cost of flexibility, it is quite possible that one will be impaled on the horns of a dilemma: either change policy, and risk losing the trust you built up by insisting that policies would not change, or carry on with the old boneheaded policies even as they prove inadequate to the task.

It goes without saying, the best way to foster trust is to be trustworthy. That is, sadly, not guaranteed to generate trust: trusted people need not be trustworthy, and trustworthy people need not be trusted. But, unfashionable as it is, it remains the surest route.

The project

The third question is what this says to the Conservative Party. The Tories have been in something of a bind for some time, torn between rottweiler attacks on Labour failures on the one hand, and sweet reason on the other – we might call these the David Davis strategy and the Oliver Letwin strategy. It is clear from the above that the latter is the one most consistent with conservatism, but equally it would be foolish to deny that aggressive tactics are often essential in politics. The key is getting a judicious mix of the two.

The Labour Party has been through more or less the same problem of trust that the Tories have now. The New Labour 'project' was Labour's response, under Mr Blair and a few close colleagues. This was always conceived as a long-term plan to build up the trust that had been lost in the years of internecine struggle. And part of Mr Blair's plan to revivify Labour was to sponsor a new way of doing politics.

> But there is one big obstacle in the way of all our plans for change. It is the greatest legacy of the Tory years – disillusion with politics itself. And if we want to remove it we must show that our politics is not theirs. Not just that our vision for Britain is different, but also our means of achieving it. A new politics – a politics of courage, honesty and trust.
>
> It means being open. It means telling it as it is, not opposing everything every other party does for the sake of it. If the government is getting it right, as over Northern Ireland, we give credit. ...
>
> People look to politicians for leadership, and leadership is about having the courage to say no as well as yes. Even this week I have heard people saying a Labour government must repeal all the Tory trade-union laws. Now there is not a single person in the country who believes that to be realistic, or that we will do it. No one believes strike ballots should be abandoned. So why do we say it? We shouldn't, and I won't.
>
> I am absolutely committed to the goal of full employment. We will develop plans to achieve it. But let's not pretend that we can deliver it overnight. Let's not seek to fool the unemployed into thinking we will walk into power on Thursday and they will walk into a job on Friday. Let us be honest, straight, realistic.
>
> Those most in need of hope deserve the truth. Hope is not born of false promises; disillusion is. They are tired of dogma. They are tired of politicians pretending to have a monopoly on the answers. They are tired of glib promises broken as readily in office as they were made on the soapbox.[19]

Well, one might wonder whether Mr Blair's promise to be trust-worthy was kept; nevertheless the general message is absolutely sound, and its pragmatic value shown by Labour's recovery. The Tories would do well to learn from this. They cannot spend too much time attacking Labour. After all, the British people voted for Mr Blair twice over; to attack Labour too hard would be something of an attack on their instincts. Mr Blair no doubt takes liberties given the size of his majority; but he can afford to take liberties. The Tories, unloved and unpopular, must be much more careful and much more painstaking. They need to think long-term; when planning attacks on Labour, they need to think less of tomorrow's headlines, less indeed of the 2005 election, as that is almost certainly lost, and more of the oppor-tunities over the next five to ten years as Labour are faced with the difficult task of preserving, or extending, Mr Blair's legacy.

Signalling trustworthiness

The issues discussed so far in this chapter have much to do with the daily rough and tumble of British politics, and with the media flurry around trust that has dominated political discourse for the last few years. But there is more here: it is my contention that conservatism has a stronger message with respect to trust than other ideologies, because of its strong connection with social continuity and epistemological scepticism. In the second half of this chapter, I want to explore some themes relevant to the sociology of trust, and to show how those themes resonate very strongly with the conservative.

To begin with, let us consider the distinction, alluded to above, between *trust* and *trustworthiness*.[20] Trustworthiness is a property of a person (or institution, or system, or anything else that makes claims about performance – for the rest of this section I will limit my discussion to the case of individuals), which is that that person will typically do what she claims she will. If she is making a claim about her identity, then that claim will be true. If she claims to be acting in another's interests, then she will be so acting.

Trust, on the other hand, is an action of an observer; the observer *imputes* trustworthiness to an actor. If I trust you, then I have *come to believe* that you are trustworthy. If you claim to act in my interests, and if I trust you, then I may leave you to defend my interests, and take no action myself. If you claim to be about to perform some action, and I trust you, then I may make my future plans on the assumption that that action will be performed.

When I trust you, I make a judgement on the basis of what I can see. I cannot, of course, trust you to mend my car after seeing you mending my car, because I have to trust you *in advance* of your doing it. So I look for by-products of trust-worthiness, things that trustworthy people tend to do, or to say, and that untrustworthy people don't. If you do or say those things, then that is a decent reason to trust you.

All very well, and there is no doubt a strong connection between trust and trustworthiness. But the connection is not solid: I may trust you without your being trustworthy; you may be trustworthy without being trusted.

Question: is it better to be trusted or trustworthy?

In a highly interactive world, being trusted is essential. Which means I had better *appear* to be trustworthy. Appearing trustworthy is an art in itself; I should smile a lot, wear a suit, look concerned at others' troubles, and so on. I should display my certificates from professional bodies. Experiments have even shown that we are more likely to trust people who have symmetric faces.

But none of these things actually *means* that I am trust-worthy. Just because I wear a suit does not mean that I will not sell you a dud car, or run off with the church funds. We associate the outer forms that trustworthy people adopt with trustworthi-ness. Such forms – suits, smiles, certificates – then become *signals* of trustworthiness. I can signal my trustworthiness by wearing a suit and smiling. But then, once the signalling system is widely adopted, others who are not trustworthy can follow my example; untrustworthy people can wear suits and smile, and then they might be trusted too. The signals can be faked. Instead of being produced accidentally by trustworthy behaviour, they are produced on purpose, to create a deliberate and often false impression.

This is the heart of the New Labour approach. Old Labour was not trusted, reasoned those behind the New Labour 'project', and the imperative was to regain trust. But, though no doubt Labour politicians wished to be trustworthy, and though no doubt most of them were, being trustworthy does not entail being trusted, and being trusted was the prerequisite of a return to power. This is the converse of the above argument; if you happen to be trustworthy, but send out too few of the generally accepted signals of trustworthiness for people to notice, then you may actually fail to be trusted.

So New Labour focused on sending out those signals of trustworthiness. Out went the beards. Out went the jeans and pullovers. New Labourites wore suits. They were neat. The party colours were toned down from red to pink. A rose was used as the new logo. Certain words were dropped from the lexicon ('socialist' perhaps the most prominent). Clause 4, which committed the party to nationalising British industry, was noisily dumped (though not even Old Labour governments took it very seriously).

This was all a very conscious effort to send out different signals from those of the unpopular rabble that was Labour in the 80s. The rationale was that, to get anything done at a policy level, it was important to be trusted enough as a party to win elections. The Labour Party, by common consent unelectable, said it had changed; that message had to be trusted if it was to get back into power. Independently of whether New Labour was actually trustworthy, it was essential that it sent out enough signals to contradict any claim that underneath it was still the same old party.

Tory campaigns against New Labour at first tried to exploit the gap between the signals and their perception of reality. The famous 'demon eyes' campaign of 1997 (Figure 4) showed the youthful, fresh-faced Mr Blair with red demonic eyes that supposedly conveyed that, however cosy he looked, he was

Figure 4: A Tory poster from the 1997 general election

really a front man for trade unionists, communists, loony lefties and so on. The posters tried to persuade us that the signals Mr Blair was so assiduously sending out concealed his real character.

Of course they failed, and the position is now reversed. It is the Tories that are not trusted, and they are trying to send signals that they have changed, that they don't hate single mothers, or gays, and that they really do think there is such a thing as society (as for example the interview that Iain Duncan Smith gave to Gyles Brandreth in 2001[21]). Labour are trying to say that those signals are bogus: 'Britain is Working: Don't Let the Tories Wreck it Again' was their less-than-mellifluous slogan in elections in 2004. What about Michael Howard? Is he still the same old hatchet man with 'something of the night' about him, the most unpopular Home Secretary for decades, as Labour claims? Or alternatively, as the Tories want us to believe, has he learned from the years of opposition and become more inclusive, more in touch with our liberal times? The argument is over the veracity of the signals Mr Howard is sending us.

This is the wrong argument. The signals Mr Howard sends, and the signals Mr Blair is sending us too for that matter, are *all* bogus. They are literally irrelevant to the question of the trust-worthiness of the two principals, because they are consciously sent in order to convince us of trustworthiness. Whether or not Messrs Howard and Blair are trustworthy has nothing to do with their public faces, which are constructed entirely by professionals to attract our trust. The signals that they send out are not by-products of their trustworthy behaviour, but instead are manufactured to imply trustworthiness. That does not mean that they are not trustworthy, only that the signals are irrelevant to the question. And when signals matter more than their causes, we have a sign of the culture of spin.

This is not intended as a criticism of Messrs Blair and Howard – if we as voters persist in voting according to the headlines rather than the facts, then we cannot blame politicians for focusing on changing the headlines rather than the facts.

It is our own fault.

Trustworthiness in politics

Trustworthiness involves much more than sending out com-forting signals. In the political context, the concept has much to do with *reliability*, with adherence to *principles*, with pursuing the *common interest*; and with a certain *predictability* based on good faith. Trust in society has much to do with predictability;[22] many social interactions, especially those which involve co-operation, are eased when the actors trust each other.

These various attributes of the trustworthy politician can come into quite stark conflict with each other. For instance, consider the pursuit of the common interest. There will always be problems, in a complex society, in defining the common interest, and politicians will often struggle to do it persuasively. Politicians have a great deal of power (given to them in trust), and they may use it in their own interests. The trustworthy politician will, on the other hand, try to calculate the general interest and make decisions accordingly. But if the politician is not trusted, then voters may come to believe that she has not made any genuine attempt to take the interests of others into account. Instead, they may believe that the politician is covertly making decisions in her own interests, be they to make her richer, or more powerful, or to help out her friends.

Quite often, of course, answering the question of whose interests a politician is pursuing is not easy. A working-class politician who promotes the interests of the working class, a businesswoman promoting the interests of the business community, a gay politician promoting the interests of the gay community; each of these is arguably promoting her own interests as well as those of a wider group of people, and disentangling the personal from the public can be little more than a matter of (often ill-informed) opinion in many cases. 'The way of even the most justifiable revolutions is prepared by personal impulses disguised into creeds.'[23] Given the complexity and inequality of most Western societies, there will also be several possible interpretations of 'the common interest', so it is not as though we can expect to discover obvious yardsticks for measuring a politician's trustworthiness.

A trustworthy politician is also, in our characterisation, supposed to be principled. Fair enough. However, it may be that she feels that actively pursuing her principles may contradict her desire to act in the common interest. For instance, it may be that trying to achieve some outcome that is in the common interest will involve some subterfuge, perhaps some dissembling, perhaps a bit of unsavoury political roughhouse. Such personal dishonesty is not very principled behaviour; however, it might make a politician more effective in the public interest. Salisbury was particularly shameless in lying for the greater good of British interests.

Indeed, it seems virtually impossible to see how a politician could function at all without some element of personal dishonesty. For example, any negotiation she undertakes will of necessity involve the concealment of information. And few politicians can be of much use without being elected, which may well demand carefully crafted representations of their work in different ways for different audiences (i.e. spin).

Conservatism, trust and tradition

Hence trustworthiness in politics, at least in the naïve sense outlined above, is trickier to produce than one might think. The question then is how trust in politics can be supported (without being misplaced), and how conservatism in particular could help that process.

If we borrow a framework from sociologist Barbara Misztal,[24] trust is a social phenomenon that performs three major functions. It helps provide social *stability*; that is, it helps people to cope in a world that is uncertain, complex, contingent and arbitrary. Second, it underpins values, faith and friendship as bonds which help society to *cohere*. Third, it enables *co-operation* between otherwise independent agents to take place.

For the conservative, stability is central. Both coherence and co-operation are possible only when people's social roles are predictable, and therefore when one can enter into long-term relationships with them with confidence that their interests aren't going to change in the interim. The aim of the conservative politician, then, is to create and foster social stability, and then to stand aside and let the bonds of coherence form, and allow people to develop forms of co-operative behaviour.

So how does stability come about, and can the conservative make the claim that he or she is better placed to create it? Since anyone can do anything at any time, and all sorts of interactions can take place, it looks like the world will be so unpredictable that it will be almost impossible to deal with. However, in societies with a modicum of social order (which happy state does not exist in all societies, of course), the impression we get is of regularity and reliability; people's actions are *legible*. People do more or less what they are expected to do, and the variation from expectations is actually kept within very strict limits. The bank manager may not do exactly what we expect; for example, he may refuse my reasonable request for a loan. But he is very unlikely to deviate from what we might consider bank-managerly behaviour; he is unlikely, for example, to spit at me, proposition me sexually, burn a £50 note under my nose or push an ice cream cone into my face. Unusual deviation from norms like these is generally reserved for comedy, the Marx Brothers or *Monty Python*. And when, in real life, people depart from norms, the result is often a story in itself; when media tycoon Richard Desmond responded to a bid for the *Daily Telegraph* from German media group Axel Springer by goosestepping round a boardroom and ordering *Daily Express* executives to sing 'Deutschland Über Alles', the story took very little time to make it into the press.[25]

> Hence, trust plays the role of a protective mechanism, which prevents chaos and disorder by helping us to cope with the volume and complexity of information. It reduces the anxiety caused by ambiguity and the uncertainty of many social situations. It also tends to endow social order with meaning and neutralizes its arbitrariness.[26]

How is this stability produced? By a number of mechanisms, some embedded in individual behaviour, some in social constraints and norms. For example, there is the idea of *habit*, of responding to a present situation more or less as one has responded in the past. Behaviour is routine, assumptions and rituals constant. Artists, teenagers and rebels of all stripes have complained about habit since time immemorial, but it provides an underlying substratum of stability which enables life to be comprehensible (and, among other things, gives rebels something against which to rebel).

People develop *reputations*, narratives of their behaviour that make sense of the chaos of their individual actions; a good reputation can take years to develop, yet can be dissipated by a single rash action. Hence if someone has invested a good deal of effort creating a good reputation for himself, then he has a clear incentive for preserving that reputation. On the other hand, the mechanism of providing such narratives can degenerate into stereotyping, or can produce opportunities for blackmail. Reputation is clearly central to trust in the public sphere.[27]

And *collective memory* is a third mechanism for producing stability. Various public objects, including texts such as histories and narratives, artworks such as statuary, traditions such as rituals, (interpretations of) phenomena such as landscape, together provide a background against which the past of a community can be made sense of, and in terms of which the present and future can be planned and understood. The identity of a community can be transmitted via such collective memories.[28] This is not to say that collective memory always provides unambiguous and consistent accounts, nor that it is never degenerate or manipulated (as, for example, in the former Yugoslavia); only that it helps provide continuity of experience.

All these mechanisms for providing trust make sense of the present in terms of the past. Social stability is rooted in a continuity that makes few cognitive demands on an individual. It goes without saying that conservatism, being the ideology specifically designed to maximise that continuity, fits well into the provision of social stability through trust. The conservative, who values that stability, happens also to value many of the mechanisms that can bring it about, such as tradition, habit, and the repression of innovation.

Conservatism, then, can make an important contribution to the restoration of trust in public life, not necessarily because conservative politicians are more trustworthy than their green, socialist, liberal, feminist or social democratic opponents, but rather because unlike those other ideologies, conservatism is compatible with many of the mechanisms within society that are known to preserve and foster trust. It is on the *content* of conservatism, not the *character* of conservatives, that the argument rests.

Conservatism and authority

There is one more aspect of trust with respect to which conservatism has a natural advantage over its ideological opposites, which is the way trust flourishes in sectors where there is an important role for *authority*. The conservative, perhaps more than all other democratic political thinkers, is a respecter of authority, and a promoter of obedience to it where it is legitimate. Indeed, the conservative, with a mixture of realism, *Realpolitik* and a love of order, even takes illegitimate authority seriously; he or she is mindful of the suffering caused by conflict, and will not treat the illegality of a seizure of power as necessarily entailing intervention. Authority can help promote trust by providing sanction and constraint for the untrustworthy. Such authority must be applied justly, of course; arbitrary authority is deeply undermining of trust.

In particular, one important area where authority has an important role to play is with the development of *group reputations*, where such a group might be a national or cultural group, or a social role (such as that of politician). A group's reputation is important social capital for members of that group in wider society.

> A group's reputation contributes to the group's continuing existence by ensuring its cohesion and increasing its members' loyalty. At the same time, the existence of the group's reputation allows outsiders, such as clients, customers and traders, to go beyond available inadequate information and to operate within a set of generalized expectations of 'proper' behaviour on the part of the reputation holder.[29]

Retaining a reputation across all members of a group requires some sense of discipline, which will presumably be furnished by various social structures within that group. The group itself, which may be very informal, will still be entirely responsible for its own reputation. It may be able to demonstrate moral commitment and the possibility of informal moral pressure exerted by members of the group against potential miscreants. There may be social pressure (perhaps ultimately of ostracism from the group). And there may be mechanisms of formal control, with rewards and punishments handed out for particular offences.

These methods will clearly be more effective in small, tight-knit groups, and in groups where the benefits of membership are high. But in all cases the role of authority, be it formal or informal, is important. Authority provides a background against which trustworthy behaviour can flourish, and a group's reputation remain solid.

That is not to say that authority by itself can ensure trust (much depends on the way authority is applied, of course), especially in our diverse and culturally fractured society. Nor is it to say that submission to over-mighty authority, whose will is law, is the same as trustworthiness. It is only to say that respect for authority does much to provide a predictable and coherent background for social behaviour, and can provide many of the elements upon which trust thrives. And, to reiterate, conservatism is arguably the most respectful, and the most sympathetic, of all the democratic ideologies to the role of authority.

Trust, change and conservatism

A relatively deep analysis of trust in modern Western democracies, then, shows that many of the important mechanisms for creating, preserving and transferring trust are, by happy coincidence, prominent themes in conservative ideology. This surely should be an important theme in political debate, while trust is such a major topic. But it is also important to make the case in ideological terms; the temptation, unfortunately, is for debates about trust and trustworthiness to personalise politics.[30]

The effect can be risible; in 2004, to coincide with the party conference, the Tory front bench produced a video in which they each revealed details of their first kiss, and which was the last CD they bought. This was part of the general effort to humanise themselves in the eyes of the electorate, though why the fact – if it is a fact – that Nicholas Soames likes Dido should cause one to trust him rather than raise an eyebrow in surprise isn't clear. Indeed, it still cannot create trust: so patrician a figure is Soames that one might merely disbelieve him, and assume that he is too wary of appearing a toff to admit he likes Wagner.

The individualism in Western political life has been under-mining of social and public trust. The rapid change character-istic of the late 20th and early 21st centuries shifted and is shifting the landscape; many old certainties and sources of stability and coherence are disappearing without being obviously replaced. This sense of loss of bearing, felt by many, may be at least in part responsible for the general malaise and melancholic outlook affecting us despite record levels of material prosperity.

On the other hand, it should be clear from this chapter, and indeed by implication from the rest of this book, that the essence of conservatism is a long way from a naïve optimism that assumes that everyone has good intentions and that good intentions are rewarded with happy outcomes. In particular, the conservative worries a lot about the inadequacy of the know-ledge that we claim to have, and is in general less trusting of experts and expertise, on the basis of the knowledge principle (Salisbury, as we have seen, exhibiting the most extreme distrust of experts). The conservative is hardly uncritical. Rather, the conservative is conscious of the benefits of trust, and the dangers to society of not trusting (withdrawing our trust from the auth-orities, without good reason, is a contravention of the change principle). But the conservative starts to worry when experts claim to be able to engineer clever outcomes in complex societies; he or she will certainly not trust uncritically in such contexts.

It may be that the crisis of trust is more rhetorical than genuine, as I noted at the beginning of this chapter. Nevertheless, the facts that people are less inclined to verbalise their trust in politicians, journalists, scientists and other people in public life, and that trust surveys frequently show unpalatable results, still point to a feeling of rootlessness, *ennui* and even unfocused anger. This is hardly a good sign. Small 'c' conservatism surely still has a role to play in helping preserve trust in a time of rapid change.

Conservatism and the Conservatives

Part One of this book described the development of a type of conservatism based on Pyrrhonism, or scepticism, and tried to show how such a model of conservatism could thrive even in the 21st century. Part Two has now fleshed out the theoretical details with some contextualisation of the ideology in the 21st-century world, looking at three of the major dilemmas of the time: how to deal with free markets and arrange our economic relationships; how to understand society and its relation to the individuals in it; and how to foster social trust. Obviously those three dilemmas are very much connected; just as obviously they hardly cover the whole of political space. Nevertheless, the aim of Part Two was to suggest what a conservative government could achieve in those areas, in such a way as to retain an ideological link to Conservative governments of the past, while simultaneously appealing to the voters who have deserted the Tories in droves to follow Mr Blair, and who might well, in the aftermath of Iraq and others of Labour's difficulties, be beginning to cast about for an alternative.

Since the catastrophic defeat of 1997, the Conservatives have half-acknowledged that the legacy of the government of 1979–97 has not been wholly positive (which does not imply, of course, that Conservatives should *repudiate* the actions of the Thatcher and Major governments; only that they might consider a different set of principles in the future). But it is fair to say that the big issue confronting all Tory leaders since 1997 has been the way to deal with that legacy, and how to appeal to an electorate which turned strongly towards Mr Blair. Failure to deal with that legacy meant the downfall of two leaders, Mr Hague and Mr Duncan Smith, and we will consider their efforts in Chapter Nine. Mr Howard, the leader at the time of writing, is as yet untested in a serious election. His politics will be considered in Chapter Ten. These two final chapters will scrutinise Tory performance in opposition, in order to see whether traditional conservative ideology has been visible in the modern Conservative Party, and whether therefore the Tories might plausibly seek to benefit in future from the arguments for conservatism that we have considered in this book.

PART THREE

ESCAPE FROM THE WILDERNESS?

Unfortunately, nine-tenths of the time of any political leader must be spent not on defeating his opponents, but on manipulating the stupidities of his own side.

Doris Lessing, *A Proper Marriage*

CHAPTER NINE

TORIES NIL DESPERANDUM TWO

The Blairite hegemony

Tony Blair, like Mrs Thatcher, has, on occasion, looked a bit wobbly in his period of office. The petrol protests threatened to undo him towards the end of his first term. Various scandals have hinted at sleaze under the surface. And he was famously booed and given a slow handclap by, of all people, the Women's Institute.

Most seriously, the conduct of the Iraq War has damaged Mr Blair. As well as the conservative worries we have already canvassed, other concerns include: the lack of weapons of mass destruction in Saddam's armoury; the obvious disconnection between the War on Terror and George Bush's pursuit of Saddam (which looked suspiciously like the continuation of a family feud); the lack of preparation for victory; the shifty-looking handout of reconstruction work to favoured firms; the undermining of the international order based on the UN Security Council; the patent lack of support for the war in the UK; the patent lack of influence of Tony Blair on George Bush; the delicate situation in Israel and the West Bank; philosophical convictions about sovereignty; and practical assessments about US/UK military capability. The death of government scientist David Kelly, who committed suicide after being pressurised for speaking out of turn to a BBC journalist, left a decidedly nasty taste in the mouth, even if Dr Kelly was to a large extent responsible for his plight. The Hutton report on the Kelly affair had the capability to bring the government down; in the event, its positive tone and virtual exoneration of Mr Blair, his spokesman Alastair Campbell (who had already resigned) and Defence Secretary Geoff Hoon merely polarised opinion. The war exposed Mr Blair to serious, well-thought-out attacks by former Foreign Secretary and Leader of the House Robin Cook; Cook, already smarting from his demotion to make room for David Blunkett at the heart of government, now finds himself happily outside the tent pissing in. In contrast, the routine carping of Clare Short is a pinprick.

But this is not all good news for the Tory Party. What stands out from any account of the Blair years is the tiny influence that Conservatives have had over events. The chief opposition to the Blair government has generally been located next door, in Chancellor Gordon Brown's office in 11 Downing Street. When there has been an opportunity, the Tories have not often been in the right place to take advantage; for example, because of their over-hastiness in supporting the Iraq War, they have had difficulty capitalising on its iffy progress.[1]

In opposition and virtually irrelevant, the Tories have had to reconsider their history, present and future. This is not easy, as they have discovered before,[2] and has not been made easier by the fact that, when they look back before 1992, they see a period of almost unparalleled success; Labour's task of re-evaluation, by contrast, was simpler: though the main party of government in 1964–79, they could see only dismal failure in actual achievement, which at least made grasping the nettle somewhat more palatable.

In this chapter, we will examine the records of William Hague and Iain Duncan Smith, to see how well they did in adapting to the post-Blair world. In particular, we will want to know whether, and if so how, the older tradition of sceptical conservatism has been visible in Tory deliberations. If the Tories are going to re-discover conservatism, how much more work is there to be done?

William Hague and the people around him

In 1997, William Hague made his grab for the Tory leadership. John Major, fed up with his fractious party, resigned immediately the extent of Mr Blair's landslide became clear, and symbolically decamped to the Oval cricket ground. Two of the three heavyweights of the time were ineligible for the contest thus precipitated: Michael Portillo, darling of the hard Thatcherite right, had stunningly lost his Enfield seat, while Deputy Prime Minister Michael Heseltine's health worsened shortly after the election. The third 'big beast', former Chancellor Kenneth Clarke, will be discussed later in this chapter; there was little doubt at the time that Mr Clarke would be the most effective opponent to Mr Blair, but his robust europhilia made it unlikely that he could unite the party.

After a brief flirtation with an unpopular former Home Secretary called, em, Michael Howard, Mr Hague, whose only serious political experience was a couple of years as Welsh Secretary, and who was still most famous for his Tory Boy appearance at a party conference twenty years before, decided to stand against Clarke, Howard and three others: John Redwood, brainy right-winger who had partly usurped Mr Portillo's position as Great Right Hope after challenging Mr Major's leadership in 1995; Peter Lilley, a thoughtful Thatcherite; and Stephen Dorrell, assumed to be a left-winger, but seen as somewhat inconsistent. Mr Dorrell quickly withdrew and put his weight behind Mr Clarke.

Mr Hague was the early favourite with the bookies, though many could not believe it. The other candidates each seemed to have something wrong with them. Mr Redwood had a reputation for being odd, which had earned him the sobriquet of 'the Vulcan'. Most people's images of him were of his misguided attempt to mime the Welsh national anthem during his own stint as Welsh Secretary, and of the news conference to publicise his 1995 candidature, surrounded by bizarrely clad members of the Tory awkward squad. Mr Howard seemed to revel in his illiberal reputation, which in May 1997 went right against the prevailing trends. Lilley's euroscepticism was regarded as too extreme, plus he was somewhat colourless. Clarke was colourful all right, though also unsound on Europe for opposite reasons.

But the advantage of not being any of the above was tactical, not strategic, as the *Economist*'s political commentator pointed out about Mr Hague during the campaign.

> He is something of a clean sheet of paper, but is pretty Eurosceptical and, most fatefully, is 36 years old and has scant experience. Against him, Mr Blair will look like an old hand. To choose him would be to concede the next election right away, which would be absurd.[3]

The Tories, as we know, did not take that advice. By 92 to 70, Mr Hague beat Mr Clarke on the final ballot, after Mr Clarke did an extraordinary and nakedly opportunistic deal with his political opposite Mr Redwood to try to scupper Mr Hague's chances. With hindsight, political commentator Mark Garnett finds it hard to understand why the youthful Mr Hague went for the leadership; surely his middle-of-the-roadness would have ensured him a serious Shadow Cabinet place whoever won the 1997 leadership election, and would have left him well placed for the next one.[4]

The *Economist*'s man had no doubt as to where Mr Hague's problems would lie.

> Even if personal relations were good, it will not be easy for the young, new leader to form a united team. Many of his campaign mistakes can be put down to youthful enthusiasm. But managing a shadow cabinet many of whose members are likely to be not only much older but far more experienced will be difficult. ...
>
> ... He must set out clear policies, not least on Europe, on which the party can unite. He must forge a united shadow cabinet from a fractious, traumatised party. And he must modernise and energise the party's grass-roots organisation, which has fallen into a woeful state of disrepair.
>
> Mr Hague, the boy wonder of British politics, has not been slow in seizing his political chances. He is an outstanding debater and has a likeable and easy manner. But glibness and charm will not be enough to lead a party as

disunited as the Tories. A sense of direction, ruthlessness and political acumen will be needed. Mr Hague has yet to show such qualities, or that he is up to the formidable task before him.[5]

The most damning judgement against Mr Hague is surely his failure to forge a united Shadow Cabinet. News items about the Tories rarely featured them against the Labour government; they tended to focus on the continuing in-fighting. Mr Clarke largely kept himself to himself, but the return to parliament of Mr Portillo discomfited Mr Hague to such an extent that he never recovered. Though he settled the European question in the party rather well, once Mr Portillo returned the cabinet dissolved into chaos.[6]

The arguments were all about where to go. Appeal to core supporters? Or try to pull a Blairite modernisation trick? The choice, dramatised by the divisions between Mr Hague's troops, seemed to be between unappealing substance and insubstantial spin. I hope that the reader of this book will by now believe, with me, that that is a false dichotomy. But to Mr Blair's delight, it is how it looked to the principals at the time.

From compassionate conservatism to the kitchen table: the American dimension

A theme began to emerge in 1997 which has accompanied Tory attempts to get back on the rails. Many Tories had found themselves very congenial company across the Atlantic, with the neo-conservative think tankers and Republican politicos within the Washington Beltway.[7] These connections were fostered during the 80s, when British Tories got themselves interested in ideology in a big way, and while Ronald Reagan's team were redefining what was possible in the US. The close personal friendship between Mrs Thatcher and Mr Reagan encouraged such exchanges. Mrs Thatcher saw much of her thought in American terms; her arguments resonated with puritanism and disdain for the morally weak.

I was an individualist in the sense that I believed that individuals are ultimately accountable for their actions and must behave like it. But I always refused to accept that there was some kind of conflict between this kind of individualism and social responsibility. I was reinforced in this view by the writings of conservative thinkers in the United States on the growth of an 'underclass' and the development of a dependency culture. If irresponsible behaviour does not involve penalty of some kind, irresponsibility will for a large number of people become the norm. More important still, the attitudes may be passed on to their children, setting them off in the wrong direction.[8]

So in 1997, it was not unnatural for the Tories to try to conceive of their predicament in American terms. Parallels were not hard to find between the Tories and the Republicans. The story went like this. Each had had a period of domestic political hegemony in the 80s, with leaders (Thatcher 1979–90, Reagan 1981–9) who had transformed their respective countries internally, while simultaneously engendering respect abroad. But these two great leaders were followed by timid courtiers hopelessly inadequate to be trusted with the great legacy (Major 1990–97, Bush Sr 1989–93). Meanwhile, useless leftie opposition had remoulded itself, at least superficially, around charismatic but fundamentally empty political geniuses (Blair 1997–, Clinton 1993–2001).

Britain's Conservatives, it was opined, were a little behind the Republicans in the cycle. Indeed, the Republicans had already tried to break out of the cycle before Mr Blair's victory, with Newt Gingrich's short-lived and ultimately disastrous Contract With America.[9] But America's multi-tiered government provides many opportunities for politicians to prove themselves in office. In particular, the local political structure mirrors federal politics. Each state is run by a governor, the analogue of the national President. And so the skills of governorship, which may involve getting things done against the wishes of bipartisan or deadlocked legislatures, do map reasonably well onto the skills required in the White House.

In almost direct opposition to Mr Gingrich's strong ideologically driven stance, various Republican governors were quietly experimenting with clever ways of dealing with the various crises of public service, steering a course between the differing moral visions of a country increasingly divided between puritan Christians and liberals. Ideology was ditched, in favour of fostering cross-party support. Prominent among these governors were Tommy Thompson of Wisconsin, John Engler of Michigan, and, not least, the two sons of George Bush Sr, George W. in Texas and Jeb in Florida. Each of these Republicans seduced large numbers of the Democrats' core supporters.[10]

George W. quickly reached a position of pre-eminence as he developed the philosophy of 'compassionate conservatism'. Much of this was a careful deployment of vocabulary, but the idea seemed to have wide appeal. In the Texan context, it generally involved reducing the involvement of government in society, exporting many of its functions to voluntary or faith-based organisations, which, it was assumed, would be less bureaucratic and more efficient at targeting resources where they were needed. Mr Bush held out a hand to the large number of Latino immigrants in his state, becoming fluent in Spanish (in the 1998 midterm elections, Mr Bush took 49 per cent of the Latino vote).[11]

In sum, compassionate conservatism pulled together many strands of American thought. It appealed to the religious right, the small government neo-conservatives, the Clintonistas who were interested in creative ways of keeping levels of public service up while saving money at the same time, and those agonising about the atomism and individualism in American society in the wake of Putnam's *Bowling Alone*.[12] Most of all, it appealed to the ordinary Texan, who was repelled by the sterility of partisan debate.

The Tories were keen. The core supporters liked the word 'conservatism'; the modernisers liked 'compassionate'. And it fitted rather nicely into the narrative of British/American parallelism. Mr Clinton was likely to be succeeded by Vice President Al Gore, a man of talent and intelligence, but who lacked the appeal of his boss, and indeed harboured a not-so-secret scepticism about much of the Clintonian agenda. Across the pond, the Gore mantle fitted Gordon Brown to a T. So, were a Republican with a big idea to win in 2000, that big idea, went the argument, could be deployed against Labour in 2001.

In the event, the narrative broke down. Mr Gore stood in 2000 as expected, and repudiated Mr Clinton's legacy in much stronger terms than the Republicans can have hoped; the election was effectively tied, Mr Bush of course coming out just on top. Given all the advantages of Mr Gore's incumbency, the election was an undoubted success for Mr Bush. Given the 50–50 split, it was assumed that Mr Bush, lacking a clear mandate, would be relatively neutral between the parties, as he had been in Texas; compassionate conservatism would be a good vehicle for such neutrality. But actually Mr Bush ran a deeply partisan White House, and ditched compassionate conservatism immediately, even before the terrible barbarism of 11 September 2001.[13] Mr Bush seemed to love polarising opinion, and became the most hated politician in the country, even while enjoying relatively good approval ratings. A cult documentary maker, Michael Moore, achieved international stardom on the back of his anti-Bush books and films. Abroad, Mr Bush put the backs up of many international leaders, and became a serious embarrassment to his supporter Mr Blair.

But in 1997–8 all that was in the future. The narrative looked good. And so, drawing upon compassionate conservatism, as well as the 'common sense conservatism' of Canadian politician Mike Harris, Mr Hague developed the philosophy of 'kitchen table conservatism'. The idea was that conservatism could be explained, or discussed, by an ordinary family around a kitchen table. It thereby rather neatly connected a number of images. First of all, it took political ideology out of the think tanks, whose pointy-headed sharp-suited denizens were not viewed with favour by voters, and brought it into people's houses. The concepts would have to be simple, clear and intuitive enough to appeal to all, not just those who owned the complete works of Hayek. Second, it resurrected the Oakeshottian idea of politics as a conversation.[14] This distanced the Hague approach from the ideologically driven Thatcherites, who were seen as arrogant and out of touch, and chimed in with the new humility of a party keen to be seen as 'listening'. Third, it subtly suggested support for the 'normal' family, the nuclear family assembled round the table at important communal moments such as breakfast and dinner, implicitly appealing to traditionalists.

But the idea did not take off.

> The party's hapless attempts to rebrand itself conquered new summits of preposterousness when Mr Hague returned from America espousing 'kitchen table conservatism', and went on to install such a table in Tory headquarters, giving shape if not clarity to this perplexing metaphor.[15]

It, and a series of planned party political broadcasts featuring young couple Chris and Debbie sitting around their – you guessed – kitchen table, were quietly canned.

What went wrong with the big idea? In the first place, the aim – to privilege particular ways of living – was always going to be hard to achieve in our secular and liberal times. No version of conservatism in a diverse democracy can be strongly linked to a 'standard' way of life. The idea of the family sitting round the kitchen table always looked a little anachronistic, but the Tories' timing was masterly. Round about the same time, the famous Oxo family, which played out a comic soap opera over several years of stonking great roasts served with mouth-watering Oxo gravy, was dropped by the advertisers, because 'family life is changing'.[16] Worse, Britain's potteries began to slump, as they continued to produce large, ornate dinner services designed for the multi-course family dinners at the table that no one was having any more. Royal Doulton's share price (Figure 5) rather mirrors the stock of kitchen table conservatism over the corresponding period.

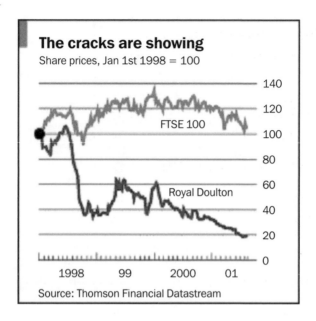

The cracks are showing
Share prices, Jan 1st 1998 = 100

Figure 5: Royal Doulton's share price, 1998–2001[17]

But the mistiming is not the real problem with kitchen table conservatism. The real problem lies in the origin of the initiative, in American policy wonkery. Why assume that the solution in America should be the same as the solution in Britain? Britain and America are very different places – obvious, but it is amazing how often one has to point it out explicitly. In particular, America has long and worthy traditions of self-reliance and philanthropic giving that Britain does not have, and cannot match. Americans give 1 per cent of GDP to philanthropic causes; Britons just 0.6 per cent (of a much smaller *per capita* figure).[18] In general, America is a much more right wing place with very different social attitudes (Figure 6).

A genuinely conservative position could take many forms, and there is no reason to think that William Hague's take on common sense could not be cast in such a mould. But it is a very unconservative line to take to transplant political ideas, with not

Divided by more than the sea

American and British public opinion
selected issues, %

	US	Britain
Oppose/disagree with an unlimited right to abortion	46	17
Proud to be "American"/"English"	97	76
Taxation is "too low"/support higher taxation (for public services)	1	62
Approve of George Bush's increase in foreign aid	53	90
Believe in the Devil	45	13
Support a ban on the possession of handguns	32	83

Selected social indicators

	US	Britain
People earning 40% or less of median income, %	14	5
Millionaires*, % of population	0.74	0.58
Gun deaths, per 100,000 people	10.6	0.3
Average number of executions, per year, 1997–2001	78	0
Defence spending per head, $	1,059	576
Government spending, % of GDP	30	39

*Investable assets of more than $1m

Sources: Gallup; MORI; Pew Research Centre; Council for Secular Humanism; *Daily Telegraph*; US Census Bureau; UK Office for National Statistics; Merrill Lynch; *British Medical Journal*; DPIC; IISS; OECD

Figure 6: Differences between America and Britain[19]

too much amendment, from the very different world of the USA and expect them to flourish and grow. And it would need a lot more work than Mr Hague's team were prepared to devote to the exercise, as Mark Garnett points out.

The inadequacies of management consultancy as an apprenticeship for politics might also be detected in Hague's attitude to slogans. Some of these – 'compassionate' or 'Kitchen Table' Conservatism, the *Common Sense Revolution, Believing in Britain*, and even 'Mainstream Majority' – were worth a sustained trial. But Hague always seemed to be looking around for a winning soundbite, when his priority from the start should have been survival, not victory. The net result was that his sales-pitch to the electorate seemed even less coherent than it really was.[20]

Populism

Mr Hague seemed to be casting around for the big idea, but never trying to make such an idea work. The problem grew worse with the splits in his Shadow Cabinet. But he had made a good start. He had been tasked by the *Economist*'s commentator to fix a clear line on Europe, and he did; he took a mild eurosceptic line and held a referendum of party members on it, which was carried suitably impressively (85 per cent to 15 per cent, with a 60 per cent turnout of members). This tactic was much derided, and it was thought that the most likely effect would be to exacerbate party divisions. In fact, the argument died down quite quickly. A number of pro-Europeans dissented, and a couple of Shadow Cabinet members resigned. But Mr Hague's move was cannier than many had thought. In the first place, the lack of response to the pro-Europeans' protests merely drew attention to their isolation within the party. And secondly, as Mr Major's period of office had shown, it was the eurosceptics who were troublesome, and who were in effect responsible for putting Mr Blair into Number 10; the europhiles were comparative pussycats.

But Mr Hague couldn't pull the same trick with the public services. His deputy, Peter Lilley, tried to edge the party away from the Thatcherite tradition with a speech in April 1999 about how market mechanisms were of limited efficacy in certain markets and for certain purposes; on this ground he attempted to rule out privatisation of education or health. The speech was moderate and sensible – and indeed the only direction the party could realistically move in, given the public consensus – but the unfortunate coincidence of the speech with a dinner to celebrate the twentieth anniversary of Mrs Thatcher's election victory, and reports that Mrs Thatcher herself had hit the roof, killed the initiative. Mr Lilley was sacked shortly afterwards.

Given the lack of an overarching political philosophy (in itself not necessarily a handicap), together with the failure of an important initiative, Mr Hague was in trouble. He was also landed with two rather nasty contingencies. First, Mr Blair's government was actually doing OK, and Mr Brown's steward-ship of the economy showed a strong continuity with the successful policies of Mr Clarke. And second, the Shadow Cabinet was unmanageable.

In the end, he decided to keep up the Tories' core vote; if all committed Tories voted, then, even though that would not be enough people to threaten Mr Blair's victory, it would still be a sufficient number to cut Mr Blair's majority, and give the youthful Mr Hague a second crack at the whip in 2005/6.

Oops.

The issues that excited Tory ultras resonated badly in the Blairite nation. Mr Hague supported the rights of Tony Martin, a farmer who had killed a burglar on his property. This was all very well, and highlighted the Tory issue of crime. But Mr Martin seems to have become obsessed with the idea of being burgled, and – to say the least – was not the sort of person that the urban professionals who had deserted the Tories could identify with in the slightest. Another dubious character with whom Mr Hague had problems was the Tory candidate for the London mayoralty election in 2000, Jeffrey Archer, a copious creator of fiction whose integrity (not widely believed to be his long suit) Mr Hague very publicly endorsed. Shortly afterwards, Mr Archer retired from the election after revelations of past perjury.

When protestors against the high price of petrol brought the country to a near standstill, Mr Hague not only supported the campaign but seemed to speak in favour of lawbreaking. He made an attack on the 'liberal elite' – much, if some accounts can be believed, to the chagrin of Michael Portillo[21] – in the wake of the Macpherson report on institutional racism in the Metropolitan Police. In the run-up to the 2001 general election, he made a speech about how Britain was becoming a 'foreign land' to its own citizens.

This last appeared to be a further sideswipe at the 'floods' of 'bogus' asylum seekers that had been the focus of Tory ire for some time. That was bad enough, as once more this was not a topic that would engage the new Blair voters; but it was interpreted by one or two on the Neanderthal right as *carte blanche* (pardon the pun) to flirt with racism in the election campaign. Outgoing Tory MP John Townend took the opportunity of lamenting the decline of the British into a 'mongrel race', and Mr Hague's dissociation of himself and his party from the remark seemed to take an age. His protestations that, as Mr Townend was retiring at the election, he was powerless to intervene struck many at the time as similar to Mr Major's failure to deal with the problem candidature of Neil Hamilton in 1997.

The final straw was the ill-fated election campaign in June 2001, which Mr Hague presented as Britain's last chance to save the pound. Events, of course, have shown the theory to be wrong, but it seemed silly even at the time. He ended up with the nickname 'Billy Bandwagon'. Rather than a pragmatic opportunism, which would be defensible and actually not that far from Mr Blair's own style, Mr Hague seemed to produce knee-jerk responses to whatever seemed to be discomfiting Mr Blair most at the time.

Opposition was ever thus. But given that the political centre had been moved leftwards by Mr Blair, it was essential that that was acknowledged by Mr Hague. If Mr Blair is seen as centrist – which he is – Mr Hague could not present himself as merely his antithesis, because that would alienate the voters he needed (compare the Labour Party's implacable opposition to Mrs Thatcher, which fired up its own supporters but was hardly likely to bring working-class Tories back). Furthermore, the presence of prominent reactionaries such as Jack Straw and David Blunkett in Mr Blair's cabinet meant that, if this became an arms race, Mr Hague would be forced further and further right, ceding the centre to Mr Blair without a fight.

Restructuring the party

The Conservative Party's ramshackle structure took a share of the blame for the poor performance in 1997 – and probably rightly. It was organisationally dispersed, spread across several independent entities (there was, in fact, no such thing as 'The Conservative Party'), which exacerbated the tensions between the different sets of interests that made up the grand coalition of members.

The sorry spectacle, certainly up to 1997, of Tory MPs squabbling among themselves, often deliberately to undermine the party leadership, provoked understandable outrage among the grass roots. The dismal performance of the leadership itself didn't help matters; nor did the fact that the leadership often seemed to take positions opposed by the majority of members. Finally, it didn't seem that long ago that the Tories were led by a woman who was in much better touch with the membership, and who swept all before her.

All these factors conspired to make the rank and file members of the party believe that their judgement was rather better than those whom they had sent to Westminster. Hence, the heady whiff of democracy was in the air; the *sans-culottes* were starting to believe that their leaders needed to be reined in, not respected.

Mr Hague, in his leadership bid in 1997, cannily put party reform high up the agenda. Just as cannily, he used his recently gained mandate to pull the Blairite trick of centralising decision-making, marginalising inconvenient views, and increasing consultation, thereby giving members the impression – in the short term at least – that their views were being taken into account. They were indeed being listened to – and largely ignored. Proposals enshrined in a white paper called *The Fresh*

Future tightened the leader's grip on the party's policy-making, finance and candidate selection.[22]

The lack of democracy in these proposals has come in for some criticism.[23] But the small 'c' conservative sees democracy as good when it is useful, bad when it is harmful. The unrepresentativeness and reactionary nature of the Conservative Party membership means Mr Hague's restriction of democracy was sensible; but unfortunately even the limited democratisation that did happen was disastrous.

The attention naturally focuses on the method of choosing the leader. The system Mr Hague inherited was that the parliamentary party chose the leader, based on a series of votes eliminating candidates until someone had a majority. He replaced that with a one-man-one-vote system in which first MPs would whittle the candidates down to two, and then after this gatekeeping the party members would vote on the finalists. Richard Kelly, writing shortly after the first use of this system in 2001, showed impressive prescience (even while equivocating!) with his analysis of what the details of the system might produce.

> Owing to Hague's voluntary departure, we are yet to gauge fully *The Fresh Future*'s effect upon challenging an incumbent leader. However, both the 1998 rules and the 2001 contest point to a clear limit upon intra-party democracy. The rules state that a vote of confidence can only be sparked by a petition signed by 15 per cent of MPs, that only MPs can vote, that a mere 51 per cent voting 'No' means the leader has lost, and – crucially – that such a leader cannot be a candidate in a subsequent contest. This means that a leader who has won overwhelming support from the grassroots could still be ousted by a numerically small fraction of party members (just eighty-four MPs according to 2001 figures). Given [new leader Iain] Duncan Smith's limited support in the MPs-only ballots of 2001, such a scenario is not implausible and was highlighted by the refusal of several prominent MPs (including Clarke, Portillo, Maude, Widdecombe and Norman) to serve in his Shadow Cabinet.

On the other hand, Duncan Smith might be secured by the new and tortuous process of finding a replacement. As we saw in 2001, leadership contests which go beyond Westminster take far longer to complete: whereas it took the Tories less than three weeks to oust and replace Margaret Thatcher, it took them over three months to find a successor to Hague. Subsequently, there may be strong incentives to leave an incumbent alone, as a drawn-out challenge (especially one as acrimonious as the Clarke/Duncan Smith battle) could damage the party even more than the continuation of a lacklustre leader.[24]

The legitimacy of the leader

There were five candidates following Mr Hague's resignation. David Davis was mainly concerned with putting a marker down for the future. His would be a particularly interesting candidacy, as he had made his name, not with a post in the Conservative Party, but rather as the tenacious and principled chairman of the House of Commons Public Accounts Committee, where he provided the most effective opposition to Gordon Brown's domination of domestic and financial politics. Michael Ancram was an unconvincing unity candidate. Neither of these looked terribly likely to trouble the big hitters Mr Clarke, Mr Portillo and Iain Duncan Smith.

But their elimination provided the first alarms that the new system had been barely thought through. In the first ballot of the MPs Mr Portillo was the clear winner, but with only 49 votes (29.5 per cent). Mr Duncan Smith was second with 39 (23.5 per cent), followed by Mr Clarke with 36 (21.7 per cent). Worst of all, though, Messrs Davis and Ancram each polled a respectable 21 votes (12.7 per cent). Mr Davis's poll was decent for someone realistically thinking four or five years ahead; Mr Ancram's was testimony to the inadequacy of the major players to create consensus. But the serious problem was that they had tied for last place: the rules of the party did not specify what would happen in such an event. Neither candidate could therefore be eliminated from the process, and the second ballot of MPs, ludicrously, was between the same five candidates. The Tory press was scathing,[25] the criticism being aimed at the system, rather than at Mr Davis or Mr Ancram for refusing to withdraw from a contest neither had a hope of winning. In the second ballot, a second tie was avoided, Mr Ancram finishing last with 17 votes (Mr Davis, on 18, chose that point to withdraw too). At the realistic end of the table, Mr Portillo again won the ballot, this time with 50 votes, though he was widely regarded to have underperformed fatally as the frontrunner (he began the race at the odds of 4–9, against second favourite Mr Duncan Smith at 100–30[26]). The excuse that many of his supporters had voted for other candidates for tactical reasons was widely and properly derided.[27]

The surprise winner of the third ballot was Mr Clarke, with 59 votes (35.5 per cent), narrowly ahead of Mr Duncan Smith (54 votes, 32.5 per cent), with Mr Portillo eliminated (53 votes, 31.9 per cent). The lack of consensus within the party was exposed. The final stage of the contest was the popular vote among the party membership between Mr Clarke and Mr Duncan Smith, with the members having been given no proper steer by the MPs. Their choice, in effect, was between ideological purity (Mr Duncan Smith) and a more popular, centrist candidate who was likely to be a more effective foil to Mr Blair (Mr Clarke). In the end, with a high turnout of 79 per cent, Mr Duncan Smith won an overwhelming victory, 155,933 to 100,864 (60.7 per cent to 39.2 per cent).

Mr Duncan Smith had the support of only a third of MPs. He had not won any of the three ballots of MPs. MPs had not been forced to make the choice between Mr Duncan Smith and Mr Clarke. And so Richard Kelly's first scenario unfolded. As the polls steadfastly refused to improve, as Mr Duncan Smith floundered and irritated many of those high up in the party, rumblings began. When attention was drawn away from Mr Blair's troubles by a minor issue over whether Mr Duncan Smith was illegitimately paying his wife a salary to which she was not entitled (a gleeful press dubbed it the 'Betsygate' scandal; Mr

'Cheer up, there'll be another
leadership contest soon'

Figure 7: The predictability of further crisis[28]

Duncan Smith was cleared of the charge), a vote of confidence
was called. Mr Duncan Smith, who had justified his disloyalty
to John Major as a matter of conscience, found himself assailed
by others doing the same thing; his appeals to loyalty unsurprisingly fell on deaf ears.

He was deposed having never been accepted by the people
he was supposed to lead; the introduction of democracy,
supposedly to increase the leader's legitimacy, actually worked
against it. The 156,000 votes of the party members were irrelevant; one problem with their overwhelming support was (one of
the premises of this book) that those party members were out of
step with the rest of society. There is a serious question in the
British party system as to whether a party leader is there to
represent the views of his or her members, or to win elections.
The two do not go – rarely have gone – hand in hand.

The American dimension revisited

The problems of the legitimacy of the leadership were doubly unfortunate for the Tories as they drew attention away from what were shaping up to be some interesting policy proposals. One disaster in particular was Mr Duncan Smith's final party conference as leader, when speculation about his position completely swamped his attempt to relaunch himself.[29]

Mr Duncan Smith unfortunately continued Mr Hague's interest in American, particularly Republican, politics (indeed, the Tory conference of 2002 was deliberately designed on American lines, with black, Asian and young people ushered on stage at various times, though Party Chairman Theresa May's kitten heels rather stole the show[30]).

The Iraq War complicated matters, but senior Tories were happy to go along with the pro-Americanism. It was a sensible stance, as not only was George Bush in the ascendant in both American and world politics, but also it was thought that British politics was beginning to look like that of America. Oliver Letwin argued as much on the ground that British political argument was about the role of the state, and how much power should be devolved from the state to lower levels of government.[31] A collection of essays, brought out under Mr Duncan Smith's *imprimatur* in 2002, was pointedly called *There Is Such a Thing as Society*, and made the connection with compassionate conservatism explicit in its subtitle.[32] Mr Duncan Smith's own contribution to the volume makes no mention of his admiration for America,[33] but leading American conservative and family-values campaigner Senator Rick Santorum was given a prominent platform in the book.[34]

The volume, interesting in many ways, ultimately fails to give a distinctly British conservative position by failing to distance itself from religio-political Americanism. To begin with, editor Gary Streeter is a prominent member of the Conservative Christian Fellowship – nothing wrong with that, of course, but it is an example of the slightly weird type of organisation that most Britons find a bit of a turn-off, and which inhibit a

Rawlsian turn in conservatism. And implicitly Mr Streeter seems to accept that, in that the book contains no mention of his involvement with CCF in either of his two mini-biographies.

Mr Streeter's hope that 'the essays represent a tremendous contribution to the renewal of the Conservative vision and its relevance to people of every background, colour and creed'[35] is a very wise hope, but undermined by the vibes the book gives out. Each chapter contains a brief biography of its author or authors, written to emphasise their ordinariness and ability to empathise with the ordinary voter – but the result is rather to emphasise how similar they all are.

For example, of the 26 authors, seven give no details of their immediate family. Of the others, eighteen are married; one has children but gives no details of marital status. Of the nineteen that mention their family, only three do not claim to have children. The mythical suburban ideal of 2.4 children seems horribly close. Only one author admits to a mere one child. But eight have two children, and a further four have three. Two have four children, including the fecund Mr Duncan Smith (whose happy family life famously led to Lord Tebbit's approving reference to his 'normality', in presumed contrast to Michael Portillo, who has admitted to having had gay experiences[36]). Pro-life campaigner and alpha male Senator Santorum leads the pack with seven.

Of course, it is easy to make mock. But the whole point about British conservative aversion to the American brand of compassionate conservatism is that it is designed, as we argued above, for a different society. America is a more religious and right wing place than Britain, and Mr Duncan Smith was as guilty of forgetting that as Mr Hague.

Tackling poverty

Mr Duncan Smith did introduce one important ideological wrinkle. He had a genuine concern for addressing the needs of those in poverty. British politics is awash with arguments about the terrible problems, of poverty, anti-social behaviour, breakdowns of social support networks, drugs, poor education and bad attitudes, in some deprived enclaves. Many lay the blame at the door of either 60s liberalism or Thatcherite market reforms; many are happy to trot out pre-digested ideologically pure solutions of either left or right. Few politicians are prepared to think seriously about how to begin to claw our way out of the hole, and most of those tend to be politicians of the mild left, such as Frank Field. Tories rarely worry much about poverty, an interesting paper by Malcolm Gooderham, one of Michael Portillo's spin doctors who was once accused of briefing the *Mirror* against William Hague,[37] being a recent exception.[38]

Mr Duncan Smith's concern was signalled with a visit to the Easterhouse estate in Glasgow in 2002;[39] the experience, and one assumes the favourable publicity, was clearly the inspiration for the *Society* volume, in which Mr Duncan Smith and his collaborators make, even if only implicitly, two important points. First of all, there is a clear need – from the conservative perspective – for the Tories to concern themselves with poverty. It is an expected function of government in Britain. Tory ideology of late has concentrated on improving the lot of the middle classes. There are good reasons for this: they are numerically preponderant in the electorate, and money injected into an economy is better injected into more productive sectors. But there was always unease about people perceived to have been left behind. Certain communities were disembowelled by the shift from manufacturing to services in the British economy; mining towns suffered massively from the wiping out of that industry. With the fading of memories of the bad old union-dominated days of the 60s and 70s, public attention has focused on ordinary people left behind, ill-equipped educationally and financially to weather the storms of unemployment.

Secondly, government is not capable of addressing the problems of poverty with any assurance.

> If Conservatives are to build on our past, we must also learn from Labour's current mistakes. Labour's most serious error is its failure to understand how society works. They

got into power by characterising the Conservative Party as only about individualism and materialism. They were wrong and that has meant that they have gone back to centralisation, as a false alternative. This is a Government that believes that it can only deliver through structures that are imposed on people, not composed of them.[40]

Huge, centralised bureaucracies are unable to handle the complexity of life and information in society. They lack the subtlety to respond to the infinitely varied needs of patients and pupils. They increasingly undermine the independence and judgement of highly qualified professionals.[41]

This of course is a serious conservative point. On the other hand, there is a tradition of governmental action to address poverty; no conservative can afford to neglect that tradition. If independent and charitable organisations do not exist in large enough numbers, the compassionate conservative argument risks being too similar to neo-liberalism. The neo-liberal says: to relieve poverty, money is required; so we should promote the economy, support wealth-creators, and not prevent the natural circulation of money. But if the compassionate conservative is perceived to be saying that governments should withdraw from social security and merely facilitate the work of non-existent support networks it looks like he or she is saying: let the rich get rich, and hope they sling some dosh at the poor.

It is essential for conservatives to address the problems of poverty. The whole conservative argument depends crucially on defending the status quo on the ground of the riskiness of innovation. But that move depends even more crucially on the status quo being acceptable; in a crummy environment, the conservative argument collapses.

The lost leaders: Clarke, Portillo, Widdecombe

The performance of the Tory Party in opposition to Mr Blair has been, on any measure, woeful. There is little argument that the two leaders discussed in this chapter, William Hague and Iain Duncan Smith, were anything other than disastrous. There are no doubt many reasons for this. One explanation, often advanced in all seriousness, is that the two men are bald. So obsessed with trivia is today's political world that that may be true; if so it is a shame to think that neither Winston Churchill nor Clement Attlee would flourish nowadays.

There are better explanations to be put in terms of poor leadership, poor tactical sense, lack of charisma (in the case of Mr Duncan Smith), lack of seriousness (in the case of Mr Hague), and so on. These personal qualities, though less important than in, say, America, where the presidential system puts a lot of emphasis on the character (assumed, of course, rather than real) of the candidates, no doubt had their effect, both on their images, and on their effectiveness as leaders.

In this book, we are not concerned with counterfactual history, as to whether any of the likely alternatives could have beaten Mr Blair, or, more realistically, dented his majority. Our concern is with ideology, specifically the conservative ideology. Neither Mr Hague nor Mr Duncan Smith met our definition. For the conservative, the interesting question – easier to answer – is not whether the alternatives would have won, but rather what they would have achieved if they had.

In this section, we will ask that question about three of the 'lost leaders' of the party, Kenneth Clarke, Michael Portillo and Ann Widdecombe. Each of them had influential supporters, each had influential enemies; there have been arguments about how acceptable to the public they would have been. Our question is much more straightforward – could they have espoused the sceptical conservatism we have developed in the course of this book?

Kenneth Clarke, successful Chancellor, stood for the party leadership on two occasions, being runner up each time. He certainly would have stood in 1995 had Mr Major been beaten by John Redwood in the first ballot, and seriously considered standing in 2003. Famously bluff, with his jazz and his Hush Puppies, indifferent to spin, style or fashion, blokey and cheerful,

Mr Clarke is not at all the sort of politician who tends to flourish nowadays. Which, in an age of mistrust of politicians, is no bad thing. Yet Mr Clarke is an intensely political animal, and would certainly have relished discomfiting Mr Blair at the despatch box.

His stewardship of the economy was almost exemplary. In fact, the major difference between his economic policy and that of his successor Gordon Brown is that Mr Brown handed control of monetary policy over to the Bank of England, a tactical masterstroke in the first days of Labour government, and arguably the logical corollary of Mr Clarke's own ideas. His chancellorship was along reasonably conservative lines, unideological and designed to allow the financial world to operate as smoothly as possible, and, as it was, Mr Brown has been able to enjoy the results of Mr Clarke's careful driving.

Yet Mr Clarke is not a conservative under the meaning of the act. There are two important indicators of that. First, he is an ardent europhile. His ambition to take Britain into the euro is deeply unconservative. This is not to say that the Tories could not be led by a europhile, though this may be true. Nor is it to say that Mr Clarke is wrong to argue against obsessive euro-phobia.[42] The point is rather that Mr Clarke is committed to important and radical changes to Britain's political and financial constitution that are not justified by any problems with that constitution, in clear breach of the change principle.

Second, Mr Clarke's real position is as a representative of the business lobby. Perhaps the most notorious example of his commitment to business was his disappearance to Vietnam to sell cigarettes for British American Tobacco as the 2001 leader-ship contest was getting under way, even missing the Queen's Speech in the newly elected Parliament.[43] Business and con-servatism often go hand in hand. Both thrive on stability, predictability; this is why the Conservative Party has always been the natural home for businessmen. But business some-times demands major change, which is not welcomed by other interests. For instance, changes to liberalise labour laws may be unwelcome to ordinary workers, or other groups such as the religious lobby (for example with respect to Sunday trading) or health professionals (for example with respect to relaxation of health and safety restrictions). One major issue, highlighted already in this book, is the relaxation of alcohol regulation entirely as a result of pressure from the powerful drink industry. It is clear that the requirements of business often depart (sometimes justifiably, sometimes not) from those of society conceived in conservative fashion.

Michael Portillo will be remembered as the leader of the modernising tendency within the Tory Party, but it wasn't always thus. His first serious shot at the leadership came in 1995. Mr Portillo was the hawkish Employment Secretary, leader of the right and favourite to succeed Mr Major, though he botched his tactics and inadvertently allowed the leadership of the right to pass to the cerebral and ideologically stiff John Redwood. Circumstances prevented him from standing in 1997 as well, when he lost his seat in the general election that precipitated the leadership vacancy. But his candidature would not have been generally welcomed. The *Economist*, in a piece written when defeat was inevitable but Mr Portillo's not, derided him as an extremist Michael Foot figure who, perish the thought, might be chosen as leader against safer hands such as Mr Clarke's or Michael Heseltine's.[44]

By the time Mr Portillo reappeared in the Commons in November 1999, though, he was a completely different person, much more 'touchy-feely', much less aggressive and right wing. He found himself the unofficial moderniser-in-chief within the Tory Party, in charge of the long-term project to ape Mr Blair's sophisticated, metropolitan tolerance and lack of ideological baggage.

Modernising the Tory Party is certainly not unconservative; it does not breach the change principle because the Party is currently so dysfunctional. And his wish to understand the state of Britain today is an absolutely correct response for the Tories in their current state. From his right wing days he preserves his euroscepticism. And, for example with his forcing a U-turn on the Tories' support for the minimum wage, he is prepared to give the opposition the benefit of the doubt when the risks they have taken pay off.[45]

But the evidence is that Mr Portillo, like Mr Clarke, is not a conservative, even though he would find many points of agreement were he ever to read this book. He seems to be an outright libertarian in crucial respects.[46] This is not necessarily unconservative; in a liberal society, any conservative would have to respect liberal principles – as American conservatives do unapologetically. Mr Portillo recognises the importance of the shifts in view of many people in our society. But his impatience with those whose views are more traditional marks him out as an ideological liberal, not a conservative.

Ann Widdecombe gained early fame as a junior minister for prisons in Mr Major's government, as an unholy row exploded between Derek Lewis, Director General of the Prison Service, and her boss Home Secretary Michael Howard.[47] Famously she took Mr Lewis's side, and almost single-handedly scuppered Mr Howard's first run at the leadership in 1997. With her forthright views, expressed without notes, she became the darling of the party conference, and after a successful spell on the Commons Privilege Committee became Shadow Health Secretary and then Shadow Home Secretary in 1999.

Miss Widdecombe's combative, even shrill style and unconventional looks earned her a deal of unfair abuse, including the nickname 'Doris Karloff'.

> Something must be done to get rid of this ghastly woman. It would take a small swing to the Tories in some marginal seats and we would have Doris for PM. Anyone who is as embarrassed by her as I am would see what a calamity this would be. Why should we suppose that it is a virtue in some insufferable bossyboots if she has given 138 interviews in the space of three summer weeks? Should we not think it is a sure sign that she is deranged, a deformed personality?[48]

It is a moot point, I think, as to how much the heavy opposition to Miss Widdecombe in 2001 was based purely on sexism, how much was due to a pragmatic calculation that her battiness and oddness would make the Tories unelectable, and how much was down to her often principled slaughter of some Tory sacred cows (if that abbatoirial image will do for someone who opposes fox hunting). In the end Miss Widdecombe retired from front line politics, declined to serve under Mr Duncan Smith, dyed her hair blonde, and reinvented herself as a novelist and media personality.

She got a reputation for being *very* stern. She was quite prepared to make blood-curdling proposals for dealing with asylum seekers, and had very little tolerance for drug addicts. Her views on the penal system were extremely traditional; she was keen for a strong punitive element. But we shouldn't lose sight of how much more acceptable her views were for being traditional. Though she promoted retribution, she also supported rehabilitation, and improvements in conditions; unlike many retributivists, she followed through the reasoning. Hers was no populist position; it laid no undue or unbalanced emphasis on either carrot or stick.

An important aspect of Miss Widdecombe's ideology is her strong religious belief; she converted to Catholicism from High Anglicanism in disgust at the arrival of women priests. This conviction actually makes her look very conservative. But we do know that a philosophy which is based on the extra-human origin of the social order cannot be genuinely conservative in the sceptical mould, because that may require too much change to be made to society itself.[49] To stand in the way of social change is to interfere in as ideologically driven a way as it would be to engineer social change artificially.

Six wasted years?

Beyond a doubt.

The Hague/Duncan Smith years were not happy ones. After the landslide of 1997, it was inevitable that the Tories would spend some time in opposition. The mathematics of the electoral system are currently stacked against them. Low turnouts and a volatile electorate make surprises possible, but the Tories did have to be prepared for at least two terms in opposition, in the absence of Labour meltdown. In particular, they should have been looking for a leader who could craft a comeback over a period of time, a Moses (or Kinnock) figure who might never see the promised land of Downing Street.

However, they seemed incapable of learning the lessons of Labour's experiences. It took Labour eighteen years to craft a centre left position that respected the changes to the country that Mrs Thatcher had brought about, yet differentiated them from their opponents.

The Tories have floundered in much the same way as Labour did initially. Though Mr Hague began his leadership well, he panicked when the opinion polls refused to budge and his programme ended up as a populist mess, like Michael Foot's 'suicide note' manifesto of 1983. Mr Hague's botched democratisation of the party in turn doomed Mr Duncan Smith. His lack of leadership skills would have always been a handicap, but he might have got away with it with the help of low expectations. He might have been able to take the necessary longer view had he been elected in a system that conferred any legitimacy on him.

A traditional, sceptical conservatism might well have had some electoral appeal in the world of Mr Blair's constant meddling and Mr Brown's performance targets. As it is, Tory policy-making has tended to equivocate between 'back to the days of Thatcher' and 'let's copy Blair in elevating style over content'. Neither is an adequate response to Blairite hegemony. A vote for Mr Blair, whatever else it is, is a rejection of much that Mrs Thatcher stood for (it may be *nothing* but that), so old-style Thatcherism is not a way forward, and as for copying Mr Blair, if Mr Blair is what you want, why on Earth vote for an ersatz version of him?

It may seem impossible that there is any acceptable position for the Tories in between these two responses; that is how it seemed to the Labour Party in the mid-80s after socialism's decisive rejection. But traditional conservatism, properly understood, is one alternative response. That is not to suggest that if the Tories adopted it they would win in 2005 – or even 2009; only that it is a way forward, not a step back.

The Conservative Party will go into the 2005 election with a new leader, Michael Howard; our final task is to examine, on the basis of the small quantity of evidence available, how he is faring, and how conservative he looks as he tries to avoid being the fourth consecutive Tory leader to be swatted aside by Mr Blair.

CHAPTER TEN

SOMETHING OF THE NIGHT

Return of the undead

The vote of confidence against Iain Duncan Smith in 2003 could have precipitated a crisis. Recall Richard Kelly's worries quoted in Chapter Nine: the 2001 contest which Mr Duncan Smith won had been very damaging for the party. The process had taken over three months, and had exposed the Tory splits over a long and damaging period. Swiss newspaper *Le Temps* even congratulated the Conservative Party in 2001 for cheering everybody up by holding their own version of *Big Brother*.

Kelly assumed that the incumbent would be strengthened by this problem; he or she couldn't realistically be challenged because of the exposure of the party to a rudderless three months during a parliament. However, Mr Duncan Smith was regarded as such a liability that, after a conference dominated by rumours of coups, and the Betsygate kerfuffle, the bandwagon for a vote of confidence eventually started rolling under its own momentum (under the appallingly under-engineered leadership rules, a mere 25 letters of complaint to the Chairman of the 1922 Committee were sufficient to trigger a confidence motion), and within a few days Mr Duncan Smith was out. It was easily the most disastrous performance of a Tory leader for over a century; there is something to be said for Balfour, Austen Chamberlain, Neville Chamberlain and Eden – not much, but something – but really very little for Mr Duncan Smith.

Candidates, though, weren't circling with quite the vulturish relish of 1997 or 2001. Hot favourite was yesterday's man,

Michael Howard. The terrifying Home Secretary of the Major years with 'something of the night' about him (Ann Widdecombe's brilliant put-down, cleverly alluding to Mr Howard's Transylvanian ancestry and sleek vampirical appearance), who had suffered the humiliation of last place in the 1997 contest, had bombed during Mr Hague's period of office, and was dropped from the Shadow Cabinet in summer 1999 (incidentally another poor managerial decision of Mr Hague, who, at a time when the Tories were not overwhelmed with talent, chose to get rid of not only Mr Howard, but Peter Lilley, Norman Fowler and Gillian Shepherd at the same time, all of whom had infinitely more experience than Mr Hague). By the 2001 landslide, he had apparently left front bench politics.

But like the Prince of Darkness himself, Mr Howard rose again. He was named Shadow Chancellor by Mr Duncan Smith in September 2001, and was judged to have performed creditably against Gordon Brown. Mr Duncan Smith was initially criticised for bringing back dead wood, and unpopular dead wood at that, but by April 2002 the *Economist* was praising Mr Howard's performance – suggesting, ironically, that because Mr Howard was too old to become party leader, he was all the more effective![1] By early 2003, when Mr Duncan Smith was causing exasperation with another botched sacking of a Tory Party official, Mr Howard was being openly discussed as a potential leader in the event of a plot, even if only as a caretaker leader who would make inroads into Mr Blair's majority and keep the seat warm for Oliver Letwin.[2]

The opposition to Mr Howard seemed unwilling to move. Mr Letwin ruled himself out, ultimately convincingly enough for the commentators. Michael Portillo seemed to have lost all appetite for the fray, though Kenneth Clarke had a good think before deciding not to go for it. The only really serious candidate was David Davis, who had been the victim of another of Mr Duncan Smith's botched sackings, but who had little chance of winning. If just two candidates stood, then the party would have been spared the full horror of a series of votes between the MPs; at least there would be only a straight fight for the votes of the party members. But Michael Ancram let it be known that he would stand if Mr Davis stood, ensuring that, if there was a contest at all, that contest would be at least a three-way fight; Tim Yeo was also discussed. That was enough for Mr Davis, who withdrew.[3] To everyone's surprise, including their own, the Tories had actually despatched their leader bloodlessly and replaced him efficiently.[4] Was this a sign that six and a half years of crazy self-destruction were over?

Full circle to the magic circle

There was one final ironic twist to the saga of Mr Duncan Smith. The Tories had had leadership elections only since 1965. The previous method – we might call it a myth – had it that a leader 'emerged' from consultations with various party officials, MPs, Lords, Cabinet members, and so on. This system of grey men in suits deciding, by a mysterious and certainly undemocratic process, who the party leader should be looked decidedly anachronistic the final time the system was used, during the unedifying spectacle of the 1963 handover, when Harold Macmillan schemed pretty shamelessly against the favourite Rab Butler, in favour of first Lord Hailsham, and then Alec Douglas-Home. Two prominent Cabinet ministers, Iain Macleod and Enoch Powell, refused to serve under Home, so appalled were they. But the real damage was done by Macleod some time later, when, now editor of the *Spectator*, he published a famous article giving his version of the story,[5] which included the following famous passage.

> Home we [i.e. Macleod and Reginald Maudling, discussing potential leaders] never mentioned in any connection. Neither of us thought he was a contender, although for a brief moment his star seemed to have flared at Blackpool. It is some measure of the tightness of the magic circle on this occasion that neither the Chancellor of the Exchequer [Maudling] nor the Leader of the House of Commons [Macleod] had any inkling of what was happening.

The phrase 'magic circle' stuck, describing the undemocratic, even mildly sinister, fixing of the contest. It stood for the illegitimacy of the practice; Home's legitimacy as leader was compromised, and after the election defeat of 1964 his days were numbered. He lasted until the following summer.

To re-confer legitimacy, a system of electing leaders by MPs only was introduced, with Edward Heath winning the first election in 1965. But the increase in democracy seemed not to solve the problem of legitimacy entirely. There was a lot of tinkering with the system to make it possible to ambush lame duck leaders; Mr Heath in 1975 and Mrs Thatcher in 1990 lost out thanks to the changes. Mr Major's legitimacy as leader wasn't accepted even after he had seen off John Redwood in 1995.

The hoped-for solution to the leadership problem was direct party democracy. The MPs had proved themselves flawed judges, and widening the franchise was seen as a way of conferring legitimacy. Mr Duncan Smith, the first and only leader elected by the whole party, used his mandate from the party members to defend his leadership right up to the end.[6] But as we have seen, the wider electorate merely undermined Mr Duncan Smith's legitimacy, because that electorate was seen to be unrepresentative and out of touch. What he had thought was the source of his legitimacy actually drained it away (ironically, as he might well have won an election of MPs – in which case he would have had a better chance of surviving until the 2005 election).

How ironic, then, that Mr Howard was accepted unopposed as leader in 2003. Tory MPs, particularly Mr Howard's rivals, realised that the only way there could be a leader universally regarded as legitimate would be to *avoid* any democratic contest! The grass roots, who nominally should decide, had to watch the spectacle of the major players desperately, and without disguise, trying to prevent them from being able to make a choice. If ever there was a public display by a party leadership to the effect that the membership was the problem, not the solution, this was it.

Be that as it may, the situation prompts an obvious question. How to move forward? We have seen how rarely a leader genuinely 'emerges'. Mr Howard, who is of an age whereby he is unlikely to stand in 2009/10, will retire. He may retire from a position of strength, in which case he could probably groom a successor – Oliver Letwin perhaps favourite at the time of writing. But if he retires from a position of weakness, another bad election defeat, say, then the question is how the Tories can avoid a contest. Dare they ditch the rhetoric of party democracy? Can they change their party quickly enough?

Howard's way*

There is clearly a difficulty with the organisation of the Tory Party – it is very hard to undo democracy once it has been introduced, but the unrepresentativeness of the party members makes one worry for the future. One way around the issue would be for the leader to produce a strong declaration of the direction the party should go in. The circumstances of Mr Howard's elevation to the leadership, acclaimed by all, meant that he had an opportunity to strike early and do this. Sure enough, at New Year 2004, Mr Howard produced a list of core beliefs:

- I believe it is natural for men and women to want health, wealth and happiness for their families and themselves
- I believe it is the duty of every politician to serve the people by removing the obstacles in the way of these ambitions
- I believe people are most likely to be happy when they are masters of their own lives, when they are not nannied or over-governed
- I believe that the people should be big. That the state should be small
- I believe red tape, bureaucracy, regulations, inspectorates, commissions, quangos, 'tsars', 'units' and 'targets' came to help and protect us, but now we need protection from them. Armies of interferers don't contribute to human happiness

---

* Apologies for the obvious pun, which everybody uses. Mark my words, it'll be *Howard's End* next.

- I believe that people must have every opportunity to fulfil their potential
- I believe there is no freedom without responsibility. It is our duty to look after those who cannot help themselves
- I believe in equality of opportunity. Injustice makes us angry
- I believe every parent wants their child to have a better education than they had
- I believe every child wants security for their parents in their old age
- I do not believe that one person's poverty is caused by another's wealth
- I do not believe that one person's ignorance is caused by another's knowledge and education
- I do not believe that one person's sickness is made worse by another's health
- I believe the British people are only happy when they are free
- I believe that Britain should defend her freedom at any time, against all comers, however mighty
- I believe that by good fortune, hard work, natural talent and rich diversity, these islands are home to a great people with a noble past and exciting future. I am happy to be their servant.[7]

This credo attracted much favourable publicity; there was an implicit contrast with Mr Blair, who, one suspects, would find it hard to produce an analogous credo of his own which differed significantly enough from Mr Howard's. The general effect was benign, patriotic, free from the shrillness over immigration, asylum and crime that the Conservative Party so often indulges in, and which so disastrously distinguishes them from the rest of the community. Has Mr Howard succeeded, or even tried, to create a conservative credo appropriate for the 21st century?

Many of the beliefs are deliberately bland and inoffensive; they could be subscribed to by virtually everybody. Who does not believe that people want health, wealth and happiness for themselves? Whom does injustice not make angry?

On the other hand, the second belief, that the duty of the politician is to remove the obstacles in the way of these ambitions, gives a subtly conservative spin to the waffle. Removing obstacles to the pursuit of natural ambition implicitly suggests that a Howard government would not actually try to secure these ambitions for people itself. That certainly distances it from, say, a socialist government. It also distances it from those ideologies, such as ecologism, where the ideology in some sense defines what 'happiness' might mean for a citizen. New Labour, which combines Mr Blair's post-Thatcher thinking with Mr Brown's social conscience and financial prudence, might have some difficulty in deciding whether or not to go along with this belief; and having decided, further difficulty in keeping its activists on board.

Many of the beliefs are interesting in what they do *not* say: since surely no one in his right mind believes that one person's sickness is made worse by another's health, the question is what the clause tries to convey. The simple message, presumably, is that people should have the right to buy private health care. That is a straightforward Tory message, uncontroversial to small 'c' conservatives. A more challenging interpretation is that Mr Howard is prepared to accept fairly radical inequalities of health care; perhaps accepting that localism in provision of health care (via the NHS) will lead to radically different outcomes, and what newspapers complain about as a postcode lottery. People in Britain seem to want overall consistency in provision of public services, or at least get outraged when disparities are pointed out. But this predilection rules out the localist solutions that many, including conservatives, Conservatives and Blairites, want in the NHS; for after all what is the point of localism if local administrators cannot set local priorities (possibly after local debate and discussion), which may differ from those of other areas?

Other statements are rather less open to conservative interpretation. He believes in the small state. That is, as we saw in Chapter Nine, an American belief rather than a British one. There is nothing intrinsically conservative about shrinking the state,[8] though most conservatives would be happy to agree that many things the state does it does pretty badly. Even given that, however, shrinking the state is something that a conservative would do slowly and cautiously. Demanding that the state be small smacks rather more of neo-liberalism than conservatism (and demanding that people be big, at the very time that the nanny state is campaigning so hard against obesity, is very liberal indeed!).

There are also interesting omissions. Mr Howard has made much of his grammar school background and immigrant parentage, to distinguish himself from posh Mr Blair.[9] Yet he did not take this opportunity to stand against discrimination, or to welcome immigrants. As we saw in Chapter Seven, such a stand would be perfectly conservative, and is becoming a political benchmark in a progressive era.

The credo of Mr Howard, then, is a balancing act, anti-regulation (and therefore implicitly pro-business), with neo-liberal and conservative overtones. It will neither stand in the way of his running a genuinely conservative administration, were he to come to power, nor commit him to doing so.

Public spending and taxes

Mr Howard's credo, it turns out, has strongly American roots, as hostile commentators enjoyed pointing out.[10] American philanthropist John D. Rockefeller's statement of his beliefs, originally made in a radio broadcast on 8 July 1941 – young Master Howard was one day old – and immortalised in a stone plaque outside the Rockefeller Center in New York, is very similar to Mr Howard's. The Tories cheerfully admitted this; after all, it is hardly a unique occurrence in British politics to borrow from America. Mr Howard's borrowings are harmless enough; the statements commit him to very little. Furthermore, Mr Howard's links with George Bush's office have been badly shaken by Mr Bush's love for Mr Blair, which caused quite a spat in 2004.[11] Nevertheless, vestiges of Americanisation remain in Mr Howard's programme.

The chief symptom in the period since 2003 is the renewed discussion of tax cuts. This has always been a Tory theme, though not necessarily a conservative one. In particular, it chimes in with a new reading of the parallels between Britain and America, according to which Mr Bush's right wing success was based not on compassionate conservatism, but rather on his trillion-dollar tax cut. Hence, Shadow Chancellor Oliver Letwin has worried about how to keep up public services without increasing taxes, and has plumped for that old favourite, the reduction of waste (Mr Brown trumpeted the results of his own search for bureaucratic waste instantly, thereby undercutting Mr Letwin). Mr Letwin claimed he could cut £35 billion more than Mr Brown by 2012.

Readers of this book who have accepted the Pyrrhonist arguments about what it is or is not possible to know in a complex, dynamic, uncertain world will already have formed an opinion about Mr Letwin's prediction. It is this: Mr Letwin's prediction of £35 billion savings by 2012 is wrong. Or if it is correct, it is by luck rather than judgement. Financial forecasts of even a year ahead, never mind eight, are always horribly wrong. So why do we see such manoeuvring by Mr Letwin?

One obvious reason is to impress subtly upon voters that the Tories are the small government party. The Tories do indeed have a low tax brand that they are wise to exploit. But lower taxes than Labour, as we argued above, should not rule out tax increases, when circumstances make that imperative (outbreak of foot and mouth, anyone? Iraq War?). The electorate is clearly uncertain that its tax pound is being well spent, but the backlash against the perception of the Thatcher years as 'tax cuts for the rich and selfish, poor public services for the poor and needy' has yet to wear itself out.

Tax politics is looking very dangerous in Britain. A legacy of the Thatcher period is that politicians are wary, probably rightly, of assuming that just because people tell pollsters that they are prepared to pay more taxes they will vote for tax-raising politicians, be the taxes ever so well costed and hypothecated. The legacy of the Blair period is that politicians are wary of saying that they will cut spending, since public services are a priority. The result is that politicians say very little on tax.

The small 'c' conservative way is surely to accept that taxes should follow spending, in general, and that spending should be as effective as possible, but that predicting levels of spending – and hence tax levels – is impossible, and indeed irresponsible. Gordon Brown talks of the 'golden rule', that the government will borrow only to invest and not to fund current spending – over the whole economic cycle. This is not only prudent, but also has the virtue of being made up of fairly elastic concepts, and hence variable in accordance with circumstances (a shorter, less kind word for this is 'meaningless'). Ironically, this is a very conservative strategy of Mr Brown's.

The Tories are being squeezed by Labour rhetoric, and by the sense that Labour are vulnerable on the issue of public services. They are being tempted to offer better services, while equally driven by their history and instincts to criticise Labour tax rises (and occasionally emboldened to talk of low taxes). It is, no doubt, possible sometimes to achieve both. But anyway voters do not believe it. If the Tories thought that the time was right for a serious debate over rates of taxes and spending, then they should offer themselves as a tax cutting party at an election; the election could be fought on the services *versus* tax cuts issue. They do not wish to do this, because their calculation, probably correctly, is that services would win. That is nothing to be ashamed of; it is the job of a conservative to assess and respect the public mood. But it puts the Tories in an awkward position; their tax-lowering rhetoric sounds hollow. In such a circumstance, a sceptical realistic conservative position, incorporating fewer value judgements about the different types of spending in the economy, surely can't do additional harm.

Inclusion

As noted, Mr Howard is well placed to comment on the notion of inclusion, being the child of immigrants. Admittedly, one has to squint with eyes half-closed and be quite sympathetic to be able to look at his previous record in this respect as Home Secretary. But his speech in Burnley about the racist British

National Party has played well, as have his visits to various areas with large immigrant populations,[12] and his unscripted addendum to his first conference speech as leader, in which he discussed his background as a son of Jewish immigrants who would not have survived the war were it not for Britain and Winston Churchill, was a great success too.[13]

As has often been pointed out, many in Britain's immigrant communities are sceptical about, or even downright hostile to, the metropolitan liberalism that underlies the policies of Mr Blair. Furthermore many in the Muslim community in particular oppose the Iraq War, or perhaps more viscerally, oppose Mr Blair's unconditional support for Mr Bush. Yet the votes of such people are going to the Liberal Democrats, not the Tories, no doubt partly because of the Tories' support for the war, but also because the Tories as a whole show little interest in the views of minority communities.

The temptation, sadly, is for the Tories to harvest the easy votes in anti-immigration and bashing asylum seekers. Such votes are trivial to pick up, since the Liberal Democrats refuse to speak to such constituencies, and those Labour politicians who dare to be illiberal, like Home Secretary David Blunkett, are hamstrung by those who do not. Ironically, it is the party of the free market, the Tories, which stands most steadfastly against a free market in labour.

Mr Howard made a splendid beginning, when a move by Mr Blunkett to put pressure on asylum seekers to leave Britain 'voluntarily' by threatening measures to take their children into care – Mr Blunkett was obviously temporarily confused about the meaning of the word 'voluntarily' – led him to complain that Labour had gone further than any civilised government should go. He was clear about the extent of his sympathy for asylum seekers, but at least his two clear principles on the topic made a lot of sense.

> Asylum policy should be based on two clear principles. First, Britain has a proud tradition of providing a safe haven for those fleeing persecution. It should continue to do so.

> But second, once a set of rules has been agreed to distinguish between such people and those without a genuine claim, then these rules should be enforced.[14]

This leaves it open as to how sympathetic one should be about such claims, and about issues such as legal aid and so on – issues ironically raised by disgraced former Tory MP Keith Best in his new, more public-spirited role as Chief Executive of the Immigration Advisory Service[15] – but has the merit of clarity.

All well and good. But Messrs Hague and Duncan Smith also began their leaderships with important messages about inclusion. Mr Hague got in a pickle over race; he ended up routinely bashing asylum seekers, and failing to slap down racist comments. Mr Duncan Smith's problem was with gays, imposing a controversial three line whip to vote against an unimportant bill to allow gay couples to adopt children (it has been suggested, unfortunately, that Mr Howard was one of the advisors who persuaded Mr Duncan Smith to make that unwise move[16]) even in the wake of a successful conference in which the Tories had made a (headline-grabbing) attempt to confront past intolerance. Then maybe we should be worried about Shadow Home Secretary David Davis's speech to the 2004 conference, which made an almost Powellite argument that uncontrolled immigration is posing a threat to the nation's values.[17] Quite apart from the facts that immigration is hardly uncontrolled, and that the nation's 'values' are highly contested and arguable, the juxtaposition of Mr Davis's speech and Mr Howard's sends an undoubtedly mixed message.

Lots of small positive mutually reinforcing messages are required, not grandstanding. The problem with being in opposition is that it is tempting to attack the government when it is vulnerable, especially to its own supporters (many of Labour's supporters are nowhere near as liberal as their representatives). But where the opposition opposes, there are arguments, and press coverage; to make the Tories' image as the party of exclusion go away, they need to oppose very carefully indeed. They certainly do not want to drive Labour rightwards.

There is nothing specifically conservative about being opposed to or wary of immigration, asylum, or homosexuality. There are perfectly sensible conservative policies on all three topics that would make the party sound like they had rejoined the rest of Britain in the 21st century.

But would that mean the Tories had stopped opposing?

The function of opposition

Mr Howard became known originally as an implacably determined, fiercely partisan politician. His decisions as Home Secretary seemed designed to appeal to his party, to put distance between his team and the opposition, to force attacks upon him. He seemed to relish living in the eye of publicity, and refusal to compromise, back down or apologise. One of his many enemies, former Director General of the Prison Service Derek Lewis, characterised him thus:

> Like many of his colleagues, Michael Howard has no experience of working with or leading people in large organizations. Time and time again this showed through – in his unwillingness to invest time in getting staff on his side, in the rarity of his visits to prisons and in his apparent belief that fear is the principal tool of motivation.
>
> He is driven by political ambition, for which he has developed the instincts of a jungle fighter. That ambition and a lack of long-term vision means that his decision-making and policy formulation are driven hither and thither by the breezes of media opinion and public mood. He is preoccupied with tactics to the exclusion of strategy, and at times appears to be cutting his suit to fit the political cloth just a little too finely.[18]

However, such confrontational macho conviction politics do not harmonise with the Clintonian/Blairite inclusive big tent *Zeitgeist*. And Mr Howard was careful to ensure that, as his political ambitions revived, a new caring and sharing side of him, hitherto unsuspected, emerged blinking in the sunrise.

I've been in parliament for 20 years now. I think I've learned a bit in that time.

I've learned that if we want to persuade people, we need to preach a bit less and listen a bit more.

I've learned that just winning an argument doesn't on its own win hearts and minds.

I've learned that politicians won't be respected by the public unless they respect each other and that people won't trust us unless we trust them.[19]

So far so good – all consistent with Mr Blair's discoveries that helped turn New Labour into the formidable election-winning machine that it still is. And Mr Howard still shows signs of having learned that lesson, notably in his closing speech to the 2004 conference, which was devoid of party political attacks.[20]

But Mr Howard does love attacking Mr Blair. He stuck to the cynical opposition to allowing universities to charge tuition fees at variable rates, preferring a bribe to the middle class to a quintessentially Tory policy. He attacked the government over the prospect of hundreds of thousands of migrant workers from Eastern Europe coming into the UK as a result of the expansion of the EU in May 2004, despite EU expansion being a long-term Tory policy, despite the supposed commitment of the Tories to free up European markets, and despite having made sensitive speeches on inclusion. His attempts to distance the Tories from the Iraq War that they originally supported seem to have been almost totally without success; the lack of headline Tory presence on the Butler committee investigating intelligence failures before that war meant that Butler, when he reported, restricted his criticism of Mr Blair to a fairly mild ticking off,[21] while Mr Howard's argument that he supported the war but would have voted against it in the Commons had he known then what he knew now was demolished comprehensively by Mr Blair in a disastrous Commons debate.[22] All of which implies that Mr Howard may have grasped intellectually the importance of differing 'with measured thought and reflection',[23] but isn't quite able to put it into practice.[24] He can talk the talk, but is having some difficulty walking the walk.

If Mr Howard was sitting on top of a motivated group of workers and voters, ready and willing to replace Labour in government, and numerically significant enough to stand a chance of doing so, then his tactics of attack would give them great cheer. The rough and tumble of politics is very exhilarating. Mr Howard is not in such a position; he needs to woo voters who have been voting regularly and for a long time for Mr Blair; given such a requirement, is attack really the way forward?

Howard's end?* Tactics and strategy

It may well be, then, that Derek Lewis's diagnosis of the problem with Mr Howard's work is correct. Mr Howard as a master tactician can sometimes put pressure on Mr Blair; unfortunately, the total strategic thrust is often difficult to discern because Mr Howard sometimes attacks from the left, sometimes from the right. Some of Mr Howard's measures look like special pleading for particular lobbies; for example the Tory attacks on speed cameras look like an extraordinary plea for the interests of lawbreakers.[25] Even if we grant the motoring lobby's contention that speed cameras are revenue-generating rather than accident-preventing (a contention that seems to be false, in that they raised a mere £73 million in 2003[26] while dramatically cutting numbers of deaths[27]), it still follows that the people who are fined are breaking the law, and fined because they are breaking the law. It is a basic principle of conservatism that the law should be obeyed. Certainly the stance fits extremely badly with initiatives – that have both a conservative and a Tory ring to them – to improve discipline in schools and tackle low-level crime by restoring respect.[28]

It is the contention of this book that the Tories have to understand that Mr Blair has moved the centre point of British politics leftward. Whereas throughout the 80s, Labour looked

* Told you.

hopelessly out of touch, it is now the Tories who are struggling to cope in a country which is leaning away from them. For the moment, the Tories are fighting on Labour ground.[29]

Many senior Tories accept this, and are willing to meet the challenge. Malcolm Rifkind, for example, spots weaknesses in Mr Blair's approach. One symptom of this is the collapse of the Labour Party's membership since it took power in 1997; the Labour Party is much less impressed by electoral success than the Tories. Consequently, few, perhaps most notably Polly Toynbee,[30] have given Mr Blair credit for the left wing policies he *has* introduced. This disconnection between the Labour Party and its supporters suggests taking the battle in that direction, says Mr Rifkind. He sees opportunity in a mild euroscepticism, and in a sympathetic view of the NHS which is seeing improvements under Labour, but at a possibly disproportionate cost. Perhaps most interestingly, he sees an opportunity to take Labour territory over civil liberties, where two reactionary Home Secretaries, Jack Straw and David Blunkett, have trampled for many years, and where the war on terror is providing ever more excuses for locking people up and throwing away the key.[31]

However, what has happened since 1997 is that panic and impatience – the friends of the tactician and the enemies of the strategist – have derailed any attempt to move the Tories back to the centre. Even as the centre shifts leftward, the Tories have tended to become mired in obsession with what Andrew Rawnsley has called the Tebbit trinity of Europe, immigration and tax.[32]

Mr Howard, despite a number of hits and some sympathetic press coverage, hasn't managed to shift this perception. A YouGov poll in 2004 asked voters to rate themselves on a left–right axis, and then to rate a number of politicians on the same scale. As this book has argued, the average British voter places him- or herself a little to the left of centre; almost exactly where Tony Blair is placed. He is further to the right than either his party or his likely successor Gordon Brown. But the worrying thing for the Tories is that they are perceived as being easily the most extreme of the three major parties.[33]

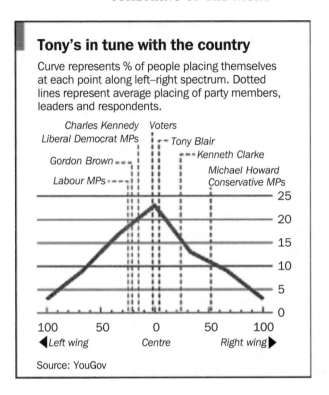

Figure 8: Voters' perceptions of themselves, the parties and the party leaders

This is a worrying position to be in, because there are pressures taking the Tories still further to the right. For example, let us consider the threat of the United Kingdom Independence Party. UKIP scored some important successes during 2004. They managed to secure celebrity backing, had a very successful election to the European Parliament in June 2004,[34] and managed to upstage the Tories' annual conference by beating them into fourth place in a by-election.[35] The claim is often made that the Tories must move rightward in order to ensure that they don't lose further votes to UKIP;[36] even commentators who deny the need to move right worry about the Tories losing votes in that direction.[37]

UKIP is indeed a threat to the Tories, but not in the way that it is generally thought. It is true that, as the Tories move towards a more moderate position on Europe, a space will open up for the obsessive brigade, so UKIP, in the short term, may well take votes away. Actually, that is not too harmful. It will do the Tories a lot of good in the longer term to have been seen to resist the temptation to placate UKIP voters. There is no chance that UKIP will be any kind of long-term threat, as it is a disorganised rabble; within a very short time of its greatest successes, it began to fall apart as the ludicrous, oddly coloured Robert Kilroy-Silk indulged in the fringe party pastime of attacking his own colleagues, before flouncing off.[38] Even its most famous member, Joan Collins, may not vote for it.[39]

So UKIP isn't going to cause any long-term problems for the Tories, who can therefore adopt a strategy of demonstrating their maturity and winning back voters over time. It is not as easy as that, however; in the short term, UKIP *will* pose problems. They may well take votes from the Tories in 2005, and many Tory MPs with slim majorities will be much more concerned about the tactical problem of maximising their vote now, than with thinking of putting the Tories back in power in five or ten years' time.

Mr Howard has so far shown much more tactical nous than strategic insight. From that point of view, UKIP are a threat. But the Tories have only been out of power for seven years; compare that with the eighteen years that Labour sat in opposition. Rebuilding the image of a self-destructive party takes a long time, and careful attention to detail. UKIP's threat is not that it will take Tory votes (though it probably will); rather its threat is that it will focus attention on 2005, and away from the more crucial election of 2009.

Michael Howard as a conservative: the balance sheet

As leader of a giant party which pursues many different sets of interests, Mr Howard has had to balance several types of policy input. This is inevitable; the skill of a great leader of a big political party is in doing that while also producing an overall sense of policy cohesion. This latter, we have argued, is where Mr Howard falls down.

There are many conservative elements in Mr Howard's thought, however. His early speeches on asylum and immigration were clever and interesting, though uncompromising. Other impressive speeches have followed, notably a speech given to the right wing think tank the Policy Exchange,[40] and one on a European theme to the Konrad Adenauer Stiftung, Berlin.[41]

The former muses on the pace of change in Britain, and the failure of government to match the pace. He sensibly contrasts the relatively straightforward imperatives of 1979, when Britain was a basket case, with the trickier tasks for arguably less powerful politicians in the 21st century. The speech contains conservative themes of the difficulties of change and improvement, alongside acceptance of the free market. And in a notable passage, he combines conservatism with social tolerance to very happy effect.

> Very few people want to lead a solitary life – to be alone. We come together in different groups of various kinds. Most of what we do every day is done together – with friends, with colleagues, at work, in our free time, as part of communities of every kind.
>
> The family remains the most immediate and important group within which people share responsibility for one another's well-being. But families are changing. Not all conform to the traditional pattern. I continue to believe that the conventional marriage and family is the best environment within which to bring up children. But many couples now choose not to marry. And more and more same sex couples want to take on the shared responsibilities of a committed relationship.
>
> It is in all our interests to encourage the voluntary acceptance of such shared responsibilities – but in some instances the State activity actively discourages it. That

should change, and I will support the Government's Civil Partnerships Bill that makes some important reforms.

But it is important to be clear about this. Civil partnership differs from marriage. Marriage is a separate and special relationship which we should continue to celebrate and sustain. To recognise civil partnerships is not, in any way, to denigrate or downgrade marriage. It is to recognise and respect the fact that many people want to live their lives in different ways. And it is not the job of the State to put barriers in their way.[42]

A perfectly reasonable statement. Ann Widdecombe is right to suggest that endless hand-wringing about the correct attitude of the Conservative Party to, say, gays, is counterproductive. But the trick is to work out a general attitude – surely including toleration – that enables the topic to be put to rest. It is no doubt salutary to be told, as the Tories were in summer 2002 by Tory front bencher and grandson of Churchill Nicholas Soames, that the party would be doomed unless it ended its 'mad obsession with gays, blacks and women'. But equally, anyone with their eye on the ball would note that those groups combined constitute 60 per cent of the population.

So there is plenty of conservative meat in Mr Howard's speeches. There is a good basis for building a conservative strategy, a disciplined, consistent body of policy work over two, three or even four parliaments in opposition, that the Tories have conspicuously lacked since 1997. Mr Howard is not a natural conservative. But he grasps, at least sometimes, that the raw economic liberalism that was so necessary in the 1980s, and the social illiberalism that fired up the Tory membership at the same time, are each *passé* in the post-Blair world. When his opportunistic streak does not get the better of him, there are many thoughtful and interesting interventions. But the point of view of strategy is long-term; Mr Howard, in his 60s, seems sadly to be all too often a man in a hurry.

POSTSCRIPT

True modesty can be nothing but a meditation on vanity.
It springs from the sight of others' mistakes, and the dread
of being similarly deceived.

Henri Bergson, *Laughter*

Sceptical conservatism: conservatism for the 21st century

The aim of this book is twofold: to understand conservatism, and to develop a specifically British conservatism for the 21st-century context. Conservatism may be a dislike of change, or an inordinate love for the status quo, or an attachment to a particular way of life or stage in society. All of these share an important handicap in ideological terms: they are hard if not impossible to convey to others. In a democracy, where political ideas spread by persuasion, the handicap is fatal.

In this book I have attempted to pare conservatism down to its essentials. Take away the adherence to particular ways of life; what is left is an attitude towards *change* and *knowledge*. I called this development of conservatism a *Rawlsian* turn, in homage to the American political philosopher who performed a similar operation on liberalism, thereby reinventing that ideology for the late 20th century. By focusing on conservatism's essentials, we move away from special preferences and provide *public* reasons. The conservative is neutral between competing conceptions of the good, and therefore can reach out to those of

329

different cultures, or non-standard lifestyles, who happen to find themselves in 21st-century Britain. The provision of such public reasoning inevitably increases inclusion, and therefore makes conservatism more attractive, and more legitimate democratically. For a conservative to make new friends, he or she has to make *fewer* assumptions about what constitutes a morally good or useful life.

Historically, that may be worrying for the conservative; conservatism traditionally rests on the privileging of certain lifestyles. But, upon examination, the essentials of conservatism turn out to be quite compatible with the Rawlsian turn of focusing on publicly justifiable reasons. The *change* principle says that a tolerable society relies on a delicate balance of forces, institutions and patterns of behaviour, and that changing any of those risks unbalancing the whole; the conservative should therefore be suspicious of change, careful and risk-averse. The *knowledge* principle says that engineering change, however desirable, will be virtually impossible. Society is so complex that the knowledge required to keep risks acceptably low will typically be unavailable to the social engineer. Indeed changing traditions or institutions actually destroys that very knowledge.

This abstract, yet highly applicable, conservatism can be traced from its roots in Ancient Greek scepticism, via Montaigne to Renaissance Europe, and thence, in different ways, to Hume and Burke. In the Conservative Party it was developed in different ways by some very different politicians, Disraeli, Salisbury and Balfour among them. The conservative tradition is an authentically Tory tradition, though it has been muted for a while. Should it, indeed can it, be revived?

Conservatism, change and the Tories

The issue of the 21st century is dislocation, powerlessness. Politicians and journalists are held in contempt because they seem unable to meet the (often excessive) expectations of their readers or voters. High standards of living do not seem to have been appreciated by those who are living them.[1] 'The rhetoric of democracy and consultation seems to make people of the 'me' generation unable to accept the loss of an argument. Every accidental setback is followed by an attempt to apportion blame, and the assumption that someone is to blame for any eventuality leads naturally to requests for compensation. Simple narratives get passed around; newspapers indulge in the most mawkish sentimentality, the most toe-curling eulogies to heroes or the dead, ludicrous cartoon patriotism.

The complexity of the world, its myriad interconnections, magnified by new technologies, cannot be rendered in black and white terms. A former President of the United States, Ronald Reagan, built a career on reducing complexities to binaries; in the cold war world which he played a vital part in ending, with the two superpowers glaring at each other and fighting proxy wars all over the place, that was a defensible strategy. That was a world that could be portrayed as the good guys against the bad guys, the men in black hats against those in white. Whether such a portrayal was accurate, of course, is a different matter; the collapse of Yugoslavia, the evils of General Pinochet and other right wing dictators and paramilitaries in Central and South America, the grim racial creed of Apartheid all suggest there was much more below the surface than Mr Reagan's sketch suggested.

If the world collapses into a clash of civilisations, of liberal Western democracies against the Chinese, or against the Muslim world, as Samuel Huntington has predicted,[2] it may be that such simplicities might be appropriate once more. But straightforward narratives can never capture the essentials of the world of globalisation, of differing trade blocs, of a single hyperpower, of a newly resurgent developing world, of a radicalised Islam, of unprecedented migrations of peoples, and of technologies simultaneously destabilising and empowering. This is a deeply complex, unpredictable world, where the effects of an action ripple effortlessly across borders.

In this world, security is a vital issue. Few enjoy risk, *pace* Hayek; most prefer defence of what they have. Where security is at a premium and complexity a constant background, conservatism, an ideology that refuses to accept simplistic assumptions about the world and society, an ideology that – in its very name – evokes the conservation of what is in hand, must surely be a viable option.

In Britain, there has not been a conservative party for some 30 years. Improvement and modernisation has been the name of the game. Indeed, few would deny that many improvements have actually occurred since the mid-70s. Yet dissatisfaction with one's lot is common through all levels of society. Intended 'improvements' seem to have had various knock-on unintended effects that have left people feeling worse off, or left behind.

The Conservative Party is widely thought to be dying, just as the Labour Party was some fifteen years ago. Maybe it is; maybe no one will ever vote for it again. There is increasing talk of a relaunch. Michael Howard has already sold off the party's old headquarters in Smith Square and moved to new offices in an attempt to give a sense of renewal.[3] Some advocate changing the name of the party, to the 'New Democrats', the 'Progressives' or 'Liberty', or changing its trademark colour from blue.[4]

That, I suppose, is a matter for the marketing men. It is, one suspects, unlikely that the same group of people turning up under a new name will have much more than a temporary effect on its fortunes, any more than changing the name of Windscale to Sellafield affected its safety record.

More important, one would think, is a change of ideology. The Conservative Party has been the traditional custodian for conservatism, and conservatism can be relevant today. The policies outlined in accordance with conservative principles in Part Two of this book will appeal to many of those who have been voting New Labour. Adoption of such an ideology would help the Conservatives back to the centre of British politics, while simultaneously differentiating them from the incessantly meddling Mr Blair.

Surely there is a place in this world in flux for a principled, sceptical conservatism, to manage the process of change and render it palatable; to allow social change to evolve with the social and global context, rather than anticipating, or worse, trying to steer, events; not to stand in the way of progress (whether one personally sees progress as good or bad); to enable people to defend the ways of life they enjoy – and to escape ways of life that are intolerable.

Such a conservatism actually crosses parties, though the tradition is much more prominent in the Conservative Party. There is currently in British politics no unambiguous spokesperson for that tradition.

Time for a change?

NOTES

1 Message in a bottle from the Slough of Despond

1 'Getting it Wrong', *Economist*, 16 June 2001.

2 John Gray, 'The Tory Endgame', in *Endgames: Questions in Late Modern Political Thought* (Polity Press, Cambridge, 1997), pp. 97–155, at pp. 124–7.

3 'Howard's Burden', *Economist*, 8 January 2004.

4 Figures taken from MORI polls, based on voting intentions of all adults naming a party, except where actual general election results (in bold) are cited.

5 Will Hutton, *The State We're In* (Vintage, London, 1996); Anthony Giddens, *The Third Way: The Renewal of Social Democracy* (Polity Press, Cambridge, 1998); Charles Leadbeater, *Living on Thin Air: The New Economy* (Viking, London, 1999); Giles Radice (ed.), *What Needs to Change* (HarperCollins, London, 1996); Ian Hargreaves and Ian Christie (eds), *Tomorrow's Politics: The Third Way and Beyond* (Demos, London, 1998). For Mulgan's work, see the output of the think tank Demos, *passim*, at http://www.demos.co.uk/catalogue/directory.aspx.

6 Enoch Powell, *Freedom and Reality* (Elliot Right Way Books, Kingswood, 1969), pp. 136–67; Simon Heffer, *Like the Roman: The Life of Enoch Powell* (Weidenfeld and Nicolson, London, 1998), pp. 225–41; E.H.H. Green, 'The Treasury Resignations of 1958: A Reconsideration', in *Ideologies of Conservatism* (Oxford University Press, Oxford, 2002), pp. 192–213.

7 Nigel Lawson, *The View from No. 11: Memoirs of a Tory Radical* (Bantam Press, London, 1992), pp. 63–5, 197–240.

8 Enoch Powell even finds himself apologising for Disraeli's government's nationalisation of the telegraph service, in *Freedom and Reality*, pp. 74–5.

9 Margaret Thatcher, *The Downing Street Years 1979–1990* (HarperCollins, London, 1993), pp. 839–40.

10 Gray, 'The Tory Endgame', pp. 99–101.

11 Simon Walters, *Tory Wars: Conservatives in Crisis* (Politico's, London, 2001).

12 Mark Garnett and Philip Lynch (eds), *The Conservatives in Crisis* (Manchester University Press, Manchester, 2003).

13 See pp. 293–7.

14 See Chapter Nine, and Gary Streeter (ed.), *There Is Such a Thing as Society* (Politico's, London, 2002).

15 John Ramsden, *An Appetite for Power: A History of the Conservative Party Since 1830* (HarperCollins, London, 1998); A.J. Davies, *We, the Nation: The Conservative Party and the Pursuit of Power* (Little, Brown, London, 1995).

16 See pp. 309–13.

17 See pp. 279–308.

18 Michael White, 'Media Coup for Howard in HQ Restructuring', *Guardian*, 21 November 2003.

19 'Top Marks for Cynicism', *Economist*, 8 January 2004.

20 See pp. 75–8 for more on Salisbury.

21 See pp. 126–8, 177–89.

22 Anthony Seldon and Stuart Ball (eds), *Conservative Century: The Conservative Party Since 1900* (Open University Press, London, 1990).

23 Michael Flanders, introductory monologue to 'The Gnu Song', from the 1959 recording of the Flanders and Swann revue *At the Drop of a Hat*.

24 Michael Freeden, *Ideologies and Political Theory: A Conceptual Approach* (Oxford University Press, Oxford, 1996), p. 318.

25 Robert Eccleshall, 'Conservatism', in Robert Eccleshall, Alan Finlayson, Vincent Geoghegan, Michael Kenny, Moya Lloyd, Iain MacKenzie and Rick Wilford (eds), *Political Ideologies: An Introduction* (3rd edn, Routledge, London, 2003), pp. 47–72, at pp. 49–50.

26 The rationale behind some of these affiliations is given at length in Roger Scruton, *The Meaning of Conservatism* (3rd edn, Palgrave, Basingstoke, 2001).

27 John Gray, 'The Undoing of Conservatism', in *Enlightenment's Wake: Politics and Culture at the Close of the Modern Age* (Routledge, London, 1995), pp. 87–119, at pp. 93–100.

28 Mark Garnett, 'A Question of Definition? Ideology and the Conservative Party 1997–2001', in Garnett and Lynch, *The Conservatives in Crisis*, pp. 107–24.

29 David Willetts, *Modern Conservatism* (Penguin, Harmondsworth, 1992), especially pp. 92–108.

30 Freeden, *Ideologies and Political Theory*, pp. 348–93.

31 W.H. Greenleaf, *The British Political Tradition Volume Two: The Ideological Heritage* (Methuen, London, 1983), p. 195.

32 Bruce Pilbeam, *Conservatism in Crisis? Anglo-American Conservative Ideology After the Cold War* (Palgrave Macmillan, Basingstoke, 2003), pp. 8–9.

33 The speech was spoofed in 'Your Guide to the Forces of Conservatism', *Observer*, 3 October 1999. The speech itself is at http://news.bbc.co.uk/1/hi/uk_politics/460009.stm.

2 The idea of human imperfection: a whistlestop tour

1 Andrew Gregory, *Eureka! The Birth of Science* (Icon Books, Cambridge, 2001).

2 Plato, *Complete Works* (John M. Cooper, ed., D.S. Hutchinson, associate ed., Hackett, Indianapolis, 1997).

3 David Sedley, 'The Motivation of Greek Skepticism', in Myles Burnyeat (ed.), *The Skeptical Tradition* (University of California Press, Berkeley, 1983), pp. 9–29.

4 The major source is a brief philosophical biography written centuries later: Diogenes Laertius, *Lives of Eminent Philosophers* (2 vols, revised edn, R.D. Hicks, trans., Loeb Classical Library, Harvard University Press, Cambridge, MA, 1931), Book IX, 61–108.

5 Though it has been convincingly argued that Pyrrhonism actually doesn't have that many resemblances to the philosophy of Pyrrho. See Richard Bett, *Pyrrho, His Antecedents, and His Legacy* (Oxford University Press, Oxford, 2000).

6 Alan Bailey, *Sextus Empiricus and Pyrrhonean Scepticism* (Oxford University Press, Oxford, 2002), pp. 100–101.

7 Various translations of this are available. The major ones are R.G. Bury (trans.), *Outlines of Pyrrhonism* (Loeb Classical Library, Harvard University Press, Cambridge MA, 1933); Julia Annas and Jonathan Barnes (eds), *Outlines of Scepticism* (Cambridge University Press, Cambridge, 2000); and Benson Mates, *The Skeptic Way: Sextus Empiricus's* Outlines of Pyrrhonism (Oxford University Press, New York, 1996).

8 Myles Burnyeat, 'Can the Sceptic Live his Scepticism?', in Myles Burnyeat and Michael Frede (eds), *The Original Sceptics: A Controversy* (Hackett, Indianapolis, 1997), pp. 25–57.

9 Michael Frede, 'The Sceptic's Beliefs', in Burnyeat and Frede, *The Original Sceptics*, pp. 1–24.

10 Jonathan Barnes, 'The Beliefs of a Pyrrhonist', in Burnyeat and Frede, *The Original Sceptics*, pp. 58–91.

11 Bailey, *Sextus Empiricus*.

12 See Gisela Striker, 'The Ten Tropes of Aenesidemus', in Burnyeat, *The Skeptical Tradition*, pp. 95–115; and Julia Annas and Jonathan Barnes, *The Modes of Scepticism: Ancient Texts and Modern Interpretations* (Cambridge University Press, Cambridge, 1985).

13 Jonathan Barnes, *The Toils of Scepticism* (Cambridge University Press, Cambridge, 1990).

14 Gregory, *Eureka!*, pp. 115–35.

15 For the debate in Greek medicine about theory and practice, see G.E.R. Lloyd, 'The Epistemological Theory and Practice of Soranus's Methodism', in *Science, Folklore and Ideology: Studies in the Life Sciences in Ancient Greece* (Cambridge University Press, Cambridge, 1983), pp. 182–200.

16 There is some debate about this. He does criticise empiricism in the *Outlines*, I, 236–7; see Bailey, *Sextus Empiricus*, pp. 92–4.

17 Diogenes, *Lives*, IX, 61, 101, 108.

18 Sextus, *Outlines*, I, 23–4 (Bury translation).

19 Herodotus, *The Histories* (Aubrey de Sélincourt and A.R. Burn, trans., Penguin, Harmondsworth, 1972). It is suggestive that Enoch Powell began his academic career studying Herodotus.

20 Diogenes, *Lives*, IX, 95.

21 Sextus Empiricus, *Against the Mathematicians*, IX, 49. Books IX and X of *Against the Mathematicians* are translated as R.G. Bury (trans.), *Against the Physicists*, in R.G. Bury (ed.), *Works of Sextus Empiricus Volume III* (Loeb Classical Library, Harvard University Press, Cambridge MA, 1936).

22 This interpretation therefore following Frede, 'The Sceptic's Beliefs', and rejecting Burnyeat, 'Can the Sceptic Live his Scepticism?', and Bailey, *Sextus Empiricus*, as being too ungenerous.

23 An important argument, I believe, developed in the context of modern science by Kieron O'Hara and Tom Scutt, 'There Is No Hard Problem of Consciousness', in Jonathan Shear (ed.), *Explaining Consciousness: The Hard Problem* (Bradford Books, Cambridge MA, 1997), pp. 69–82, at pp. 72–4.

24 Luciano Floridi, *Sextus Empiricus: The Transmission and Recovery of Pyrrhonism* (Oxford University Press, New York, 2002), pp. 20–22.

25 I Corinthians 8:1.

26 Floridi, *Sextus Empiricus*, p. 27.

27 C.B. Schmitt, 'The Rediscovery of Ancient Skepticism in Modern Times', in Burnyeat, *The Skeptical Tradition*, pp. 225–51, at p. 236.

28 Montaigne, *The Complete Essays* (M.A. Screech, ed., Penguin, Harmondsworth, 1991).

29 See for instance 'On the Cannibals', *Essays*, pp. 228–41, though there are dozens of examples.

30 Montaigne, 'On Presumption', *Essays*, pp. 718–52, at p. 745.

31 Peter Burke, *Montaigne* (Oxford University Press, Oxford, 1981), p. 28.

32 David Lewis Schaefer, *The Political Philosophy of Montaigne* (Cornell University Press, Ithaca, 1990).

33 Schaefer, *The Political Philosophy of Montaigne*, p. 154.

34 Montaigne, 'On Habit: and on Never Easily Changing a Traditional Law', *Essays*, pp. 122–39, at p. 135.

35 Edmund Spenser, *The Faerie Queene*, V.ii.36. I have taken the liberty of modernising the spelling.

36 I have discussed this aspect of Shakespeare's work elsewhere at greater length. See Kieron O'Hara, *Trust: From Socrates to Spin* (Icon Books, Cambridge, 2004), pp. 36–42.

37 Anthony Holden, *William Shakespeare: His Life and Works* (Abacus, London, 1999), pp. 281–3.

38 Richard H. Popkin, *The History of Scepticism From Erasmus to Spinoza* (4th edn, University of California Press, New York, 1979).

39 Sir Thomas Browne, *The Works of Sir Thomas Browne Volume III* (Sir Geoffrey Keynes, ed., Faber and Faber, London, 1964), p. 290.

40 Sir Thomas Browne, 'Religio Medici' in C.A. Patrides (ed.), *Sir Thomas Browne: The Major Works* (Penguin, Harmondsworth, 1977), pp. 55–161.

41 *Religio Medici*, p. 66.

42 *Religio Medici*, pp. 147–8.

3 The Conservative Party as the custodian of the conservative tradition

1 Samuel P. Huntington, 'Conservatism as an Ideology', *American Political Science Review*, vol. 51 (1957), pp. 454–73; Michael Freeden, *Ideologies and Political Theory: A Conceptual Approach* (Oxford University Press, Oxford, 1996), pp. 335–8.

2 That right wing comedians are funnier than left wing ones is a fact acknowledged even in the *Guardian*: Andrew Anthony, 'Why Does the Devil Have All the Best Gags?' *Guardian*, 15 April 2004.

3 Louis I. Bredvold, *The Intellectual Milieu of John Dryden: Studies in Some Aspects of Seventeenth-Century Thought* (University of Michigan Press, Michigan, 1934).

4 John Dryden, 'The Medall', ll. 247–50.

5 John Dryden, *Absalom and Achitophel*, ll. 795–800.

6 Basil Williams, *The Whig Supremacy 1714–1760* (2nd edn, C.H. Stuart, rev., Oxford University Press, Oxford, 1960).

7 Edmund Burke, *Reflections on the Revolution in France* (Conor Cruise O'Brien, ed., Penguin, Harmondsworth, 1968).

8 Conor Cruise O'Brien, 'Introduction', in Burke, *Reflections*, pp. 9–76, at pp. 34–41.

9 Private communication.

10 See e.g. Thomas Paine, *The Rights of Man*, Part One, abridged in Michael Foot and Isaac Kramnick (eds), *The Thomas Paine Reader* (Penguin, Harmondsworth, 1987), pp. 201–364, especially pp. 201–62.

11 O'Brien, 'Introduction', pp. 56–62.

12 Burke, *Reflections*, pp. 89–90.

13 From a letter to Lord Charlemont on 9 August 1789, from Thomas W. Copeland (ed.), *The Correspondence of Edmund Burke Volume VI.* According to O'Brien, this is Burke's earliest known comment on the French Revolution.

14 Burke, *Reflections*, p. 207.

15 Burke, *Reflections*, p. 140.

16 René Descartes, 'Meditations on First Philosophy', in John Cottingham, Robert Stoothoff and Dugald Murdoch (eds), *The Philosophical Writings of Descartes Vol. II* (Cambridge University Press, Cambridge, 1984), pp. 1–62, especially pp. 12–23.

17 See in particular *A Treatise of Human Nature*, *An Enquiry Concerning Human Understanding* and *Dialogues Concerning Natural Religion*.

18 David Hume, *A Treatise of Human Nature* (L.A. Selby-Bigge and P.H. Nidditch, eds, Oxford University Press, Oxford, 1978), I.iv.i, pp. 180–81.

19 Richard H. Popkin, 'David Hume: His Pyrrhonism and his Critique of Pyrrhonism', in Richard H. Popkin, *The High Road to Pyrrhonism* (Richard A. Watson and James E. Force, eds, Hackett, Indianapolis, 1980), pp. 103–32.

20 David Hume, *Dialogues Concerning Natural Religion* (Henry D. Aiken, ed., Hafner, New York, 1948), XII, p. 87.

21 Richard H. Popkin, 'David Hume and the Pyrrhonian Controversy', in *The High Road to Pyrrhonism*, pp. 133–47.

22 Hume, *Treatise*, I.iv.vii, p. 269.

23 Robert Blake, *The Conservative Party from Peel to Thatcher* (Fontana, London, 1985), pp. 1–9.

24 For an innovative and usable online resource covering the age of Peel, see Marjie Bloy's *Peel Web*: http://dspace.dial.pipex.com/town/terrace/adw03/peel/marjie.htm.

25 John Ramsden, *An Appetite for Power: A History of the Conservative Party Since 1830* (HarperCollins, London, 1998), pp. 47–9.

26 Blake, *The Conservative Party*, pp. 19–27.

27 Blake, *The Conservative Party*, pp. 58–9.

28 Blake, *The Conservative Party*, pp. 18–19, 53–4.

29 See David Willetts, 'The Three Rights of Public Services', speech delivered 9 December 2003 at the Viennese Institute of Human Science. Available from http://www.davidwilletts.org or http://www.conservatives.com.

30 Benjamin Disraeli, *Coningsby* (Sheila M. Smith, ed., Oxford University Press, Oxford, 1982), II.5, p. 87.

31 Benjamin Disraeli, *Sybil* (Thom Braun, ed., Penguin, Harmondsworth, 1980).

32 Maurice Cowling, *1867: Disraeli, Gladstone and Revolution* (Cambridge University Press, Cambridge, 1967).

33 Blake, *The Conservative Party*, pp. 98–103 summarises the controversy.

34 Anthony Trollope, *Phineas Redux* (John C. Whale, ed., Oxford University Press, Oxford, 1983).

35 Sir Robert Ensor, *England 1870–1914* (Oxford University Press, Oxford, 1936), pp. 20–22.

36 Paul Smith, *Disraelian Conservatism and Social Reform* (Routledge, London, 1967).

37 Quoted in Ramsden, *An Appetite for Power*, p. 530.

38 Blake, *The Conservative Party*, pp. 131–2.

39 Salisbury writing in 1872 about the Irish question; he was also to serve as Secretary of State for India under Disraeli. The passage is taken from Lady Gwendolyn Cecil, *The Life of Robert Marquess of Salisbury Vol. II* (Hodder and Stoughton, London, 1921), pp. 38–9, and quoted in Blake, *The Conservative Party*, p. 133.

40 Andrew Roberts, *Salisbury: Victorian Titan* (Weidenfeld and Nicolson, London, 1999), pp. 85–6.

41 Roberts, *Salisbury*, pp. 282–7.

42 Ramsden, *An Appetite for Power*, p. 537.

43 Ramsden, *An Appetite for Power*, p. 180.

44 Arthur James Balfour, *A Defence of Philosophic Doubt: Being an Essay on the Foundations of Belief* (new edn, Hodder and Stoughton, London, 1920), p. viii; Kenneth Young, *Arthur James Balfour: The Happy Life of the Politician, Prime Minister, Statesman and Philosopher 1848–1930* (G. Bell and Sons Ltd., London, 1963), p. 48.

45 Balfour, *Defence*, pp. 296–8.

46 Balfour, *Defence*, pp. 322–3. This position is not a million miles away from ideas of the leading 20th-century conservative philosopher Michael Oakeshott, e.g. 'The Voice of Poetry in the Conversation of Mankind', in Michael Oakeshott, *Rationalism in Politics and Other Essays* (new and expanded edition, Timothy Fuller, ed., Liberty Fund, Indianapolis, 1991), pp. 488–541.

47 Rt. Hon. Arthur James Balfour, *The Foundations of Belief: Being Notes Introductory to the Study of Theology* (Longmans, Green and Co., London, 1895).

48 Young, *Balfour*, p. 153.

49 This is an argument very reminiscent of Enoch Powell's defence of the hereditary principle during his campaign opposing the reform of the House of Lords in 1969. Simon Heffer, *Like the Roman: The Life of Enoch Powell* (Weidenfeld and Nicolson, London, 1998), pp. 496–7.

50 For these arguments see Balfour, *Foundations*, p. 194ff.

51 Balfour, *Foundations*, pp. 226–30.

52 Balfour, *Defence*, pp. 138–53.

53 Balfour, *Foundations*, p. 230.

54 As discussed by Willetts, 'The Three Rights of Public Services'.

55 Freeden, *Ideologies and Political Theory*, pp. 139–314.

56 Isaiah Berlin, 'Two Concepts of Liberty', in Anthony Quinton (ed.), *Political Philosophy* (Oxford University Press, Oxford, 1967), pp. 141–52.

57 Willetts, 'The Three Rights of Public Services'.

58 See E.H.H. Green, '"No Settled Convictions"? Arthur Balfour, Political Economy, and Tariff Reform: A Reconsideration', in E.H.H. Green, *Ideologies of Conservatism* (Oxford University Press, Oxford, 2002), pp. 18–41.

59 Blake, *The Conservative Party*, pp. 168–9.

60 Quoted in Young, *Balfour*, p. 214.

61 Robert Eccleshall, 'Conservatism', in Robert Eccleshall, Alan Finlayson, Vincent Geoghegan, Michael Kenny, Moya Lloyd, Iain MacKenzie and Rick Wilford (eds), *Political Ideologies: An Introduction* (3rd edn, Routledge, London, 2003), pp. 47–72.

62 W.H. Greenleaf, *The British Political Tradition Volume Two: The Ideological Heritage* (Methuen, London, 1983), p. 195.

63 Quintin Hogg, *The Case for Conservatism* (Penguin, West Drayton, 1947), pp. 51–3.

64 J. Enoch Powell, speech to the Royal Society of St George, 22 April 1961, in J. Enoch Powell, *Freedom and Reality* (John Wood, ed., Elliot Right Way Books, Kingswood, 1969), pp. 337–41, at pp. 338–40.

65 Powell, speech at Docking, Norfolk, 21 April 1964, in *Freedom and Reality*, pp. 32–4, at pp. 33–4.

66 J. Enoch Powell, 'Theory and Practice', in G.M.K. Hunt (ed.), *Philosophy and Politics* (Cambridge University Press, Cambridge, 1990), pp. 1–9, at pp. 5–6.

67 Powell, 'Theory and Practice', p. 7.

68 Powell, speech at Birmingham, 20 April 1968, in *Freedom and Reality*, pp. 281–90.

69 Heffer, *Like the Roman*, p. 484.

70 Blake, *The Conservative Party*, p. 301. The predecessors were: Winston Churchill (Prime Minister 1940–45, 1951–5), Anthony Eden (Prime Minister 1955–7), Harold Macmillan (Prime Minister 1957–63) and Alec Douglas-Home (Prime Minister 1963–4).

71 J. Enoch Powell, 'Superwhig?' *Spectator*, 1 March 1980.

72 Andrew Denham and Mark Garnett, *Keith Joseph* (Acumen, Chesham, 2001), pp. 245–53.

73 Blake, *The Conservative Party*, pp. 339–40.

74 Andrew Blowers, 'Transition or Transformation? – Environmental Policy Under Thatcher', *Public Administration*, vol. 65 (1987), pp. 277–94.

75 Ian Gilmour, *Dancing With Dogma: Britain Under Thatcherism* (Simon and Schuster, London, 1992), p. 8.

76 See e.g. Steve Buckler and David P. Dolowitz, 'Theorizing the Third Way:

New Labour and Social Justice', *Journal of Political Ideologies*, vol. 5 (2000), pp. 301–20.

4 What is conservatism?

1 John Rawls, *A Theory of Justice* (Oxford University Press, Oxford, 1971), especially pp. 136–42.

2 Andrew Gamble, *The Free Economy and the Strong State: The Politics of Thatcherism* (Macmillan, London, 1988).

3 Mike Harris, 'The New Right', in Adam Lent (ed.), *New Political Thought: An Introduction* (Lawrence and Wishart, London, 1998), pp. 53–71, at pp. 55–6.

4 Harris, 'The New Right', pp. 56–61.

5 Robert Eccleshall, 'Conservatism', in Robert Eccleshall, Alan Finlayson, Vincent Geoghegan, Michael Kenny, Moya Lloyd, Iain MacKenzie and Rick Wilford (eds), *Political Ideologies: An Introduction* (3rd edn, Routledge, London, 2003), pp. 47–72, at p. 53.

6 Stuart Sim, *Fundamentalist World: The New Dark Age of Dogma* (Icon Books, Cambridge, 2004), pp. 102–34.

7 Argued by Robert Nozick, for example, in *Anarchy, State and Utopia* (Blackwell, Oxford, 1974).

8 Eccleshall, 'Conservatism', p. 53.

9 W.H. Greenleaf, *The British Political Tradition Volume Two: The Ideological Heritage* (Methuen, London, 1983), pp. 272–3.

10 David Willetts draws attention to the 'fragmentation, rivalry and jealousy' of the period that prompted the setting up of a 'legion of leagues' in David Willetts with Richard Forsdyke, *After the Landslide: Learning the Lessons from 1906 and 1945* (Centre for Policy Studies, London, 1999), pp. 14–15.

11 Andrew Roberts, *Salisbury: Victorian Titan* (Weidenfeld and Nicolson, London, 1999), p. 283.

12 E.H.H. Green, 'Conservatism, the State, and Civil Society in the Twentieth Century', in E.H.H. Green, *Ideologies of Conservatism* (Oxford University Press, Oxford, 2002), pp. 240–79, at p. 257.

13 Eccleshall, 'Conservatism', pp. 54–5.

14 Greenleaf, *The Ideological Heritage*, p. 195, in a passage already quoted in Chapter One, p. 28.

15 Harold Macmillan, *At the End of the Day: 1961–1963* (Macmillan, London, 1973), p. 37. He quotes from his own diary, from 21 September 1961.

16 Chapter One.

17 Mike Brewer, Alissa Goodman, Michal Myck, Jonathan Shaw and Andrew Shephard, *Poverty and Inequality in Britain: 2004* (Institute for Fiscal Studies, London, 2004).

18 Tony Burns, 'John Gray and the Death of Conservatism', *Contemporary Politics*, vol. 5 (1999), pp. 7–24.

19 John Gray, 'The Tory Endgame' in *Endgames: Questions in Late Modern Political Thought* (Polity Press, Cambridge, 1997), pp. 97–155, at pp. 114–15.

20 Michael Freeden, *Ideologies and Political Theory: A Conceptual Approach* (Oxford University Press, Oxford, 1996), pp. 47–95.

21 Eccleshall, 'Conservatism', p. 49.

22 Roger Scruton, *The Meaning of Conservatism* (3rd edn, Palgrave, Basingstoke, 2001), p. 10.

23 Lawrence Lessig, *Code and Other Laws of Cyberspace* (Basic Books, New York, 1999), *passim*, but particularly pp. 30–60; Kieron O'Hara, *Trust: From Socrates to Spin* (Icon Books, Cambridge, 2004), pp. 106–9.

24 H. Schuman, R.F. Belli and K. Bischoping, 'The Generational Basis of Historical Knowledge', in James W. Pennebaker, Dario Paez and Bernard Rimé (eds), *Collective Memory of Political Events: Social Psychological Perspectives* (Lawrence Erlbaum, Mahwah, NJ, 1997), pp. 47–78.

25 Scruton, *The Meaning of Conservatism*, p. 11.

26 Freeden, *Ideologies and Political Theory*, pp. 332–3.

27 Michael Oakeshott, 'On Being Conservative', in *Rationalism in Politics and Other Essays* (new and expanded edn, Liberty Fund, Indianapolis, 1991), pp. 407–37, at pp. 410–11.

28 See Edmund Dell, *A Strange Eventful History: Democratic Socialism in Britain* (HarperCollins, London, 2000).

29 Freeden, *Ideologies and Political Theory*, p. 334.

30 Freeden, *Ideologies and Political Theory*, pp. 348–83.

31 Scruton, *The Meaning of Conservatism*, pp. 10–12.

32 Scruton, *The Meaning of Conservatism*, pp. 88–90.

33 Scruton, *The Meaning of Conservatism*, pp. 39–41.

34 Scruton, *The Meaning of Conservatism*, pp. 65–6.

35 Scruton, *The Meaning of Conservatism*, pp. 182–94.

36 Scruton, *The Meaning of Conservatism*, pp. 79–82.

37 Scruton, *The Meaning of Conservatism*, pp. 127–47.

38 Scruton, *The Meaning of Conservatism*, pp. 64–86.

39 F.A. Hayek, *The Constitution of Liberty* (Routledge and Kegan Paul, London, 1960), pp. 397–411.

40 Daniel Kahneman, Paul Slovic and Amos Tversky (eds), *Judgement Under Uncertainty: Heuristics and Biases* (Cambridge University Press, Cambridge, 1982).

41 James C. Scott, 'Geographies of Trust, Geographies of Hierarchy', in Mark E. Warren (ed.), *Democracy and Trust* (Cambridge University Press, Cambridge, 1999), pp. 273–89.

42 Bureaucracy has been, for many, the key to modernity. The classic

account is in the sociological works of Max Weber (1864–1920), such as in Hans H. Gerth and C. Wright Mills (eds), *From Max Weber: Essays in Sociology* (Oxford University Press, New York, 1948). See also O'Hara, *Trust*, pp. 55–8, 224–31.

43 George Eliot, *Felix Holt, The Radical* (Panther, London, 1965), ch. 29, p. 262.

44 'The Trouble with Targets', *Economist*, 26 April 2001.

45 'Targetitis', *Economist*, 12 December 2002.

46 O'Hara, *Trust*, pp. 35–6.

47 Elliott Krause, *Death of the Guilds: Professions, States and the Advance of Capitalism, 1930 to the Present* (Yale University Press, New Haven, 1996).

48 John Vickers, *Competition in Professions* (Office of Fair Trading, London, 2001), which can be downloaded from http://www.oft.gov.uk/News/Press+releases/2001/PN+10-01.htm.

49 'Silks' Purses', *Economist*, 8 March 2001.

50 Marshall Meyer, 'The Performance Paradox', in B.M. Staw and L. Cummings (eds), *Research in Organizational Behavior Vol. 14* (JAI Press, Greenwich, CT, 1994), pp. 309–69.

51 'Missing the Point', *Economist*, 26 April 2001.

52 O'Hara, *Trust*, pp. 157–61.

53 F.A. Hayek, 'The Use of Knowledge in Society', *American Economic Review* vol. 35 (1945), pp. 519–30.

54 Hayek, 'The Use of Knowledge in Society', p. 523.

55 Mary Douglas, *How Institutions Think* (Routledge and Kegan Paul, London, 1986).

56 Kieron O'Hara, *Plato and the Internet* (Icon Books, Cambridge, 2002), pp. 32–7, 59–60.

57 David Willetts, *Modern Conservatism* (Penguin, Harmondsworth, 1992), pp. 93–108.

58 See Chapter Six.

59 R. Eyerman and B. Turner, 'Outline of a Theory of Generations', *European Journal of Social Theory* vol. 1 (1998), pp. 91–106.

60 Barbara A. Misztal, *Theories of Social Remembering* (Open University Press, Maidenhead, 2003), pp. 91–8.

61 John N. Adams and Roger Brownsword, *Understanding Law* (3rd edn, Sweet and Maxwell, London, 2003), pp. 46–53.

62 Adams and Brownsword, *Understanding Law*, pp. 82–145.

63 Bruce Pilbeam, *Conservatism in Crisis: Anglo-American Conservative Ideology at the End of the Cold War* (Palgrave Macmillan, Basingstoke, 2003), p. 8.

64 Freeden, *Ideologies and Political Theory*, p. 337.

65 Karl Mannheim, *Conservatism: A Contribution to the Sociology of Knowledge* (Routledge and Kegan Paul, London, 1986).

66 Roberts, *Salisbury*, pp. 86–98.

67 Phil Marfleet, 'Islamist Political Thought', in Lent, *New Political Thought*, pp. 89–111.

68 Martin Durham, 'The Christian Right', in Lent, *New Political Thought*, pp. 72–88.

69 Pilbeam, *Conservatism in Crisis?* pp. 97–9.

70 Quintin Hogg, *The Case for Conservatism* (Penguin, West Drayton, 1947), p. 18.

71 Roberts, *Salisbury*, p. 23.

72 Pilbeam, *Conservatism in Crisis?* pp. 173–85.

73 Edmund Burke, *Reflections on the Revolution in France* (Conor Cruise O'Brien, ed., Penguin, Harmondsworth, 1968), pp. 194–5.

74 John Aspinall, *The Best of Friends* (Macmillan, London, 1976), p. 139.

75 John Gray, 'Beginnings', in *Endgames*, pp. 156–86, at pp. 168–70.

76 See Pilbeam, *Conservatism in Crisis?* pp. 142–68.

5 Is conservatism dead?

1 Michael Andrews featuring Gary Jules, 'Mad World', composed by Roland Orzabal, published by Chrysalis Music, © 2001.

2 Alan Bennett, 'A Shameful Year', *London Review of Books*, 8 January 2004.

3 Kieron O'Hara, *Trust: From Socrates to Spin* (Cambridge: Icon Books, 2004).

4 Ulrich Beck, *Risk Society* (Sage, London, 1992).

5 Robert Putnam, *Bowling Alone* (Simon and Schuster, New York, 2000).

6 As I argued in *Trust*, pp. 239–69.

7 Amy Chua, *World on Fire: How Exporting Free-Market Democracy Breeds Ethnic Hatred and Global Instability* (William Heinemann, London, 2003).

8 Richard Layard, 'Happiness: Has Social Science a Clue?' Second Lionel Robbins memorial lecture, London School of Economics (2003), http://cep.lse.ac.uk/events/lectures/layard/RL030303.pdf.

9 Michael Oakeshott, 'On Being Conservative', in *Rationalism in Politics and Other Essays* (new and expanded edn, Liberty Fund, Indianapolis, 1991), pp. 407–37, at p. 408.

10 John Gray, 'The Undoing of Conservatism', in *Enlightenment's Wake: Politics and Culture at the Close of the Modern Age* (Routledge, London, 1995), pp. 87–119, at p. 93.

11 Gray, 'The Undoing of Conservatism', p. 106.

12 Gray, 'The Undoing of Conservatism', pp. 99–100.

13 Enoch Powell, speech to Royal Society of St George, 22 April 1961, in *Freedom and Reality* (John Wood, ed., Elliot Right Way Books, Kingswood, 1969), pp. 337–41.

14 Quintin Hogg, *The Case for Conservatism* (Penguin, West Drayton, 1947).

15 Roger Scruton, *England: An Elegy* (Pimlico, London, 2001).

16 See for instance, *Freedom and Reality*, pp. 281–314; speech at Wolverhampton, 11 June 1970, in John Wood (ed.), *Powell and the 1970 Election* (Elliot Right Way Books, Kingswood, 1970), pp. 97–104; *Still to Decide* (John Wood, ed., Batsford, London, 1972), pp. 189–212; *A Nation or No Nation? Six Years in British Politics* (Richard Ritchie, ed., Batsford, London, 1978), pp. 160–74.

17 Linda Colley, *Britons: Forging the Nation 1707–1837* (Yale University Press, New Haven, 1992), pp. 24–37.

18 Enoch Powell, *The Common Market: Renegotiate or Come Out* (Elliot Right Way Books, Tadworth, 1973), pp. 66–90.

19 Robin Young, 'Best of British Guts a Nation', *The Australian*, 29 April 2004.

20 Anthony Giddens, *Runaway World: How Globalisation Is Shaping Our Lives* (2nd edn, Profile Books, London, 2002), p. 39.

21 Eric J. Hobsbawm and Terrence O. Ranger (eds), *The Invention of Tradition* (Cambridge University Press, Cambridge, 1983).

22 Giddens, *Runaway World*, pp. 42–3.

23 Giddens, *Runaway World*, p. 45.

24 Giddens, *Runaway World*, p. 38.

25 Barbara A. Misztal, *Theories of Social Remembering* (Open University Press, Maidenhead, 2003), p. 91.

26 Misztal, *Theories of Social Remembering*, p. 92. She cites T.W. Luke, 'Identity, Meaning and Globalization', in P. Heelas, S. Lash and P. Morris (eds), *Detraditionalization: Critical Reflections on Authority and Identity* (Blackwell, Oxford, 1996), pp. 109–33, at p. 115, in this passage.

27 Marshall McLuhan, *The Gutenberg Galaxy* (University of Toronto Press, Toronto, 1962).

28 Misztal, *Theories of Social Remembering*, pp. 96–7.

29 Jamie Wilson and Sue Quinn, 'Millionaire's Libel Case Against *Guardian* Fails', *Guardian*, 20 May 1999.

30 Michael Oakeshott, 'Political Education', in *Rationalism in Politics*, pp. 43–69, at p. 58.

31 Kirsty Scott, 'Scrambled Dreams on Isle of Eigg', *Guardian*, 4 August 2003.

32 Bruce Pilbeam, *Conservatism in Crisis? Anglo-American Conservative Ideology After the Cold War* (Palgrave Macmillan, Basingstoke, 2003), pp. 196–7.

33 The gender aspects of this change were caught fascinatingly in an old British comedy film, as I argued in '*Carry On Cabby*, Gender and the Local Industrial Power Nexus', *Journal of Popular Culture* vol. 31, no. 3 (1997), pp. 81–104. Sid James's cabbies were no match for Hattie Jacques and the Glamcabs.

34 Arthur Aughey, Greta Jones and W.T.M. Riches, *The Conservative Political Tradition in Britain and the United States* (Pinter, London, 1992), pp. 1–31, is an interesting argument about the extent to which this is true.

35 John Parker, 'Us Against Us', *Economist*, 6 November 2003.

36 Ronald Inglehart and Wayne E. Baker, 'Modernization, Cultural Change, and the Persistence of Traditional Values', *American Sociological Review* vol. 65 (2000), pp. 19–51.

37 Inglehart and Baker, 'Modernization, Cultural Change, and the Persistence of Traditional Values', p. 29.

38 Pilbeam, *Conservatism in Crisis?*; Aughey et al., *The Conservative Political Tradition*.

6 Conservatism and markets

1 F.A. Hayek, *The Constitution of Liberty* (Routledge and Kegan Paul, London, 1960), p. 228.

2 J. Enoch Powell, speech at Wolverhampton, 25 September 1964, reprinted in *Freedom and Reality* (John Wood, ed., Elliot Right Way Books, Kingswood, 1969), pp. 35–9, at pp. 38–9.

3 J. Enoch Powell, speech at Bromley, 24 October 1963, *Freedom and Reality*, pp. 8–17, at p. 9.

4 J. Enoch Powell, speech at Wolverhampton, 6 March 1964, *Freedom and Reality*, pp. 92–4, at p. 94.

5 Powell, speech at Bromley, p. 13.

6 J. Enoch Powell, speech at Lytham St Annes, 10 October 1968, reprinted in *Still to Decide* (John Wood, ed., Batsford, London, 1972), pp. 23–5, at pp. 23–5.

7 Hayek, *The Constitution of Liberty*, p. 400.

8 J. Enoch Powell and Keith Wallis, *The House of Lords in the Middle Ages* (Weidenfeld and Nicolson, London, 1968), p. xi.

9 Philip Coggan, *The Money Machine: How the City Works* (5th edn, Penguin, London, 2002), pp. 56–8.

10 'Time, Please', *Economist*, 16 April 1998.

11 *Britain's Ruin* (Alcohol Concern, London, 2000).

12 'Drinking Disorder', *Economist*, 18 May 2000.

13 'Reclaiming the Night', *Economist*, 10 August 2000.

14 'Reclaiming the Night'.

15 'In a Pickle', *Economist*, 18 March 2004.

16 Hayek, *The Constitution of Liberty*, p. 400.

17 Kenneth J. Arrow, *The Limits of Organization* (W.W. Norton, New York, 1974), p. 20.

18 J. Enoch Powell, speech at Harrogate, 6 July 1966, reprinted in *Freedom and Reality*, pp. 159–61, at pp. 160–61.

19 Arrow, *The Limits of Organization*, p. 21.

20 Richard Layard, 'Happiness: Has Social Science a Clue?' Second Lionel Robbins memorial lecture, London School of Economics (2003), http://cep.lse.ac.uk/events/lectures/layard/RL030303.pdf.

21 Andrew Roberts, *Salisbury: Victorian Titan* (Weidenfeld and Nicolson, London, 1999), pp. 279–87.

22 Mark Lawson, 'This Revenge Is Very Sour', *Guardian*, 15 May 2004.

23 Richard Sennett, *The Corrosion of Character: The Personal Consequences of Work in the New Capitalism* (W.W. Norton, New York, 1998).

24 Oliver Letwin, 'The Problems of Household Debt Cannot Be Ignored', speech of 23 April 2004, at http://www.conservatives.com/news/article.cfm?obj_id=98696&speeches=1.

25 F.A. Hayek, *Law, Legislation and Liberty Volume 2: The Mirage of Social Justice* (Routledge and Kegan Paul, London, 1976), p. 110.

26 David Willetts, *Modern Conservatism* (Penguin, Harmondsworth, 1992), pp. 107–8.

27 Barry Smart, *Economy, Culture and Society* (Open University Press, Buckingham, 2003), pp. 100–101.

28 Kieron O'Hara, 'We Don't Trust Them an Inch', *New Statesman*, 26 April 2004, pp. 27–8.

29 Smart, *Economy, Culture and Society*.

30 Julian Le Grand, *Motivation, Agency and Public Policy: Of Knights and Knaves, Pawns and Queens* (Oxford University Press, Oxford, 2003). As will be clear, this section is deeply indebted to this essential work.

31 Le Grand, *Motivation, Agency and Public Policy*, pp. 15–17.

32 Le Grand, *Motivation, Agency and Public Policy*, pp. 23–38, which reviews the empirical literature about this.

33 See the discussion of the performance paradox in Chapter Four above.

34 Kieron O'Hara, *Trust: From Socrates to Spin* (Icon Books, Cambridge, 2004), pp. 157–205.

35 Le Grand, *Motivation, Agency and Public Policy*, pp. 31–2.

36 Le Grand, *Motivation, Agency and Public Policy*, pp. 163–8.

37 David Willetts, 'How to Reform the Public Services', speech of 5 April 2004 to the Social Market Foundation, available at http://www.davidwilletts.org.uk/record.jsp?type=speech&ID=46&sectionID=3.

38 David Willetts, *Who Do We Think We Are?* (Centre for Policy Studies, London, 1998), pp. 10–11.

39 Willetts, *Modern Conservatism*, p. 108.

40 John Gray, 'The Undoing of Conservatism', in *Enlightenment's Wake: Politics and Culture at the Close of the Modern Age* (Routledge, London, 1995), pp. 87–119; 'The Tory Endgame', in *Endgames: Questions in Late Modern Political Thought* (Polity Press, Cambridge, 1997), pp. 97–155.

41 David Willetts, 'The Three Rights of Public Services', speech delivered 9 December 2003, at the Viennese Institute of Human Science. Available from http://www.davidwilletts.org or http://www.conservatives.com.

42 David Willetts with Richard Forsdyke, *After the Landslide: Learning the Lessons from 1906 and 1945* (Centre for Policy Studies, London, 1999), pp. 82–96.

43 Willetts, *Modern Conservatism*, pp. 95–6; J. Enoch Powell, speech at Kensington, 30 November 1970, reprinted in *Still to Decide*, pp. 11–13.

44 'Liberalism Lives', *Economist*, 31 December 1998.

45 Alan Travis and Matt Wells, 'Nationalise Railtrack, Says Public', *Guardian*, 26 October 1999.

46 David Willetts, *Why Vote Conservative?* (Penguin, Harmondsworth, 1997), pp. 7–9.

7 Conservatism and societies

1 Interview in *Woman's Own*, 31 October 1987.

2 Margaret Thatcher, *The Downing Street Years 1979–1990* (HarperCollins, London, 1993), p. 625.

3 Thatcher, *The Downing Street Years*, p. 626.

4 David Willetts, *Modern Conservatism* (Penguin, Harmondsworth, 1992), p. 48.

5 David Willetts, *Why Vote Conservative?* (Penguin, Harmondsworth, 1997), p. 15.

6 Willetts, *Why Vote Conservative?* p. 20.

7 Gary Streeter (ed.), *There Is Such a Thing as Society* (Politico's, London, 2002).

8 Oliver Letwin, 'For Labour There Is No Such Thing as Society, Only the State', in Streeter, *There Is Such a Thing as Society*, pp. 38–51, at p. 39.

9 Gyles Brandreth, '"Your Strengths Are Like Hague's and You're Bald – Why Should You Do Any Better?"' *Sunday Telegraph*, 2 September 2001.

10 Nicholas Watt, 'Howard Plans Gay Summit as Tories Eye the Pink Vote', *Guardian*, 25 February 2004.

11 Toby Helm, 'Tory MPs Give Pro-Gay Summit a Miss', *Daily Telegraph*, 30 March 2004.

12 Simon Walters, *Tory Wars: Conservatives in Crisis* (Politico's, London, 2001), pp. 72–85.

13 Explored at greater length in Iain McGill and Colin Robertson, 'Drugs Undermine Human Dignity', in Streeter, *There Is Such a Thing as Society*, pp. 84–95.

14 'The Decline of the English Burglary', *Economist*, 29 May 2004.

15 Brandreth, '"Your Strengths Are Like Hague's and You're Bald"'.

16 Julian Le Grand, *Motivation, Agency and Public Policy: Of Knights and Knaves, Pawns and Queens* (Oxford University Press, Oxford, 2003), pp. 1–19.

17 David R. Olson, *Psychological Theory and Education Reform: How School*

Remakes Mind and Society (Cambridge University Press, Cambridge, 2003).

18 Richard Garner, '"Scandal" of Elitism Still Exists, Says Chief Schools Inspector', *Independent*, 20 May 2004.

19 Alison Wolf, *Does Education Matter? Myths About Education and Economic Growth* (Penguin, London, 2002).

20 'Jack of No Trades', *Economist*, 27 June 2002.

21 'Get Bac', *Economist*, 23 January 2003.

22 'Skills Filled', *Economist*, 5 February 2004.

23 'The New Blacks', *Economist*, 20 May 2004.

24 Robert Stevens, *University to Uni: The Politics of Higher Education in England Since 1944* (Politico's, London, 2003).

25 Le Grand, *Motivation, Agency and Public Policy*, pp. 163–4.

26 Sean Williams, *Alternative Prescriptions: A Survey of International Healthcare Systems* (Conservative Policy Unit, London, 2002).

27 Stephen Evans and Sean Williams, *The Wrong Prescription: A Critique of Labour's Management of the NHS* (Conservative Policy Unit, London, 2002).

28 See *Hansard* online, at http://www.publications.parliament.uk, for 23 April 2002.

29 Sheila Leatherman and Kim Sutherland, *The Quest for Quality in the NHS* (The Stationery Office, London, 2003).

30 'Haunted House', *Economist*, 30 October 2003.

31 Michael Howard, speech at Dundee, 15 May 2004, available at http://www.scottishtories.org.uk/conf04-howardspeech.htm.

32 Andrew Roberts, *Salisbury: Victorian Titan* (Weidenfeld and Nicolson, London, 1999), p. 494.

33 Philip Lynch, 'The Conservatives and Europe, 1997–2001', in Mark Garnett and Philip Lynch (eds), *The Conservatives in Crisis* (Manchester University Press, Manchester, 2003), pp. 146–63.

34 'Foreign, Redirected Investment', *Economist*, 29 May 2004.

35 Andy McSmith, 'Howard Sacks Peers for Endorsing UKIP', *Independent on Sunday*, 30 May 2004.

36 Roberts, *Salisbury*, p. 506.

37 J. Enoch Powell, 'Theory and Practice', in G.M.K. Hunt (ed.), *Philosophy and Politics* (Cambridge University Press, Cambridge, 1990), pp. 1–9, at pp. 7–8.

38 J. Enoch Powell, speech at Birmingham, 20 April 1968, in J. Enoch Powell, *Freedom and Reality* (John Wood, ed., Elliot Right Way Books, Kingswood, 1969), pp. 281–90, at p. 283.

39 See for instance J. Enoch Powell, speech at Wolverhampton, 11 June 1970, reprinted in John Wood (ed.), *Powell and the 1970 Election* (Elliot Right Way Books, Kingswood, 1970), pp. 97–104.

40 Paul Foot, *The Rise of Enoch Powell* (Penguin, Harmondsworth, 1969).

41 Powell, speech at Wolverhampton, p. 282.

42 *Enoch: A Life in Politics* (Brooks Productions, 1987).

43 Census figures taken from *Encyclopædia Britannica Book of the Year 2004* (Encyclopædia Britannica, Chicago, 2004), p. 721.

44 'The Natives Are Restless', *Economist*, 9 October 2003.

45 'A World of Exiles', *Economist*, 2 January 2003.

46 Peter Marsden, *The Taliban: War, Religion and the New Order in Afghanistan* (Oxford University Press, Karachi, 1998).

47 Michael Ignatieff, 'Is Nothing Sacred? The Ethics of Television', in *The Warrior's Honor: Ethnic War and the Modern Conscience* (Chatto and Windus, London, 1998), pp. 9–33, at p. 21.

48 Quoted in Roberts, *Salisbury*, p. 508.

8 Conservatism and trust

1 Jürgen Habermas, 'Modernity – an Incomplete Project', in Hal Foster (ed.), *Postmodern Culture* (Pluto Press, London, 1985).

2 John Rawls, *A Theory of Justice* (Oxford University Press, Oxford, 1971).

3 Robert Putnam, *Bowling Alone* (Simon and Schuster, New York, 2000).

4 Francis Fukuyama, *Trust: The Social Virtues and the Creation of Prosperity* (Free Press, New York, 1995). See Kieron O'Hara, *Trust: From Socrates to Spin* (Icon Books, Cambridge, 2004), pp. 67–9.

5 O'Hara, *Trust*, pp. 75–91.

6 Fukuyama, *Trust*.

7 O'Hara, *Trust*, pp. 95–119, 121–56, 157–205 and 207–38 respectively.

8 Onora O'Neill, *A Question of Trust: The BBC Reith Lectures 2002* (Cambridge University Press, Cambridge, 2002), pp. 44–5.

9 Kieron O'Hara, 'Conflict Overrules Consensus', *Times Higher Education Supplement*, 25 June 2004.

10 Nevil Johnson, 'Constitutional Reform: Some Dilemmas for a Conservative Philosophy', in Zig Layton-Henry (ed.), *Conservative Party Politics* (Macmillan, London, 1980), pp. 126–55, at pp. 135–6.

11 Kieron O'Hara, 'We Don't Trust Them an Inch', *New Statesman*, 26 April 2004.

12 Polly Toynbee, 'Voting's Too Good for 'Em', *Guardian*, 4 June 2004.

13 O'Hara, 'We Don't Trust Them an Inch'.

14 Kieron O'Hara, 'Why It's OK to Be Bliar', *New Statesman*, 8 September 2003.

15 O'Hara, *Trust*, pp. 271–6.

16 Michael Howard, 'A Government Which Is Honest. A Government You Can Trust', speech at Bournemouth, Conservative Party conference, 7 October 2004, http://www.conservatives.com/tile.do?def=news.story.page&obj_id=116484&speeches=1.

17 Michael Howard, 'Timetable for Action', available from http://www.
conservatives.com/tile.do?def=policy.listing.page.

18 Michael Ancram, 'Conservatives Will Restore Trust in Britain's Foreign
Policy', speech at Harrogate, Conservative Party spring conference, 7
March 2004, http://www.conservatives.com/tile.do?def=news.story.page
&obj_id=91783&type=springforum.

19 Tony Blair, speech to the Labour Party conference, Blackpool, 4 October
1994.

20 O'Hara, *Trust*, p. 283.

21 Gyles Brandreth, '"Your Strengths Are Like Hague's and You're Bald –
Why Should You Do Any Better?"' *Sunday Telegraph*, 2 September 2001.

22 Barbara A. Misztal, *Trust in Modern Societies* (Polity Press, Cambridge,
1996), pp. 102–20.

23 Joseph Conrad, *The Secret Agent* (Martin Seymour-Smith, ed., Penguin,
Harmondsworth, 1984), p. 102.

24 Misztal, *Trust in Modern Societies*, pp. 95–101.

25 Lisa O'Carroll, Nicholas Watt and Matt Wells, 'Nazi Tirade Stream of
Abuse by *Express* Owner Provokes Walkout', *Guardian*, 23 April 2004.

26 Misztal, *Trust in Modern Societies*, p. 97.

27 O'Hara, *Trust*, pp. 71–3.

28 Barbara A. Misztal, *Theories of Social Remembering* (Open University
Press, Maidenhead, 2003).

29 Misztal, *Trust in Modern Societies*, p. 121.

30 See e.g. Jackie Ashley, 'I Confess: I've Had Enough of All This Personal
Politics', *Guardian*, 7 October 2004; Andrew Rawnsley, 'The Big Idea Is
Now Small Ideas', *Observer*, 10 October 2004.

9 Tories nil desperandum two

1 Toby Helm, 'Unhappy Howard Fails to Squeeze an Apology from Blair',
Daily Telegraph, 21 July 2004.

2 Stuart Ball, 'The Conservatives in Opposition, 1906–79: A Comparative
Analysis', in Mark Garnett and Philip Lynch (eds), *The Conservatives in
Crisis* (Manchester University Press, Manchester, 2003), pp. 7–28.

3 'Who Can Rescue the Tories?' *Economist*, 29 May 1997.

4 Mark Garnett, 'Win or Bust: The Leadership Gamble of William Hague',
in Garnett and Lynch, *The Conservatives in Crisis*, pp. 49–65.

5 'Gambling on William Hague', *Economist*, 19 June 1997.

6 Simon Walters, *Tory Wars: Conservatives in Crisis* (Politico's, London,
2001).

7 The ideological commonalities between the British and American right
are described, in what I believe is somewhat exaggerated form, in Bruce
Pilbeam, *Conservatism in Crisis? Anglo-American Conservative Ideology
After the Cold War* (Palgrave Macmillan, Basingstoke, 2003).

8 Margaret Thatcher, *The Downing Street Years 1979–1990* (HarperCollins, London, 1993), pp. 626–7.

9 Edward Ashbee, 'The US Republicans: Lessons for the Conservatives?' in Garnett and Lynch, *The Conservatives in Crisis*, pp. 29–48, at pp. 30–34.

10 Ashbee, 'The US Republicans', pp. 39–41.

11 Ashbee, 'The US Republicans', pp. 41–2.

12 Robert Putnam, *Bowling Alone* (Simon and Schuster, New York, 2000).

13 'On Target, So Far', *Economist*, 26 April 2001.

14 Michael Oakeshott, 'The Voice of Poetry in the Conversation of Mankind', in *Rationalism in Politics and Other Essays* (new and expanded edn, Liberty Fund, Indianapolis, 1991), pp. 488–541.

15 'Something for the Kitchen Table', *Economist*, 29 April 1999.

16 Sandra Barwick, 'Last Supper as Oxo Family Finally Crumbles', *Daily Telegraph*, 31 August 1999.

17 'The China Syndrome', *Economist*, 23 August 2001.

18 Matthew Bishop, 'Giving Something Back', *Economist*, 14 June 2001.

19 'A Tale of Two Legacies', *Economist*, 19 December 2002.

20 Garnett, 'Win or Bust', p. 62.

21 Walters, *Tory Wars*, p. 101.

22 Richard Kelly, 'Organisational Reform and the Extra-parliamentary Party', in Garnett and Lynch, *The Conservatives in Crisis*, pp. 82–106, at pp. 87–90.

23 For the criticism, see Kelly, 'Organisational Reform and the Extra-parliamentary Party'. For a short response, see Lord Parkinson, 'The Reform of the Conservative Party', in Garnett and Lynch, *The Conservatives in Crisis*, pp. 217–20. Lord Parkinson was Conservative Party Chairman under Mr Hague during 1997–8.

24 Kelly, 'Organisational Reform and the Extra-parliamentary Party', p. 101.

25 Paul Eastham, 'Tory Hopefuls Face Rerun', *Daily Mail*, 11 July 2001.

26 'The Form', *Economist*, 21 June 2001.

27 Eastham, 'Tory Hopefuls Face Rerun'.

28 'Matt' cartoon, *Daily Telegraph*, 14 September 2001.

29 Toby Helm and Benedict Brogan, 'Chief Whip Tells Rebels to Sign Up or Quit Party', *Daily Telegraph*, 10 October 2003.

30 Rachel Sylvester, 'Duncan Smith Tries On the Leopard-Print Kitten Heels', *Daily Telegraph*, 12 October 2002; Colin Brown and Francis Elliott, 'The Week the Kitten Heel Trod on the Polecat', *Daily Telegraph*, 13 October 2002; Benedict Brogan, 'Theresa Given her Own Range of Shoes', *Daily Telegraph*, 22 November 2002.

31 'A Tale of Two Legacies'.

32 Gary Streeter (ed.), *There Is Such a Thing as Society: Twelve Principles of Compassionate Conservatism* (Politico's, London, 2002).

33 Iain Duncan Smith, 'The Renewal of Society', in Streeter, *There Is Such a*

Thing as Society, pp. 30–37.

34 Rick Santorum, 'The New Wave of Compassionate Conservatism', in Streeter, *There Is Such a Thing as Society*, pp. 60–67.

35 Gary Streeter, 'Conservatives Must Change to Help the Vulnerable', in Streeter, *There Is Such a Thing as Society*, pp. 1–10, at p. 10.

36 Andy McSmith, 'Tebbit Praises "Family Man" Duncan Smith', *Daily Telegraph*, 12 June 2001.

37 Walters, *Tory Wars*, p. 49.

38 Malcolm Gooderham, 'A Tory War on Poverty: Fighting Deprivation, Drugs and Despair', in Edward Vaizey, Nicholas Boles and Michael Gove (eds), *A Blue Tomorrow: New Visions for Modern Conservatives* (Politico's, London, 2001), pp. 184–91.

39 Duncan Smith, 'The Renewal of Society'; Auslan Cramb, 'Tories Must Travel a Long, Hard Road', *Daily Telegraph*, 25 March 2002.

40 Duncan Smith, 'The Renewal of Society', p. 35.

41 Oliver Letwin, 'For Labour There Is No Such Thing as Society, Only the State', in Streeter, *There Is Such a Thing as Society*, pp. 38–51, at p. 45.

42 Walters, *Tory Wars*, pp. 220–21.

43 Walters, *Tory Wars*, pp. 210–11.

44 'Are the Tories Dead and Buried?' *Economist*, 1 May 1997.

45 Walters, *Tory Wars*, pp. 25–6.

46 Mark Garnett, 'A Question of Definition? Ideology and the Conservative Party 1997–2001', in Garnett and Lynch, *The Conservatives in Crisis*, pp. 107–24, at pp. 117–19.

47 Derek Lewis, *Hidden Agendas: Politics, Law and Disorder* (Hamish Hamilton, London, 1997); 'Howard's End?' *Economist*, 15 May 1997. Only the question mark at the end of the title of the *Economist* article stops it being a huge miscalculation!

48 A.N. Wilson, *Evening Standard*, 23 August 1999.

49 See pp. 114–18.

10 Something of the night

1 'In Praise of Older Men', *Economist*, 18 April 2002.

2 'Mr Nasty and Mr Nice', *Economist*, 27 February 2003.

3 Benedict Brogan, '"Dance of Death" Sees Off Davis the Kingmaker', *Daily Telegraph*, 30 October 2003.

4 'Over to Howard', *Economist*, 30 October 2003.

5 Iain Macleod, 'The Tory Leadership', *Spectator*, 17 January 1964.

6 Iain Duncan Smith, 'I Know I Have the Confidence of the Grass Roots', *Daily Telegraph*, 29 October 2003.

7 Michael Howard, 'I Believe', *The Times*, 2 January 2004.

8 Roger Scruton, *The Meaning of Conservatism* (3rd edn, Palgrave, Basingstoke, 2001), pp. 39–41.

9   George Jones, 'Blair Gets the Third Degree over Fees', *Daily Telegraph*, 4 December 2003.

10 Nicholas Watt, 'Tories' New Credo Has US Roots', *Guardian*, 3 January 2004.

11 Melissa Kite, 'Howard Tells Bush: I Don't Care If You Won't See Me', *Daily Telegraph*, 29 August 2004.

12 'Howard's New Way', *Guardian*, 20 February 2004.

13 George Jones, 'I'll Be Straight with You, Says Howard, We've Got to Earn Trust Through Action', *Daily Telegraph*, 6 October 2004.

14 Michael Howard, 'I Wouldn't Go That Far', *Guardian*, 28 November 2003.

15 Raekha Prasad, 'Best of Both Worlds', *Guardian*, 17 December 2003.

16 'Where Did it All Go Wrong?' *Economist*, 7 November 2002.

17 Philip Johnston, 'Davis Talks Tough on the Need to Control Migration', *Daily Telegraph*, 7 October 2004.

18 Derek Lewis, *Hidden Agendas: Politics, Law and Disorder* (Hamish Hamilton, London, 1997), p. 119.

19 Michael Howard, speech announcing his candidacy for the leadership of the Conservative Party, October 2003.

20 George Jones, '"I'll Give You a Government You Can Trust"', *Daily Telegraph*, 8 October 2004.

21 'All For One, One For All', *Economist*, 15 July 2004.

22 'The Birthday Boy', *Economist*, 22 July 2004.

23 Howard, speech of October 2003.

24 'Howard's Way', *Economist*, 4 March 2004.

25 George Jones, 'Tories Pledge to Reverse Spread of Speed Cameras', *Daily Telegraph*, 4 August 2004.

26 'Fast and Loose', *Economist*, 6 May 2004.

27 'More Cameras, Less Speed', *Economist*, 16 August 2001.

28 Toby Helm, 'Howard Talks Tough on Crime to Lift the Tories', *Daily Telegraph*, 9 August 2004.

29 Andrew Rawnsley, 'Is There Anywhere for the Tories to Turn?' *Observer*, 1 August 2004.

30 Polly Toynbee, 'Don't Collaborate With Our Enemies to Tear Blair Down', *Guardian*, 17 March 2004; 'Would-be Protest Voters Need to Get a Grip on Reality', *Guardian*, 9 June 2004.

31 Malcolm Rifkind, 'Blair's Tory Policies Have Failed: But Ours Won't', *Observer*, 1 August 2004.

32 Rawnsley, 'Is There Anywhere for the Tories to Turn?'

33 'Dead Centre', *Economist*, 30 September 2004.

34 Nicholas Watt, 'Ukip Soars in Voter Backlash', *Guardian*, 14 June 2004.

35 Patrick Wintour, 'Tories Pushed into Fourth Place as Labour Holds On to Hartlepool', *Guardian*, 1 October 2004.

36 For example, 'Redwood Puts Europe Back on the Tory Agenda', *Daily Telegraph*, 22 September 2004; 'Tories Must Win Back the Right to be Believed', *Daily Telegraph*, 4 October 2004.

37 'Spoilers', *Economist*, 27 May 2004.

38 David Gow and Nicholas Watt, '"You're All Barmy." Exit Kilroy from Ukip Group', *Guardian*, 28 October 2004.

39 Matthew Tempest, 'Patron Joan Collins "May Not Vote Ukip"', *Guardian*, 28 October 2004.

40 Michael Howard, speech to the Policy Exchange, 9 February 2004.

41 Michael Howard, 'A New Deal for Europe', speech given to the Konrad Adenauer Stiftung, Berlin, 12 February 2004.

42 Howard, speech to the Policy Exchange.

Postscript

1 Nicholas Pyke and Malcolm Fitzwilliams, '1954 v 2004 No Contest: We Are Cleaner, Healthier and Better Off (But Men Still Won't Do the Housework)', *Independent*, 21 November 2004.

2 Samuel P. Huntington, *The Clash of Civilizations and the Remaking of the World Order* (Simon & Schuster, London, 1997).

3 George Jones, 'Tories Have New HQ for Election Campaign', *Daily Telegraph*, 22 July 2004.

4 Marc-Henri Glendenning, 'Prada and Prejudice: Designing a Toryism for the Pavement Not the Penthouse', in Edward Vaizey, Nicholas Boles and Michael Gove (eds), *A Blue Tomorrow: New Visions for Modern Conservatives* (Politico's, London, 2001), pp. 203–12; Toby Helm, 'Poll Defeat Could Mean a New Name for Tories', *Daily Telegraph*, 7 August 2004.

CREDITS

The author and publisher wish to thank the following for their permission to reprint copyright material:

Robert Eccleshall et al., *Political Ideologies: An Introduction* (3rd edn, Routledge, London, 2003). Reproduced with permission.

Michael Freeden, *Ideologies and Political Theory* (Oxford University Press, Oxford, 1996). Reproduced by permission of Oxford University Press.

John Gray, *Enlightenment's Wake: Politics and Culture at the Close of the Modern Age* (Routledge, London, 1995). Reproduced with permission.

F.A. Hayek, *The Constitution of Liberty* (Routledge and Kegan Paul, London, 1960). Reproduced with permission.

'Reclaiming the Night', *Economist*, 10 August 2000 © The Economist Newspaper Limited, London 2000.

Margaret Thatcher, *The Downing Street Years 1979–1990* (HarperCollins, London, 1993). Reprinted by permission of HarperCollins Publishers Ltd. © Margaret Thatcher 1993.

Figures 2 and 7: Reproduced by permission of The Telegraph.

Figure 3: Reproduced by permission of the American Sociological Association.

Figures 5, 6 and 8: Copyright © The Economist Newspaper Limited, London (2001, 2002, 2004).

Although every effort has been made to contact copyright holders, there are instances where we have been unable to do so. If notified, the publisher will be pleased to acknowledge the use of copyright material in future editions.

Index